The Social Dimensions of Early Buddhism

For
Upali, Siddhartha, and Anand

The Social Dimensions of Early Buddhism

UMA CHAKRAVARTI

DELHI
OXFORD UNIVERSITY PRESS
BOMBAY CALCUTTA MADRAS
1987

Oxford University Press, Walton Street, Oxford OX2 6DP
New York Toronto
Delhi Bombay Calcutta Madras Karachi
Petaling Jaya Singapore Hong Kong Tokyo
Nairobi Dar es Salaam
Melbourne Auckland
and associates in
Beirut Berlin Ibadan Nicosia

SBN 19 562069 0

Typeset by Taj Services Limited, Noida, U.P.
Printed in India at Jay Print Pack (P) Ltd., New Delhi 110015
and published by S.K. Mookerjee, Oxford University Press
Y.M.C.A. Library Building, Jai Singh Road, New Delhi 110001

Contents

associated with agriculture – The *brāhmana-gahapati* – *Gahapati, seṭṭhi*, and *seṭṭhi-gahapati* – *Gahapati* as employer of labour – *Gahapati* as a status term – The *gahapati's* association with wealth – The *gahapatis* as extenders of popular support to Buddhism – The *gahapati's* special relationship with the *saṅgha* – *Gahapati* and *gāmanī* – *Gahapati*: from householder to agriculturist – The social organization of the *gaṇa-saṅghas* – Landholding in the *gaṇa-saṅghas* – Tension within the *gaṇa-saṅghas* – Two types of *saṅghas* – Some implications of clan ownership of land – Clan ownership of land, *khattiyas* and the *gaṇa-saṅghas* – The *gahapaṭi*, the family, agriculture and the private control of land

IV. Social Stratification as Reflected in the Buddhist Texts 94

The problem – Buddhism and caste – Two schemes of categorization in the Buddhist texts – Terms of categorization – High and low strata in Buddhist texts – Regional dimension of stratification – The relationship of *kula, kamma,* and *sippa* – Empirical relevance of *vaṇṇa, jāti,* and *kula* – The Buddhist view of stratification: the *saṅgha* – Stratification outside the *saṅgha* – Principles of stratification based on *kula, kamma* and *sippa* – Evidence of stratification from Ceylon – The importance of the *gahapati* in the Buddhist view of stratification

V. The Social Background of the Early Buddhists 122

The problem – The method – The *saṅgha* – Social origins of important *bhikkhus* – Important *bhikkhus* of *khattiya* origin – The laity – The *brāhmaṇa* component of the laity – Important *gahapati* supporters of the Buddha – Other prominent supporters of the Buddha – *Khattiya, brāhmana,* and *gahapati*: key figures in the Buddhist texts – Wealthy supporters of Buddhism – The importance of kinship ties in the extension of support to Buddhism – Analysis of the social composition of the early Buddhists

VI. The King in Early Buddhism 150

General ideas on kingship – The origin of kingship in

the Buddhist genesis myth – Seven symbols of sovereignty – Despotic kingship at the time of the Buddha – Legitimate exercise of power – Arbitrary exercise of power – Normative kingship: the *cakkavatti dhammiko dhammarāja* – The creation of just social order – The king and the *saṅgha*

Abbreviations

A.N.	*Aṅguttara Nikāya*
B.O.D.	*Book of Discipline*
B.S.O.A.S.	*Bulletin of the School of Oriental and African Studies*
D.B.	*Dialogues of the Buddha*
D.N.	*Dīgha Nikāya*
D.P.P.N.	*Dictionary of Pāli Proper Names*
G.S.	*Gradual Sayings*
J.B.B.R.A.S.	*Journal of the Bombay Branch of the Royal Asiatic Society*
J.B.R.S.	*Journal of the Bihar Research Society*
J.E.S.H.O.	*Journal of the Economic and Social History of the Orient*
J.R.A.S.	*Journal of the Royal Asiatic Society*
K.S.	*Kindred Sayings*
M.L.S.	*Middle Length Sayings*
M.N.	*Majjhima Nikāya*
P.T.S.	*Pāli Text Society*
S.B.E.	*Sacred Books of the East*
S.N.	*Saṁyutta Nikāya*

Note: The system of transliteration followed here is based on the Pāli-English Dictionary of the Pāli Text Society. For the sake of consistency most words appear in their Pāli variant.

Glossary

abhiseka Consecration
añña titthiya Buddhist term for wandering groups other than their own
araññа Forest
ārāma A private park given to the *saṅgha* for the benefit of the *bhikkhus*
ariya sāvaka Ideal disciple of the Buddha
āvāsa Dwelling place, residence
ayya putta An aristocratic gentleman, a worthy gentleman
brahmadeya Grant of land, usually to *brāhmaṇas*, from the king's domain
brahmaloka The world of the celestials, the highest world
cakkavatti Emperor, head of the social world
dakkhiṇā Fee given to *brāhmaṇas* for the performance of sacrifice; also a gift or a donation
daḷidda Poor, needy
dāna Gift
dāsa A slave, one who is in servitude (masculine)
dasī Feminine of above
gaṇa-saṅgha Clan oligarchy usually of one or more *khattiya* clans, republican territory; more precisely a political unit where there is collective control over land and collective exercise of power
gaṇana One who is skilled in counting
gaṇācariyo A teacher of a group, one who has many followers
gorakkhā Cattlekeeping
hīna Inferior, low
isi Seer
janapada Inhabited territory, a province, district or country
jaṭila One who wears a *jaṭa* or matted hair, a type of ascetic
kamma Work
kammakara One who works for a master, a labourer
kasī Agriculture
kula Good family, collection of agnates and cognates, clan
kulaputta A clansman, a young man of good family
lekha Writing

mahānagara A seat of government, an important centre of trade
nīca Low, inferior, humble
nikāya Collection of *suttas*
pañca sīlas Five items of good behaviour
paribbājaka One who has renounced the status of a householder, a wandering religious mendicant
parisa An assembly of people
pātimokkha Fortnightly assembly of monks, also texts containing rules which are recited at the assembly
santhāgāra Council Hall
samaṇa A wanderer, a recluse
śastra Arms, weapons
sippa Craft
sutta Chapter, division, dialogue, discourse
tathāgata An epithet of *arahant*, he who has won through to the truth
thera A senior monk
theri A senior nun
titthiya A non-conformist sect
ucca High
ukkaṭṭha Exalted, high, prominent
upāsaka Lay follower (masculine)
upāsikā Feminine of above
upasampadā Higher ordination, admission to the privileges of recognized *bhikkhus*
uposatha Days preceding four stages of the moon's waxing and waning, utilized by the Buddhists for the recitation of the *pātimokkha*
vārta Economic activities
vaṇa Forest, wood, place of pleasure or sport
vāṇija Merchant, trader
vassā-vāsa A place to spend the rainy season
yañña A Brahmanic sacrifice
yajamāna A person on whose behalf a sacrifice is performed

Acknowledgements

To the University Grants Commission for the grant of a fellowship which enabled me to pursue the work uninterruptedly for three years; to Professor D. Devahuti, my supervisor, for just the right combination of encouragement, enthusiasm, and caution which improved the quality of the work; to the late Professor A.L. Basham for encouragement before the work was undertaken and after it was completed; to Professor S. J. Tambiah for commenting on an earlier draft of the work; to Jagdish for locating books in the maze of the Central Library, Delhi University; to Anand Doraswami for editorial assistance; to Lola Chatterji for helping to prepare the index; to my parents for launching me into a career in history; and to Anand, Upali, and Siddhartha for bearing with the preoccupations and the demands of research.

CHAPTER I

Introduction

The problem

The sixth century B.C. has left its mark on Indian history mainly because it witnessed an intense preoccupation with philosophical speculation. Among the various thinkers contributing to this unique phase was the Buddha, who more than any other historical personage born in India has compelled the attention of the world. Consequently, there is no dearth of writing on the Buddha and on Buddhism as a whole. But while an intimate connection between ideas and the societies which give rise to them would be readily conceded, there is a lacuna in historical writing, especially in the field of social history dealing with the major concerns of the Buddha, the society in which he lived, and the connection between the two.

The absence of such a focus of study is particularly noticeable because contemporary interest in Buddhism is in a large measure based on its social appeal. Within India Buddhism has appeared as an alternative to the hierarchical and inegalitarian ideology and practice of Hinduism. In contrast Buddhism is viewed as a system which was more sympathetic to oppressed groups and it has been considered an economic, political, and social solution to the problem of caste oppression. Buddhism in other Asian countries has also taken on the character of a socio-political movement in recent times.[1] It has been described as a humanistic ethic seeking full embodiment in a socio-political community'.[2] Despite this interest in the social dimensions of Buddhism there is no full-length study of the society in which Buddhism had its genesis or the social groups that constituted it. While it has become evident that early Buddhist society was rapidly changing and becoming sharply stratified[3] the form in which that stratification was expressing itself

[1] Adele M. Fiske, 'Buddhism in India Today' in Heinrich Dumoulin and John C. Maraldo (eds), *Buddhism in India Today*, p. 142.

[2] Trevor Ling, *The Buddha*, p. 286.

[3] See D.D. Kosambi, *An Introduction to the Study of Indian History*, pp. 147–62; *The*

needs to be analysed. Further certain broad generalizations regarding the close association between Buddhism and specific social groups[4] have to be tested mainly because the conclusions have not been founded on any rigorous analysis of the sources available for early Buddhist society. There is therefore considerable scope for a study that intensively analyses the nature of society in which Buddhism originated and shows the relationship between the two. This work is an attempt in that direction.

The sources

One of the major problems faced by a historian attempting an analysis of Buddhism and the society in which it originated is that of the stratification of the Pāli texts. Very few secondary works show any regard for the relationship between a particular text and the probable period that it represents. This may have been because traditionally Buddhist texts *as a whole* formed the unit of study, as distinct from the Brahmanical texts. While this may have been a viable focus of study in itself, it has at least partially been responsible for the broad generalizations that followed from treating the Buddhist texts as a homogeneous unit. Texts ranging from approximately the fifth century B.C. to the fifth century A.D. are often capsuled by scholars into one category. In the initial stages of historical writing such an approach may have been justified, but the trend has continued even after the appearance of specialist studies, including the study of social history. More than any other branch of specialist studies this area requires a proper time perspective for the accurate analysis of social and economic categories. Thus Fick, Mehta, and Bose all treat the evidence from the *Vinaya* and *Sutta Piṭakas* and the *Jātakas* as reflecting the same society.[5] To some extent this confusion was inevitable, given the inadequate state of knowledge on the internal stratification of the texts. Although the pace of studies on

---

Culture and Civilization of Ancient India in Historical Outline, pp. 100–4; R.S. Sharma, *Material Culture and Social Formations in Ancient India*, pp. 106–10.

[4] H. Oldenberg, *The Buddha: His life, His Doctrine, His Order*, p. 17; T.W. Rhys Davids, *The Dialogues of the Buddha*, p. 102; M. Weber, *The Religion of India*, pp. 225–7; R. Thapar, *History of India*, Vol. 1, p. 68; R.S. Sharma, *Material Culture and Social Formations in Ancient India*, p. 124.

[5] R. Fick; *The Social Organization of North-East India in Buddha's Time*; Ratilal Mehta, *Pre-Buddhist India*; A.N. Bose, *The Social and Rural Economy of North-East India*.

the subject of stratification of the texts is far from satisfactory, some progress has been made in recent years. We outline below the present knowledge on the stratification of the Buddhist texts.

Rhys Davids, Winternitz, and Law[6] place the *Vinaya* and the first four *Nikāyas* in approximately the same chronological stratum, and treat them as having more or less reached their present shape before the Mauryan period, although they do so for different reasons. This dating has been arrived at on the basis of the internal unity of the texts. Rhys Davids places the works mentioned above as having been compiled approximately a hundred years after the Buddha's death.[7] An important factor in the pre-Mauryan dating of the *Vinaya* and the first four *Nikāyas* of the *Sutta Piṭaka* is the reference to seven selected passages of the Pāli canon in the Bhābhra edict of Aśoka. According to Rhys Davids, two of the titles are ambiguous, four others are from the four *Nikāyas*, and the remaining one is from the *Sutta Nipāta*.[8] Rhys Davids argues that the literature in which the passages are found are older than the inscriptions themselves. It has also been suggested that the fifth *Nikāya* of the *Sutta Piṭaka*, which contains miscellaneous texts, does not appear to have been recognized by schools other than the *Theravāda*,[9] and is therefore likely to have been a later supplementary *Nikāya*.

More recent research has refined the work of Rhys Davids, Winternitz and Law but has confirmed the pre-Mauryan dating of the bulk of the *Vinaya* and *Sutta Piṭaka*. Pande has devoted considerable attention to the problem of the stratification of the Pāli canon and places the *Nikāyas* of the *Sutta Piṭaka*, in particular, to a period when the sects, at least in all important doctrinal matters, were still one. Pande dates them before the convening of the Third Council in the third century B.C. Since the *Vinaya* does not mention the Third Council he suggests that it too had reached completion in the first two centuries after Buddha. However, Pande also points out that particular versions of the *Nikāyas* contain much editorial retouching, addition, and expurgation. In addition, Pande has

[6] T.W. Rhys Davids, 'Early History of the Buddhists' in E.J. Rapson (ed.), *Cambridge History of India*, Vol. I, p. 171; M. Winternitz, *A. History of Indian Literature*, Vol. II, p. 15; B.C. Law, *History of Pāli Literature*, Vol. I, p. 42.

[7] T.W. Rhys David, op. cit., p. 171.

[8] Ibid., pp. 171–2.

[9] G.C. Pande, *Studies in the Origin of Buddhism*, p. 7; N.N. Wagle, *Society at the Time of the Buddha*, p. 2.

attempted to analyse the earlier and later strata within the *Nikāyas*.[10]

Similarly, on the basis of a study of Pāli metre, Warder has suggested that a comparison with the Prākrit inscriptions shows that the Pāli language is closest to the early records and may therefore be regarded as having flourished in, and probably before, the Mauryan period. According to him, 'The canonical texts have the appearance of standing close to a living language rather than that of an artificial production in a dead language like their commentaries, and would therefore seem to belong to a period when the language flourished.'[11]

Following Pande and Warder, Wagle has accepted the major portions of the *Sutta Piṭaka* and *Vinaya Piṭaka* as pre-Aśokan. He treats the first four *Nikāyas* and the *Vinaya* material as being a reliable guide to conditions between 500–300 B.C. In addition, Wagle has accepted the *Sutta Nipāta*, a text listed in the *Khuddaka Nikāya*, as belonging to the earliest stratum of Buddhist literature[12] on the basis of a study of the *Sutta Nipāta* by Jayawickrame. Jayawickrame remarks, 'The social conditions reflected in the *Sutta Nipāta* regarding people and castes, countries and towns, *brāhmaṇas* and sacrifices are no different from those in the *Nikāyas*'.[13] The identification of one of the passages of the Aśokan inscription with the *Sutta Nipāta* may be cited as an additional reason to include the *Sutta Nipāta* among the earliest strata of Buddhist literature.

This study follows a similar division of the Pāli canon as outlined by Pande, Warder, Wagle and Jayawickrame. The main sources for the present analysis are the *Vinaya Piṭaka*; the first four *Nikāyas* of the *Sutta Piṭaka*, i.e., the *Dīgha Nīkāya, Majjhima Nikāya, Saṁyutta Nikāya*, and the *Aṅguttara Nikāya*; and the *Sutta Nipāta*. We have also occasionally used the *Jātakas*, the commentaries on the Pāli canon; and the later chronicles, but this is done with the utmost caution and each instance of their use is specifically pointed out. The factor of internal unity is the major clue to the dating of the texts and is particularly relevant in the chapter on the *gahapati* and for understanding social categories generally.

[10] G.C. Pande, *Studies in the Origins of Buddhism*, pp. 12–16.

[11] A.K. Warder, *Pāli Metre*, p. 5.

[12] N.N. Wagle, *Society at the Time of the Buddha*, p. 3.

[13] N.A. Jayawickrame, *Analysis of the Sutta Nipāta*, cited in N.N. Wagle, *Society at the Time of the Buddha*, pp. 2–3.

When we first began this study we examined in considerable detail the parallel sources available in the Brahmanical and Jaina traditions. Unfortunately we have been unable to use this material exhaustively because the focus of our work, as it developed, required a degree of specificity which led us to concentrate on the Buddhist literature. We have however attempted to draw parallels or contrasts with the Brahmanical and Jaina sources wherever possible. We have also used the earliest body of inscriptions available although they belong to the period 200 B.C. to 200 A.D. This material has been used to substantiate the conclusions on social stratification derived from the early Pāli literature. The regional spread of the texts takes account mainly of eastern U.P., Bihar and central India, while the inscriptions were found scattered over central and western India.

Key terms in the Buddhist sources

The progress made in the field of textual studies has been particularly relevant for our analysis of the Buddhist texts. It has helped us isolate some of the key terms which appear in Buddhist literature and to analyse their significance as fundamental concepts in Buddhism. Many of these terms were part of a floating vocabulary common to all the religious traditions of the sixth century B.C. However the unique feature of the period is the particular use of certain terms which a specific religious tradition adopted in the language of its discourse. A few examples will reiterate our point here.

The Buddhist and Jaina literature use a variety of terms to denote a spiritually elevated person, such as: *arahant, tathāgata, brāhmaṇa, jina, mahāvīra* and *tīrthaṅkara*, among others. Of these *arahant* and *tathāgata* became identified with Buddhist discourse, and *jina* and *mahāvīra* with the Jaina.

The term *brāhmaṇa* was used by both systems as representing a spiritually elevated person. The word *brāhmaṇa* occasionally appeared in this sense in Brahmanical literature, but most often it represented just a social category. In Buddhist and Jaina literature the term appears in both senses. Each system had clearly invested the terms with their own special connotation.

The use of the term *tīrthaṅkara* is even more interesting. Its literal meaning is 'ford-maker', or one who helps to bridge a ford. In the process of its adoption the word came to be particularly associated with the Jainas, who used it in its literal sense for a great man, but especially for the leaders of the Jainas. The Buddhists, on the other hand, derived the term *titthiya* from it, probably because of its clear identification with the Jainas, and used the term to describe a rival body of teachers and their sects who were also opposed to the Brahmanical system, like the Buddhists thinkers. However the *titthiyas* between them advocated a variety of philosophical teachings. The Buddhists therefore used the term *añña titthiya* to indicate sects other than their own, which suggests that they considered themselves to be *titthiyas* along with the others, but also regarded themselves as distinct from the other sects at the same time. Since *añña titthiyas* were clearly rivals of Buddhists, the latter managed to convey both their identity and their separation from the other sects through the use of the term *titthiya*.

Similarly, the words *ārya* and *cakkavatti* already existed in sixth century B.C. vocabulary, but the Buddhists gave both terms a special colour. *Ārya* always represented a value and referred to noble virtues, rather than to race. The ideal disciple, for example, was called an *ariyasāvaka*. The word *cakkavatti* which, along with other terms such as *samrāṭ* and *sārvabhauma*, denoted a universal ruler or a king who established his sovereignty to the physical limits of India, became a key concept in Buddhism. The term *cakkavatti* was popularized by Buddhists, and it ultimately became the most widely used word for a paramount sovereign in the Indian tradition.

The terms *gahapati* and *seṭṭhi*, on the other hand, were notable for another phenomenon: the need for the vocabulary of the sixth century B.C. to adapt itself to contemporary requirements. In both cases their connotation changed; from being words which had originally been devoid of any economic implications they came to represent clear economic categories. The new socio-economic situation required specific terms to denote the emerging economic categories. Coining new words is a conscious process which was less likely to occur in a gradually developing situation. Adaptation of words on the other hand could imperceptibly and naturally occur, transforming the original meaning of words in the course of time. This development is an indication not only of the needs of a given society but reflects also the process by which the terms acquired their new meaning, and reveals the relationship between the old connotation and the new one.

CHAPTER II

The Political, Economic, Social, and Religious Environment at the Time of the Buddha

SECTION I: THE POLITICAL BACKGROUND OF BUDDHISM

Monarchies, gaṇa-saṅghas *and state formation*

The political system at the time of the Buddha was characterized by the existence of two distinct forms of government: monarchical kingdoms and republican territories (*gaṇa-saṅghas*). Sixteen such political units are mentioned in Buddhist and Jaina literature. The *Aṅguttara Nikāya* depicts the country as being divided into '*solasa mahājanapada*',[1] and a variant of this appears in the *Bhagavatī Sūtra* of the Jainas,[2] although the Jaina evidence has been described as a later version and therefore a depiction of later times.[3] The geographical location of these units is itself interesting with the monarchical kingdoms occupying the Ganga-Yamuna valley and the *gaṇa-saṅghas* being located closer to the foothills of the Himalaya. The largest of the *gaṇa-saṅghas* was the Vajjian confederacy[4] which controlled the whole of the area north of the river Ganga and east of the river Gandak. The origin of these distinct republican units has been explained as a reaction against the growing power of the monarchies in the later Vedic period and the divinity beginning to be attributed to the king. The republican tradition of the earlier Ṛg-Vedic period may not have submitted to this change, and a section of the people probably moved away eastwards in order to preserve their political system. This became manifest in the republican

[1] *A.N.*, III, pp. 349–50, 353, 357; *A.N.*, I, p. 197. The sixteen kingdoms are Aṅga, Magadha, Kāsī, Kosala, Vajji, Mallā, Ceti, Vaṁsa, Kuru, Pañcāla, Machchha, Surasena, Assaka, Avānti, Gandhāra, and Kamboja.

[2] H.C. Ray Choudhari, *Political History of Ancient India*, p. 85.

[3] Ibid., p. 86.

[4] The exact composition of the Vajjian confederacy is a matter of controversy although there is general consensus regarding its status as a confederacy.

institutions that flourished during the period of the Buddha and would account for Megasthenes' view that some of the republics had been ruled by kings in the past.[5]

Of the monarchies listed among the *solasa mahājanapada*, four appear to have been more important than the others.[6] These were Magadha, Kosala, Vaṁsa, and Avānti, and three of them occupied contiguous territory in the Ganga-Yamuna valley. All four were in conflict with each other, and this conflict forms the main feature of the political history of the period. There was also conflict between the monarchies and the *gaṇa-saṅghas*. The picture that emerges from the Buddhist and Jaina literature is one of expanding horizons and political consolidation, the beginnings of a process which ended with the establishment of the Mauryan empire.[7] This process of political consolidation and expansion led to the need for an efficient administrative system, through which political control could be effectively exercised. Apart from the increasing references to *amātyas*, the period marks the beginnings of a vast bureaucracy. Bimbisāra, the king of Magadha, is depicted as assembling 80,000 *gāmikas* or village superintendents and issuing instructions to them.[8] He also kept track of the state's resources, including the timber in the forests, and on one occasion censured the *bhikkhu*, Dhaniya, for encroaching upon it.[9] Bimbisāra appears to have been the first known king in India to realize the value of an efficient bureaucracy. In the light of this understanding it is not surprising that Megasthenes identified the overseers and councillors as a distinct social group.[10] They were obviously a large enough category to make their separate presence noticeable.

In this movement towards expansion and consolidation the keynote was politics unhampered by moral restraint. This is exemplified by Ajātasattu, who eliminated his father[11] in order to gain political control of the embryonic Magadhan empire, after which he embarked upon a career of aggressive expansionism. According to the *Bhaddasāla Jātaka*, Viḍūḍabha did the same with his father

[5] J.P. Sharma, *Ancient Indian Republics*, p. 239.

[6] T.W. Rhys Davids, *Buddhist India*, pp. 1–2.

[7] According to N.R. Ray the developments in the Ganga basin during the period between 600 B.C. and 320 B.C. represent the long and arduous process of state formation (N.R. Ray, 'Technology and Social Change in Early Indian History', *Purātattva*, Vol. VIII, 1975–6, p. 136). See also R. Thapar, *From Lineage to State*.

[8] *Mahāvagga*, p. 199. [9] *Pārājika*, pp. 53–4.

[10] R.C. Majumdar, *Classical Accounts of India*, p. 226.

[11] *Mahāvagga*, pp. 290–1; *D.N.*, I, p. 75.

Pasenadi, the king of Kosala.[12] It is significant that marriage alliances were an aid to the expansion of the kingdom, but kinship ties were no barrier to war and political expansion. Ajātasattu carried on a long battle[13] with King Pasenadi of Kosala, who was his uncle,[14] and destroyed the Vajjians even though a Vajjian princess was one of his father's queens.

The pattern of expansion indicates the compulsions of economic and strategic factors. Kāsī, one of the sixteen *mahājanapadas*, seems to have already lost its independence at the time of the Buddha, since it features among the dominions of Pasenadi.[15] Subsequently, possession over Kāsī was the bone of contention between Kosala and Magadha. Kāsī was a flourishing city famed for its luxury items, particularly fine cloth, and therefore important for its revenue. It was also famed for its *mālās* (garlands), *gandha* (perfume), *vilepana* (lotion), and *candana* (sandal wood).[16] Its strategic location on the Ganga would have added to its significance. The conflict between Magadha under Ajātasattu and the Vajjians can be traced to similar compulsions of physical control over a port located on the Ganga over which both territories laid their claim.[17] A long and protracted, but planned,[18] war was fought by Ajātasattu before the Vajjians could be subjugated.[19] Earlier, Bimbisāra had already annexed Aṅga where he had granted lands to a *brāhmaṇa*.[20] Further, Magadha appears as a joint territory along with Aṅga in the *Dīgha Nikāya*.[21] The annexation of Aṅga had enabled Bimbisāra to gain control over its wealthy river port of Campa, which is listed as one of the six great cities of north-eastern India.[22] Later Pāli sources say it was famed for its flourishing trade with Suvaṇṇabhūmi.[23] The

[12] *The Jātakas*, tr. by H.T. Francis, Vol. III, pp. 95–6.

[13] *S.N.*, I, p. 82.

[14] According to one version Pasenadi was Ajātasattu's maternal uncle (*Jātaka*, ed. by V. Fausboll, Vol. III, p. 121).

[15] The *Aṅguttara Nikāya* says, 'as far as the Kāsī-Kosalans extend, as far as the rule of Pasenadi the Kosalan *rāja* extends, therein Pasenadi the Kosalan *rāja* is reckoned Chief' (*G.S.*, V., p. 40; *A.N.*, IV, p. 145).

[16] *M.N.*, II, p. 358.

[17] A.L. Basham, 'Ajātasattu's War with the Lichchhavis', *Studies in Indian History and Culture*, p. 73.

[18] This is evident from the references to the fortification of Pātaligāma in the *Dīgha Nikāya* (*D.N.*, II, p. 70).

[19] A.L. Basham, 'Ajātasattu's War with the Lichchhavis', *Studies in Ancient History and Culture*, p. 75.

[20] *D.N.*, II, p. 152. [21] *D.N.*, I, p. 97. [22] *D.N.*, II, p. 113.

[23] G.P. Malala-Sekhara, *Dictionary of Pali Proper Names*, Vol. I, p. 856.

location of all these places indicates the value of complete control over the Ganga river system, which was heightened in an era when river transport was certainly cheaper and easier than transport by land.[24]

The conflict between the monarchical kingdoms and the *gaṇa-saṅghas* had an additional dimension in that the *gaṇa-saṅghas* were fighting with their backs to the wall, in order to preserve their distinct political and socio-economic structure. Buddhist and Jaina literature indicates their gradual decline in the face of the aggressively expansionist policies of the kingdoms of Kosala and Magadha. The process probably began with the acceptance of overlordship of a monarchy by the *gaṇa-saṅghas* as the first stage of its loss of independence. This appears to have occurred in the case of the Bhaggas of Suṁsumāragiri, in whose territory Bodhi *rājakumāra* of Vaṁsa had already built a palace at the time of the Buddha.[25] The kingdom of Kosala which had possibly exercised overall sovereignty over many of the *gaṇa-saṅghas* in its vicinity began a campaign under Viḍūḍabha for tighter control, as indicated by his somewhat wanton attack upon the Sākyas.[26]

There are indications that the *gaṇa-saṅghas* were conscious of the implications of the expansionist policies of the kingdoms. Determined to preserve their own way of life and constitution, which they saw being seriously threatened, they formed a confederation of *gaṇa-saṅghas* to resist the imperialist ambitions of the new rulers of Kosala and Magadha.[27] According to Basham, the attack on the Sākyans by Viḍūḍabha probably had the effect of rousing the suspicion and hostility of other tribal republican tributary units of Kosala, including the Mallās, who were incensed at the destruction of the Sākyans. Unwilling to accept Kosala's tightening control, they took advantage of Viḍūḍabha's death to throw off their allegiance and allied themselves to the Vajjians, who were by far the largest and strongest *gaṇa-saṅgha* in the region.[28] It is likely that the refer-

[24] See also A.L. Basham, 'Ajātasattu's War with the Lichchhavis', *Studies in Indian History and Culture*, p. 77.

[25] *M.N.*, II, p. 318; *D.P.P.N.*, Vol. II, p. 316.

[26] *Jātaka*, tr. by H.T. Francis, Vol. IV, p. 96. Also see A.L. Basham, 'Ajātasattu's War with the Lichchhavis', *Studies in Indian History and Culture*, p. 76

[27] H.C. Raychoudhari, *Political History of Ancient India*, p. 188.

[28] A.L. Basham, 'Ajātasattu's War with the Lichchhavis', *Studies in Ancient History and Culture*, pp. 76–7.

ence in Jaina literature to the eighteen *gaṇa-rājās* of Kāsī and Kosala[29] joining the Vajjian confederation against Ajātasattu resulted from a common recognition by the *gaṇa-saṅghas* of the dangers they faced, especially from the expanding monarchical kingdoms.

Although there is considerable controversy on the nature and extent of the democratic content within the *gaṇa-saṅghas*,[30] there is no doubt that they represented a political system distinct from that of the monarchical kingdoms.[31] The *Avadāna Śataka* speaks of merchants from Northern India, who, when visiting a southern kingdom, were asked by a king, 'who is the king there?' The merchants replied, 'Some countries are under *gaṇas* and some are under kings' (*kechid deśā gaṇādhīnāh: kechid rāj-ādhīnā iti*).[32] Jayaswal holds that this statement shows royal rule to be opposed to *gaṇa* rule,[33] and Bhandarkar suggests that the political rule of one is being contrasted with that of the many.[34] Similarly, in the *Ācārāṅga Sūtra*, Jaina monks and nuns were prohibited from visiting an *arāya* (country without a king), a *juva rāya* (country with a young king), a *do rajja* (government by two rulers), and a *gaṇa-rāya* (where the *gaṇa* or multitude is the ruling authority).[35] From a passage in the *Majjhima Nikāya* it is clear that these distinct political units were sovereign bodies since their sovereignty is equated with that of the kings of Kosala and Magadha.[36] This distinct form of government came to be referred to by the terms *gaṇa* and *saṅgha* in the sixth century B.C.[37] Some scholars seek to distinguish between the *gaṇa* and

[29] *Kalpa Sūtra*, tr. by Hermann Jacobi, *Jaina Sūtras*, S.B.E., Vol. XXII, p. 266; *Nirayāvalikā Sūtra*, ed. by A.S. Gopani and V.J. Choksi, p. 19.

[30] A considerable body of literature exists on the political structure of the *gaṇa-saṅghas*, in spite of which controversy persists. Those who have written on the subject include K.P. Jayaswal, *Hindu Polity*; A.S. Altekar, *State and Government in Ancient India*; D.R. Bhandarkar, *Ancient History of India*; and J.P. Sharma, *Ancient Indian Republics*.

[31] We are concentrating here on a review of the political system of the *gaṇa-saṅghas* to the exclusion of the monarchical kingdoms which will feature in the chapter on Kingship (Chapter VI).

[32] *Avadāna Śataka*, ed. by J.S. Speyer, Vol. II, p. 103.

[33] K.P. Jayaswal, *Hindu Polity*, p. 26.

[34] D.R. Bhandarkar, *Ancient History of India*, p. 147.

[35] *Ācārāṅga Sūtra*, tr. by Hermann Jacobi, *Jaina Sūtras*, S.B.E., Vol. XXII, 1973, p. 138.

[36] *M.N.*, I, p. 284.

[37] J.P. Sharma, *Ancient Indian Republics*, p. 9.

saṅgha,[38] but the terms are used synonymously in the *Majjhima Nikāya*, and in the *Aṣṭādhyāyī* of Pāṇini,[39] as well as in the Sanskrit version of the *Mahāparinibbāna Sutta*.[40] Altekar has argued that the terms *gaṇa* and *saṅgha* were used in the same sense to denote a form of government where power was vested in a group of people, as opposed to monarchy where power was vested in one person.[41] We have used the term jointly to denote a form of government in which sovereign power was vested in a collectivity rather than in the individual.

Khattiya *clans and the* gaṇa-saṅghas

The most striking feature of the *gaṇa-saṅghas* was their association with the *khattiyas*. From a statistical analysis of the early Buddhists,[42] it appears that the majority of the identifiable *khattiyas* in early Buddhist texts are located in the *gaṇa-saṅghas*; only a few references occur to *khattiyas* as members of the *rāja kulas* in the monarchical kingdoms. The *Arthaśāstra* also refers to an association between *khattiyas* and the Lichchhavis and Vajjis, referring to them as having equal rank and position with the great *kṣatriyas* of northern India, i.e. the Madras in the west, the Kuru-Pañcālas in the central region, and the Mallās in the east.[43] Varma has hinted at the possibility of a connection between the *kṣatriyas* and the republican form of government.[44] The *khattiyas* in the *gaṇa-saṅghas* are almost invariably referred to by their respective clan names, such as Lichchhavi, Sākya, Mallā, etc., but there is no doubt about their status as *khattiyas*. In the *Mahāparinibbāna Sutta* various clans come forward and demand a share of the Buddha's ashes on the ground that they were *khattiyas* like the Buddha. It is significant that all the *khattiya* claimants except Ajātasattu were associated with the *gaṇa-saṅghas*.[45] Numerous other instances can be cited. For example, the Buddha is referred to as a high-born *khattiya* in the *Sutta Nipāta*,[46]

[38] K.P. Jayaswal, *Hindu Polity*, p. 24.
[39] *Aṣṭādhyāyī of Pāṇini*, ed. and tr. by S.C. Vasu, Vol. I, p. 513.
[40] J.P. Sharma, *Republics in Ancient India*, p. 10n.
[41] A.S. Altekar, *State and Government in Ancient India*, pp. 109–10.
[42] See Chapter V below and Appendix C for details.
[43] *Arthaśāstra of Kauṭilya*, ed. by R.P. Kangle, Vol. I, p. 244.
[44] V.P. Varma, *Hindu Political Thought and its Metaphysical Foundations*, p. 31.
[45] *D.N.*, II, pp. 126–7.
[46] *Sutta Nipāta, Khuddaka Nikāya*, Vol. I, pp. 68–9.

and Trisalā, sister of the Lichchhavi leader of Vesāli, is called *kṣatriyānī*, and her husband Siddhārtha of the Ñatrikas is also described as a *kṣatriya* in the *Kalpa Sūtra*.[47]

We may draw attention to the fact that the territories of the *gaṇa-sangha* were actually known by the clans that occupied them. Significantly, the use of the clan name was a prerogative only of the *khattiyas* and it was never used for other inhabitants of the *gaṇa-saṅgha*, such as the artisans and the *brāhmaṇas*, whose occasional presence is noticed there. Thus Upāli the barber is not called a Sākyan[48] although he lived in Sākyan territory. Nor is Cunda the *kammāraputta* (son of a metal-smith worker) referred to as a Mallā.[49] Similarly, the *brāhmaṇas* of Khomadussa in the Sākyan territory are not referred to as members of the Sākyan clan.[50] It has also been argued that collective power in these territories was vested in the *khattiya* clan composing the *gaṇa-saṅgha*, and that they had sovereignty over other social groups inhabiting the territory of the *gaṇa-saṅgha*.[51] Sovereignty therefore extended over the territory and not merely over the members of the clan.[52]

The prerogative of the use of the clan name only to the *khattiyas* is related to the right to exercise power, which the *non-khattiyas* did not possess. On the basis of a reference in Pāṇini, Agrawala has suggested that not all members of the *saṅgha* were entitled to exercise political power, which was the privilege only of the governing class. He says: 'It appears that the descendants of the pioneer *kṣatriyas* who had settled on the land and founded the *janapada* treated political sovereignty as their privilege which they transmitted in

[47] *Kalpa Sūtra*, *Jaina Sūtras*, tr. by Hermann Jacobi, S.B.E. Vol. XXII, p. 226. More instances of *khattiyas* are recorded in Chapter V.

[48] *Cullavagga*, p. 281.

[49] *D.N.*, II, pp. 98–9.

[50] *S.N.*, I, p. 183. The *brāhmaṇas* of Khomadussa seem to have had definite identity of their own since they had their own *santhāgāra* or assembly hall in which they met. This suggests that they did not participate in the deliberations of the Sākyan assembly. The existence of the *santhāgāra* was itself a special feature of the *gaṇa-saṅghas*. It is a technical term which never appears in the context of the monarchies. All the *santhāgāras* were located in the capitals of the territories of the respective clans (T.W. Rhys Davids, *D.B.*, I, p. 113n.). It may also be noted that unlike the Sākyans the *brāhmaṇas* of Khomadussa were antagonistic to the Buddha. They addressed the Buddha as *mundaka and samaṇaka* to indicate their disapproval of him (*S.N.*, I, p. 183).

[51] K.P. Jayaswal, *Hindu Polity*, p. 394.

[52] D.R. Bhandarkar, *Ancient History of India*, p. 161.

their families from generation to generation'.[53] While it is probable that only descendants of the pioneer *khattiyas* wielded power, all *khattiyas* in a *gaṇa-saṅgha* were related to each other and believed themselves to be descended from a common ancestor.[54] All would therefore be descendants of the pioneer *khattiyas*. This is very evident from Buddha's references to his Sākyan kinsmen who appear to be very closely connected to each other in a network of relationships. Drekmeier has pointed out that the lineage principle was the basis of the political system in tribal organizations (or the *gaṇa-saṅghas*), and that territory generally corresponded to kinship ties.[55] He elucidates his argument with the example of certain societies such as the Nuer, Tallensi and Logoli in modern Africa where kinship ties play an important role in political organization, although political relations are not necessarily coterminous with kinship organization. We endorse this view as an important characteristic of the *gaṇa-saṅghas*. In the light of the discussion outlined here, it appears that all *khattiya* clan members were associated with the collective exercise of power although the exact method may be unclear to us.

In this connection a passage in the *Bhaddasāla Jātaka* is noteworthy. It depicts the existence of a specially protected tank at Vesāli which was used for the *abhiseka* (consecration) of the families of the *gaṇa-rāja*. The passage which reads *vesāli nagare gaṇa rāja kulānang abhiseka maṅgala pokkharaṇī*[56] has been understood as describing the consecration of the *rāja kulas* of the *gaṇa* (*gaṇasya rāja kula*); but Adhir Chakravarti argues that it should be understood as *gaṇarājasya kulānang* or families of the *gaṇa rāja*.[57] According to him, this also explains a passage in the *Lalita Vistara* which states that every Lichchhavi regards himself as a *rājā* in the Vajjian republic.[58] In our opinion *all* Lichchhavi families of the Vajjian *gaṇa-saṅgha* participated in the *abhiseka* ceremony because all Lichchhavi families

[53] V.S. Agrawala, *India as known to Pāṇini*, p. 428.

[54] *D.N.*, I, p. 51; see also A.S. Altekar, *State and Government in Ancient India*, p. 136.

[55] Charles Drekmeier, *Kingship and Community in Early India*, p. 93n.

[56] *Jātaka*, ed. by V. Fausboll, p. 148.

[57] Adhir Chakravarti, 'The Federal Experiment in India', *Journal of Ancient Indian History*, Vol. XI, 1977–8, p. 34.

[58] *Ekaika eva mānyate ahaṁ rājā ahaṁ rājeti* (*Lalita Vistara*, ed. by Lefmann, Vol. I, p. 21).

would be equally entitled to participate in the collective exercise of power.

The suggestion that power was wielded only by the *khattiya* clan members is supported by the evidence of the *Jātakas*. In a dispute between the *dāsa-kammakaras* of the Sākyan and Koliyan clans, the *dāsa-kammakaras* go back and report to their respective masters, who then deliberate on the problem. There are no indications that the *dāsa-kammakaras* participated in the deliberations.[59] Jayaswal deduces from his reading of the sources that the slaves and workmen who were inhabitants of *gaṇa-saṅghas* were categories to whom citizenship or political participation did not apply.[60] The political structure of the *gaṇa-saṅghas* was also related to their social structure, but this is an aspect which will be discussed in greater detail in Chapter III. What should be noted here is the fact that the social organization of the *gaṇa-saṅghas* was comparatively simple—with a preponderantly *khattiya* population, and a marginal non-*khattiya* population composed primarily of *brāhmaṇas*, artisans and the *dāsa-kammakaras*. Of the three non-*khattiya* categories in the *gaṇa-saṅghas*, the *dāsa-kammakaras* were numerically more significant since they represented the base of the working population in the *gaṇa-saṅghas*.

It may thus be argued that, at least in the Buddhist literature, the *khattiyas* actually exercise power, either as members of the *gaṇa-saṅghas* where they wield collective power, or by association as members of the *rāja kulas* in the monarchical kingdoms. In this context we may draw attention to a passage in the *Ambaṭṭha Sutta* where it appears that all *khattiyas* were entitled to receiving the consecration of the *abhiseka* ceremony which was normally associated with the actual sanction to rule (*khattiyā khattiyābhisekana abhisiñcheyyang*).[61] This association conforms to the original meaning of *kṣatriya* as derived from *kṣatra*, which Keith translated as sovereignty, and which Hocart renders as the Roman imperium.[62] Hocart has pointed out that the tradition of describing the *kṣatriya* as a warrior is based upon later texts and that the primitive meaning is connected with kingship, or, in other words, with power.[63] Var-

[59] The *Jātakas*, ed. by V. Fausboll, Vol. II, p. 413.

[60] According to K.P. Jayaswal citizenship was a prerogative of 'free' men (*Hindu Polity*, p. 98; see also J.P. Sharma, *Republics in Ancient India*, p. 112).

[61] *D.N.*, I, p. 85.

[62] A.M. Hocart, *Caste*, p. 37.

[63] Ibid., p. 34.

ma treats Keith's translation of sovereignty as acceptable if it is used in the general sense of power,[64] and this is exactly the way in which the *khattiya* is represented in the Buddhist texts. This feature of the *khattiyas* was also noticed by Fick who, in many scattered references, implied that the *khattiyas* were associated with the actual exercise of power.[65]

The most significant political phenomenon, to which the Buddha was a witness, was the gradual decline of the *gaṇa-saṅghas*, and the corresponding rise of territorial units led by the kingdoms of Kosala and Magadha. Both features played a crucial role in the development of Buddhist political thought and of the Buddhist *saṅgha*. Whereas in the past the shift had been from monarchies to *gaṇa-saṅghas*, in the sixth century B.C. a shift was taking place in the reverse direction. Ling has suggested that the growth of individualism[66] was responsible for the decline of the *gaṇa-saṅghas*, but there were other socio-economic forces which explain their collapse and we must now turn to an analysis of these forces.

Explanation of decline of gaṇa-saṅghas and rise of territorial units.

SECTION II: ECONOMY AND SOCIETY AT THE TIME OF THE BUDDHA

Expansion of agriculture

A striking feature of the economic and social system of the period is the tremendous expansion of the economy. In many ways the period provided the basis for the kind of economic development that occurred over the next 500 years. It was characterized by important agrarian changes which, in turn, influenced the social and political forces of the time. There is considerable evidence of agriculture having now firmly become the pivot of the economy. The clearing of the land and its preparation for cultivation had been facilitated by the increasing availability and use of iron, a fact attested by numerous archaeological excavations and their historical analyses. A great deal of attention has been focused on the theme since Kosambi[67] argued that the large-scale clearing of forests in the

[64] V.P. Varma, *Hindu Political Thought and its Metaphysical Foundations*, p. 49.

[65] R. Fick, *The Social and Economic Organisation of North-East India in Buddha's Time*, pp. 79–81.

[66] T. Ling, *The Buddha*, p. 62.

[67] D.D. Kosambi, 'Ancient Kosala and Magadha', *J.B.B.R.A.S.*, Vol. XXVII, 1952, pp. 180–213; and 'The Beginning of the Iron Age in India', *J.E.S.H.O.*, Vol. VI, pt. III, 1963, pp. 309–18.

Gangetic valley could not have been undertaken without the use of iron.[68] The point has been restated since then by other scholars and we need merely summarize the findings of archaeologists and historians on this theme.

Early recognition of the relationship between iron and the beginnings of a new civilization was suggested by Y.D. Sharma.[69] Later it was pointed out that the archaeological evidence for iron predates the emergence of Northern Black Polished ware (hereafter NBP ware) pottery in the Ganga Valley,[70] and that NBP ware itself is associated with the second urbanization in India. NBP ware is also characteristic of the age of the Buddha. Sharma says: 'In upper India a number of widely distributed sites of this period are marked by the occurrence of a highly individual shiny ware, often black, known to archaeologists as NBP ware'. Its duration is roughly defined between 500 and 300 B.C. (although some archaeologists now tend to push the date back by a couple of centuries), and Sharma points out that the Ganges plain was the centre of its dispersal. He also suggests that, broadly speaking, it was co-eval with the supremacy of Magadha.[71]

Expansion in agricultural produce is similarly related to the enhanced use of iron implements, including ploughshares, the sickle,

[68] N.R. Ray ('Technology and Social Change in Early Indian History', *Purāttatva,* Vol. VIII, 1975–6, p. 133) has questioned the conclusion that large scale clearing of the Gangetic valley could not have taken place without the use of iron. He argues against the assumption that the introduction of iron technology and iron implements in the Ganga-Yamuna valley, before 320 B.C., were of such a scale as to induce the sort of social changes which are held to have been triggered off by the technological changes associated with the use of iron (R.S. Sharma, 'Material Milieu of the Birth of Buddhism', paper presented at the 29th International Congress of Orientalists, Paris, 16–22 July 1973). According to Ray, archaeological evidence available to date does not indicate any large scale clearance of the jungles through the use of iron technology. He argues that iron technology was neither qualitatively nor quantitatively diversified enough to bring about significant social changes. Earlier D.K. Chakrabarti had pointed out that iron was responsible for stabilizing agriculture rather than initiating it. According to him, it was the basic technological element only from the sixth century B.C. onwards and not before (D.K. Chakrabarti, 'Beginning of Iron and Social Change in India', *Indian Studies Past and Present,* Vol. XIV, no. 4, 1973, pp. 336–8).

[69] Y.D. Sharma, 'Exploration of Historical Sites', *Ancient India,* Vol. IX, 1956, pp. 118–9.

[70] V.D. Misra, *Some Aspects of Indian Archaeology,* p. 85.

[71] Y.D. Sharma, 'Exploration of Historical Sites', *Ancient India,* Vol. IX, 1956, p. 119.

hoe and chopper, which are supported by archaeological evidence.[72] A survey of references relating to iron in early Indian literature has revealed beyond dispute the association of iron with the common people and thus with agriculture in the Gangetic Valley by about 700 B.C.[73] Further, it is suggested that there is a case for putting the beginnings of the use of iron in the Indo-Gangetic divide to about 800 B.C.[74] Buddhist texts also allude to the use of the iron plough for cultivation. The *Kasībhāradvāja Sutta of the Sutta Nipāta* gives the analogy of a ploughshare which having become heated during the day, hisses and smokes when plunged into water.[75] The analogy is repeated in the *Mahāvagga*.[76] Its use indicates a widespread familiarity with the iron plough and suggests that it was regularly employed in agriculture by the time of the Buddha.

The extension of agriculture in the middle Ganga plains is reflected in a variety of ways in Buddhist literature. A large range of crops has been tabulated by G.S.P. Misra, who has also collected information on the classification of land, the implements used, and the cycle of operations on the basis of references in the *Vinaya Piṭaka*.[77] The frequent use of agricultural similes[78] reinforces the importance of agriculture in society. Many of the *vinaya* rules themselves relate to crops, and the institution of the *vassā-vāsa* or the rain retreat was permitted by the Buddha when people complained against the damage caused to the new crops by the *bhikkhu's* incessant touring in the rainy season.[79] Although cattle keeping did not decrease very radically, it clearly became a subsidiary and ancillary occupation of agriculture. A passage in the *Saṁyutta Nikāya* reflects the Buddha's recognition of the importance of agriculture. In a conversation between a *deva* (deity) and the Buddha, the *deva* upholds the traditional view and remarks on the significance of cattle.

[72] S.P. Gupta, 'Two Urbanizations in India', *Purātattva*, Vol. VII, 1974, p. 55.

[73] D.K. Chakrabarti, 'Iron in Early Indian Literature', *J.R.A.S.*, 1979, no. I, p. 24.

[74] Ibid.

[75] *Sutta Nipāta, Khuddaka Nikāya*, Vol. I, p. 282.

[76] *Mahāvagga*, p. 241.

[77] G.S.P. Misra, *The Age of the Vinaya*, pp. 243–50.

[78] *M.N.*, I, p. 200; *A.N.*, I, pp. 213, 222, 224; *S.N.*, II, pp. 77, 284, 370. See also J.W. de Jong, 'The Background of Early Buddhism', *Journal of Indian Buddhist Studies*, Vol. XII, 1964, p. 39.

[79] *Mahāvagga*, p. 144.

In his reply, the Buddha favours agriculture as against pastoralism, and in this he was clearly reflecting the new values of the period.[80] Consequently, the possession of fields become an extremely valuable asset and is frequently reflected in the Buddhist texts.[81]

The extension of agriculture in the mid Ganga plains was primarily a rice phenomenon since the area was eminently suited to rice cultivation, particularly because of the year-long supply of water from the river Ganga. The method of paddy transplantation was probably learnt during this period.[82] The increase in rice cultivation and the decline in cattle rearing resulted in major dietary changes. On the basis of population research Ling suggests that there is a definite relationship between rice growing areas and a higher fertility rate, since the consumption of rice gruel allows children to be weaned earlier, thus enabling the mother to conceive again.[83] The Buddhist literature suggests that the increase in population is a sign of development and prosperity. The narratives speak of teeming cities with people jostling each other and of numerous settlements in the countryside, all of which are an index of a flourishing and prosperous kingdom.[84] The kingdom of Magadha is described as consisting of 80,000 *gāmas* but of course the significant point is that the economy could support the population even as it expanded.[85]

The period also witnessed the second urbanization of India. Archaeological evidence confirms the existence of a number of historical sites in the central Gangetic basin associated with the Buddhist tradition, and it is notable that most of them also disclose the presence of NBP ware.[86] Some excavations have been identified as places referred to in Buddhist literature such as Jetavana at Sāvatthi (Sahet-Maheth) and the Ghositārāma at Kosambī.[87] Other excavations in Raja Vishal Ka Garh (Basarh) in Muzzafarpur and Piprawa have been identified as the Vesāli and Kapilavatthu of

[80] *S.N.*, I, p. 8.

[81] *M.N.*, II, 136; *A.N.*, IV, p. 208. See also *Ācārāṅga Sūtra*, *Jaina Sūtras*, tr. by Hermann Jacobi, S.B.E., Vol. XXII, p. 19.

[82] R.S. Sharma, *Śūdras in Ancient India*, p. 95.

[83] Trevor Ling, The *Buddha*, p. 50.

[84] *D.N.*, II, p. 130; *G.S.*, III, p. 158.

[85] *Mahāvagga*, p. 199.

[86] Y.D. Sharma, 'Exploration of Historical Sites', *Ancient India*, Vol. IX, 1956, p. 142. It has been suggested that Buddha's alms bowl, seen by Fa-hien and described by him, was probably of NBP ware (M.D.N. Sahi, 'Stratigraphical Position of the NBP ware in the Upper Ganga Basin and its Date', *Purātattva*, Vol. VI, 1974, p. 93).

[87] Ibid., p. 145.

Buddhist literature.[88] The *Mahāparinibbāna Sutta* mentions six *mahānagaras* which were populated by many wealthy people. These were Campā, Rājagaha, Sāvatthi, Sāketa, Kosambī and Kāsi. Ānanda considers these *mahānagaras* worthy of being the scene of the Buddha's *parinibbāna*.[89] Similarly, Buddhist literature frequently mentions the existence of well fortified towns with city gates and wise wardens to watch over the entry and exit points.[90] There was considerable contact between these urban centres, and people are often described as visiting others cities on various kinds of business.[91] There are examples of people travelling for professional reasons too. The physician Jivaka went from Rājagaha to Taxila to train for his vocation.[92] On his way back he was able to sustain himself by curing patients living in the urban centres along the highway.[93] He was also especially sent for by princes and other wealthy urban dwellers in the large cities once he had established his reputation as a great physician.

The second urbanization

The expansion of agriculture and, consequently, of the economy as a whole was a major factor in the new phenomenon of urbanization. Cities cannot exist without some form of agricultural surplus, and it has been pointed out that there was some degree of movement in foodgrains along with other items of trade[94] during this period. In fact, the emergence of money itself has been related to the exchange or barter of agricultural produce. According to Joshi, the term for currency in early India, ***kārshāpaṇa*** or ***kahāpaṇa***, is derived from the verbal roots ***krish*** (to cultivate) and ***paṇ*** (to exchange, barter or bargain).[95]

The emergence of a more complex economy with a greater degree of specialization and the appearance of metallic money in the form of punch-marked coins also contributed to the expansion of trade. The beginnings of the corporate organization of trade are evident in the use of terms such as *saṅgha, gaṇa, seṇi* and *pūga*.[96]

[88] Ibid., p. 146. [89] *D.N.*, II, p. 113.
[90] *A.N.*, III, pp. 234–5; *G.S.*, I, p. 64; *K.S.*, V, p. 139.
[91] *Pācittiya*, p. 136. [92] *Mahāvagga*, p. 287. [93] Ibid., p. 288.
[94] S.P. Gupta, 'Two Urbanizations in India', *Purāttatva*, Vol. VII, 1974, p. 55.
[95] M.C. Joshi, 'Early Historical Urban Growth in India: Some Observations', *Purāttatva*, Vol. VII, 1974, p. 91n.
[96] *Pācittiya*, p. 302.

Trade routes were established and were called *vaṇippaṭhas*,[97] and caravan traffic made its appearance.[98] A number of market towns grew up along the trade routes forming linking points. Joshi has pointed to a verse in the *Sutta Nipāta* which enumerates a number of market towns on the trade route connecting Assaka with Magadha.[99] A number of similar trade routes connected the major trading centres, such as the route to the south from Rājagaha,[100] which in turn gave a decided fillip to urbanization.[101] Joshi has argued that urbanization began with the adoption of monetary exchange, and this was part of an economic phenomenon which transformed the barter-based economy of a vast rural area and linked it with the exchange structure of those days.[102] While the importance of economic and social factors, such as an agricultural base, increased importance of trade, growth of a merchant and artisan class, etc., are conceded as obvious features of any urban scene, Chakrabarti has argued that the spark that set off the process of early historical urban growth in cities such as Rājagaha, Vārānasi, Kosambī and Ujjayini was the factor of political power. He argues that the socio-economic factor could be effectively integrated within one social complex and given a centralized direction only under the aegis of a consolidated power structure.[103] This reasoning receives support from the examples of urbanization in the *gaṇa-saṅghas*. We have earlier mentioned the six *mahānagaras* of Buddhist literature—significantly all six cities were in monarchical kingdoms. Although Vesāli otherwise appears to be an important city it does not feature in the list. Perhaps it was not as large a trading centre as the six other cities. This would add support to our point that the *gaṇa-saṅghas* had a simpler social organization than the monar-

[97] *Mahāvagga*, p. 244. [98] *Pārājika*, p. 294.

[99] M.C. Joshi, 'Early Historical Urban Growth in India: Some Observations', *Purāttava*, Vol. VII, 1974, p. 90; *Sutta Nipāta, Khuddaka Nikāya*, I, p. 419.

[100] *Pācittiya*, pp. 113, 176.

[101] While the beginnings of trade made a definite appearance in our period it was to reach great heights and have its full impact only in the following era. Our period reflects what could be termed the 'take-off' stage for trade and commerce. This is consistent with the notion that an expansion in agricultural output has to precede an expansion in trade and commerce.

[102] M.C. Joshi, 'Early Historical Urban Growth in India: Some Observations', *Purāttatva*, Vol. VII, 1974, pp. 90–1.

[103] D.K. Chakrabarti, 'Some Theoretical Aspects of Early Urban Growth', *Purāttatva*, Vol. VII, 1974, p. 88.

chies, and that they did not produce a wide range of goods. But a more important reason for none of the cities of the *gaṇa-saṅghas* being listed as a *mahānagara* was that the *gaṇa-saṅghas* were suffering from problems of internal collapse. In contrast, the monarchies were marked by a period of political consolidation which probably provided a boost to the process of urbanization.

Of the six *mahānagaras* which were major political and commercial centres, the most important appear to have been Sāvatthi and Rājagaha. In the lifetime of the Buddha, Sāvatthi probably had an edge over Rājagaha, and it was there that the Buddha spent a large part of his teaching career. However, by the time he died, Rājagaha seems to have grown in importance because it was here that the first Buddhist Council was held.

Craft production and trade

Other concomitants of an expanding economy also began to make an appearance, and some of these features were used as similes by the Buddha. They include trade, interest and debts.[104] There are several references in the texts to metallurgy,[105] the construction of permanent structures,[106] and a very wide range of goods. Textiles, both silk and cotton,[107] leatherwork,[108] fine pottery,[109] ivory work,[110] and woodwork[111] all figure in the literature. This increase in the production of material goods was reflected in the numerous rules about the permitted articles of possession for the *bhikkhus* that also made their appearance in the texts.[112] A natural outcome of this growing complexity of the economy was expressed in the degree of specialization which became apparent during the period. The *Samaññaphala Sutta* of the *Dīgha Nikāya* lists a number of occupations that were commonly pursued.[113] There are 25 such occupations listed by the king, and these include a wide range of specialized skills.

Types of settlement

Apart from newly developed large urban centres, there were va-

[104] *A.N.*, II, p. 86; *A.N.*, I, p. 107; *A.N.*, III, pp. 65–7.
[105] *Cullavagga*, p. 225; *A.N.*, II, p. 286.
[106] *Cullavagga*, pp. 239–49. [107] *Pārājika*, p. 321.
[108] *Mahāvagga*, pp. 204–49.
[109] *Pārājika*, p. 348. [110] *Pācittiya*, p. 221. [111] *M.N.*, II, p. 371.
[112] *Cullavagga*, pp. 195ff. [113] *D.N.*, I, p. 52.

rious other settlements such as the *gāma, nigama* and *nagara*. According to Wagle,[114] although the *gāma* is treated as being equivalent to a village, in practice it was merely the smallest unit of settlement and could imply a ward, a hamlet, or even a temporary settlement. A *nigama* represented a settlement which was between a *gāma* and *nagara* and represented a large and more complex unit than the *gāma*. The *nagara* was a town which was frequently a fortified settlement and apart from the *mahānagaras*, was the largest unit of settlement in a *janapada*. Between each of these settlements, each of which was a unit of social recognition and constantly growing as a result of the expanding economy, lay the forest areas into which the *bhikkhus* frequently retreated for solitude. The *Vinaya* definition of the *arañña* states that, leaving aside the *gāma* and the outskirts of the *gāma*, the surrounding land was *arañña*.[115] Many of the towns mentioned in the texts had a *mahāvana* in the vicinity, but with the expansion of the cultivated area the forests were gradually diminishing, making way for new settlements.

The pattern of landholding

The expansion of agriculture brings us to an extremely significant aspect of the economy: the pattern of landholding. The problem of ownership of land continues to be one of the unresolved controversies of ancient India. However there are certain observations which have struck us during the course of our study, but in making them we shall restrict ourselves to the question of landholding.[116] Individual holdings had definitely appeared by the time of the Buddha, and most of the land was being farmed in this manner, at least in the monarchical kingdoms, as is evident from the *Aggañña Sutta* in which kingship originates with the emergence of separate fields. According to it the violation of rights to ownership of the fields leads to the need for a king. The idea of separate fields is reiterated in a parable which derides the folly of a man who neglects his own fields but thinks of weeding his neighbour's.[118] The *Milindapañha* gives us at least one method by which the rights over land origin-

[114] N.N. Wagle, *Society at the Time of the Buddha*, pp. 13–37.

[115] *Pārājika*, p. 62.

[116] J. Jolly has pointed to the distinction between ownership and possession in the law of property (J. Jolly, *Hindu Law and Custom*, p. 196).

[117] *D.N.*, III, pp. 72–3.

[118] A.N. Bose, *Social and Rural Economy of North India*, Vol. I, p. 17.

ated. It says that, when a man clears the land of its forest and prepares it for cultivation he establishes rights over it: '*yathā . . . koci puriso vanaṁ sodhetvā bhūmim nīharati tassa sā bhūmi ti jano voharati na cesa bhūmi tena pavatita taṁ bhūmiṁ kāranaṁ katvā bhūmi sāmiko nāma hoti*'[119] ('It is as when a man clears away the jungle and sets free a piece of land and the people say 'that is his land'. Not that the land is made by him. It is because he has brought the land into use that he is called the owner of the land.'[120]) This statement represents a very important principle in relation to private property and associates it with that of labour. It suggests that a person becomes entitled to the land *primarily* because he has put labour into it.[121] While a considerable amount of land was in the possession of peasant proprietors, which according to Mrs Rhys Davids represented the bulk of the holdings,[122] the king also appears to have been in direct control of some of it. This probably consisted of all the wastelands, forests and mines.[123] From this category of land the kings of Kosala and Magadha began to grant *brahmadeya* lands to the *brāhmaṇas*[124] which make their appearance in the Pāli canon. Such a view is supported by Radhakrishna Choudhary, who argues that *brahamadeya* lands were granted out of the royal domain or the crown lands, and these had nothing to do with the lands held by cultivators.[125] It may be noted that all the *brahmadeya* lands mentioned in the Pāli texts were granted by Pasenadi and Bimbisāra. The fact that these lands were a distinct category carrying a special connotation is evident from a stock passage in the Pāli canon describing *brahamadeya* lands as follows: '*tena kho pana samayena brāhmaṇo pokkarasādi ukkaṭṭang ajjhāvasati sattussadang, satinakaṭṭhodakang, sadhaññang, rājabhogang, rañña pasendinā kosalena dinnang rājadāyang brahmadeyyang*'.[126] ('At that time there dwelt at Ukkaṭṭha the *brāhmaṇa* Pokkharasādi, a spot teeming with life, with much grassland and woodland and

[119] *Milinda pañha* ed. by V. Trenckner, p. 219.

[120] A.N. Bose, *The Social and Rural Economy of North East India*, Vol. I, p. 15.

[121] Jayamal Rai, *The Rural-Urban Economy and Social Changes in Ancient India*, p. 15.

[122] C.A.F. Rhys Davids, 'Economic Conditions according to Early Buddhist Literature' in E.J. Rapson (ed.), *Cambridge History of India*, Vol. I, p. 176.

[123] A.S. Altekar, *State and Government in Ancient India*, p. 275.

[124] *D.N.*, I, p. 109; *D.N.*, I, p. 96; *M.N.*, II, p. 427; *D.N.*, I, p. 76.

[125] Radhakrishna Choudhary, 'Ownership of Land in Ancient India', *J.B.R.S.*, Vol. LIII, p. 32.

[126] *D.N.*, I, p. 76

corn, on a royal domain, granted him by King Pasenadi of Kosala as a royal gift, with power over it as if he were king'.)[127] The commentary to the *Majjhima Nikāya* explains *brahmadeya* as *seṭṭhadeya*, the best gift; and adds that once given the gift could not be taken back again.[128]

The implication of the statement *rāja bhogang* is not completely clear. It has been suggested that the lands were rent free and that the grantee was entitled to full usufructuary rights on it, rather than carrying administrative and political rights with the grant.[129] Rhys Davids suggests that the lands were tax free, being a grant of the king's half share as tax, although he believes that the *brahmadeya* carried with it judicial and executive rights too. He further suggests that the grant would cover only the king's rights, and that the right of the peasants to the other half and to the use of the common wasteland would remain with them.[130] It should be noted that *brahmadeya* lands in the Pāli canon are always located in a *brāhmaṇa gāma*. In addition to the single *brahmadeya* holder, such as the *brāhmaṇas* Pokkharasādi, Soṇadaṇḍa, or Caṅkī, there are a large number of *brāhmaṇa-gahapatis* who also constitute the *brāhmaṇa gāma*. This point is discussed in greater detail in the following chapter.

Another controversial point related to the question of landholding and land ownership is that of the transfer, sale and gift of land. Anāthapiṇḍika's purchase of Jetavana from the prince Jeta Kumāra is well known, although not entirely free of controversy. It should be noted that the transfer of Jetavana represents orchard land or woodland, and not agricultural land, of which type of transfer we do not find a single instance in early Pāli literature. Similarly, although numerous gifts of land were made to the *saṅgha*, each consisted of the gift of a *vana* or orchard land.[131] Even though this may not have been actual forest land, it probably represented partially cleared, or even uncleared land on the outskirts of urban centres[132] like Sāvatthi, Rājagaha, Sāketa, Kosambī[133] and other smaller set-

[127] *D.B.*, Vol. I, p. 108. [128] *M.L.S.*, II, p. 354n.

[129] *D.B.*, I, p. 108n. [130] Ibid.

[131] The *Vinaya* defines an *ārāma*, the usual term for the gift of land to the *saṅgha*, as a flower garden (*puppharāmo*), or orchard (*phalarāmo*). See Horner (*B.O.D.*, II, p. 2n; *Pārājika*, p. 61). The *Aṅguttara Nikāya* bans the *saṅgha* from the possession of agricultural land (*A.N.*, IV, p. 266).

[132] S. Dutt, *Buddhist Monks and Monasteries of India*, p. 59.

[133] For example, Jetavana, Veḷuvana, Añjanavana and Ambavana. The natural or

tlements, which were meant to be used as units of settlements for residential purposes for the *bhikkhu-saṅgha*. We believe that this indicates that the sale or gift of agricultural land had not yet appeared in society. Even the land gifted by the king to *brāhmaṇas* as *brahmadeya* is likely to have been uncleared or partially cleared land which was part of the royal lands. This is suggested by the description of much wood, grass and insects inhabiting the grassland which does not give the impression of already cleared agricultural land. The presence of large numbers of *brāhmaṇa-gahapatis* in these *brāhmaṇa-gāmas* could imply that the land was prepared for cultivation through the initiative of the former.

Emergence of a stratified society

The growing complexity of the economy as it expanded was naturally expressed through the emergence of a more stratified society. While most of the land may have been in the hands of peasant proprietors, some large units of land had also come into existence. The most striking example is that of the *brāhmaṇa* Kasībhāradvāja of the village of Ekanāḷā, who is described as using 500 ploughs.[135] While the figure 500 need not be taken too seriously, the fact that it represented a large holding should be noted. In contrast to this, the period also marks the beginning of hired labour on a fairly large scale. Pāli texts frequently mention *dāsas*, *kammakaras*, and *porisas*,[136] who appear to be employed within households as well as working the land. It is pertinent that the words *vetan* and *vaitanika* appear for the first time in Pāṇini's *Aṣṭādhyāyi*,[137] and this characterizes the emergence of wage labour. It can be argued that these terms began to occur in this period only because large agricultural holdings did not exist in the past, whereas they had begun to appear at the time of the Buddha. Of the three categories of *dāsa*, *kammakara*, and *porisa*, the *dāsas* may actually have been better off since they were integrated into the family that owned them.[138]

---

virgin nature of these lands is suggested by the names themselves. For example, Veḷuvana is a bamboo grove.

[134] There is no indication of the ritual injunction against the *brāhmaṇas*' participation in agriculture in the Buddhist texts. The *brāhmaṇa* Kasībhāradvāja, for instance, is directly involved in managing agricultural operations on his land (*Sutta-Nipāta*, *Khuddaka Nikāya*, Vol. I, p. 281).

[135] Ibid., p. 281. [136] *Pācittiya*, p. 108; *S.N.*, I, p. 94.

[137] S.C. Vasu, *Aṣṭādhyāyī of Pāṇini*, Vol. I, p. 811.

[138] D.N. Chanana, *Slavery in Ancient India*, 1960, pp. 58, 162.

The term *dalidda*[139] also appears frequently in the Pāli texts to denote extremely poor people who led miserable and deprived existences, and were 'needy, without enough to eat or drink, without even a covering for the back'.[140] In contrast, there were people who lived very comfortably or even luxuriously, possessing gold, silver, grain, a carriage, and a beautiful house[141] with servants to work for them.[142] Bose has pointed to the pronounced social contrast between classes expressed through the familiar Pāli phrases *mahābhoga kula* and *daḷidda kula, sadhana* and *adhana; sugata* and *duggata*.[143] The texts also reflect a pragmatic recognition of the power of wealth. The *Aṅguttara Nikāya* mentions a poor man who would have to go to jail for non-payment of debt, whereas a person of wealth could escape the same fate.[144]

The sharp differentiation between the two categories created the beginnings of social tension. The *Vinaya Piṭaka* refers to the *dāsa-kammakaras* of the Sākyans attacking their masters' womenfolk as an act of revenge when the women were alone in the woods.[145] The recognition of exploitation had also emerged. The *Majjhima Nikāya* relates a very significant incident[146] of a *dāsi* called Kāḷī, and her mistress, a *gahapatnī* called Vaidehi, who was reputed to be even tempered and gentle. Kāḷī, however, attributed her mistress' supposed even temper to the fact that her own exemplary behaviour gave the mistress no cause for anger. Kāḷī was meek, submissive and hard-working normally, but she decided to test her mistress' real temper by rising late and ignoring her calls three mornings in succession. This was too much for the mistress whose temper cracked up under the strain of the incident and she physically assaulted the *dāsi*. The whole incident is narrated as a sarcastic comment on the behaviour of the rich mistress. While the *dāsas* were sometimes treated reasonably well, the normal food for the *dāsa-kammakaras* was broken rice and sour gruel.[147] The *dāsa-*

[139] See *Pācittiya*, p. 108 for a *daḷidda kammakara*, and *Cullavagga*, p. 254 for a *daḷidda tunavāya*. Also see *M.N.*, II, p. 89; *A.N.*, III, p. 84.

[140] *M.N.*, III, p. 240; *M.L.S.* III, p. 215.

[141] *M.N.*, III, p. 248. [142] *Cullavagga*, p. 249.

[143] A.N. Bose, *The Social and Rural Economy of North-East India*, Vol. II, p. 270.

[144] *A.N.*; I, p. 232.

[145] Significantly this is also one of the first written records of women being the obvious targets in the case of antagonism between two social groups (*Pācittiya*, p. 241).

[146] *M.N.*, I, pp. 167–8. [147] *A.N.*, I, p. 134.

kammakara-porisa, or those who laboured for others, formed the lowest economic strata in society. Evidently, even in an era of expanding agriculture, there was not enough land to go round for everyone. Further as the economy became more complex the availability of land and the ability to provide labour were not enough to begin agriculture. A certain minimum of capital in the form of bullocks for ploughing and the basic requirements of farming had made their appearance so that those without the means to raise this capital had to sell their labour in order to survive.

Another interesting facet from the early Pāli texts is the idea that there was only a fixed surplus available in any household, which placed the *samaṇa-brāhmaṇa* in a relationship of opposition to the *dāsa-kammakara*. The *Saṁyutta Nikāya* indicates that the share gifted to the *samaṇa-brāhmaṇas* as alms could have gone instead to the *dāsa-kammakaras*. A *seṭṭhi-gahapati* of Sāvatthi is described as giving alms to *samaṇa-brāhmaṇas* but subsequently regretting his action and arguing that he should have given it to the *dāsa-kammakaras* instead.[148] This opposition between the *samaṇa-brāhmaṇa* on the one hand and the *dāsa-kammakaras* on the other, in relation to the *gahapati*, is also noticeable in the *Sigalovāda Sutta*. The *samaṇa-brāhmaṇa* is placed at the zenith (*uparimādisā*) and the *dāsa-kammakara* is placed at the nadir (*heṭṭhimādisā*) in a structure of relationships in which the *gahapati* is the nodal point.[149] This appears to imply an opposition based on the principle that the *dāsa-kammakaras* provided labour and thereby formed the base of the productive system and of society. In contrast, the *samaṇa-brāhmaṇa* withdrew from labour and economic activity as also from society and lived off the labour and economic activity of others. Since the *samaṇa-brāhmaṇa* was outside society, although supported by it, he was placed at the zenith. The *dāsa-kammakara* was an integral part of the economy and society, forming its very foundation. It was primarily through his effort that the surplus was generated but since he had no control over it he was placed at the bottom or nadir. The placement of the two groups is indicative of the basic values of the system itself. It has been generally assumed that India's economy in the sixth century B.C. was producing enough surplus[150] to feed a substantial sec-

[148] *S.N.*, I, p. 91. [149] *D.N.*, III, pp. 147–8.

[150] It should however be noted that the existence of surplus all the time cannot be taken for granted. Occasional shortages of food are mentioned (see *S.N.*, III, p. 286 and *A.N.*, II, p. 330). Also the *Vinaya* speaks of food being the product of hard labour (*Cullavagga*, p. 223).

tion of the people who had withdrawn from economic activity. Even so, Buddhist texts reveal that this became possible only at the expense of the *dāsa-kammakaras*, or those who provided their labour to produce the surplus. The surplus itself was relative since it could have been redistributed among the *dāsa-kammakaras* themselves.

Occupational groups and the process of tribal assimilation

The proliferation of the number of occupational groups which resulted from the expansion of the economy was probably one way in which many tribal groups were being assimilated into society. We shall deal with the problem of social stratification as reflected in Buddhist literature in Chapter III where we shall consider the terms *vaṇṇa* and *jāti*. However here we shall discuss briefly the Brahmanical theory of *varṇasaṃkara*. The theory, which features in the *Dharma-Sūtra* literature[151] composed roughly during the period of Buddhist literature that we are analysing, depicts a process of social adaptation. Since the Brahmanical system of stratification was a hierarchical or linear order, every new group or occupation had to be fitted into the scheme of the social order in relation to the total system. This empirical reality of assimilation had to be given a conceptual formulation which was provided by the *varṇaśaṃkara* theory. The process by which this assimilation took place has been suggested by N.K. Bose[152] on the basis of similar tribal assimilation in nineteenth century India. He has argued that, with the gradual expansion of organized society and the consequent lack of space available to the tribals, their economy could no longer effectively support them. This resulted in the tribal group beginning to specialize in a particular occupation like basket-weaving or hunting, and then joining the larger productive system of the Hindus. They were then absorbed into Hindu social organization at the lower end[153] and became a distinct caste. This was done as far as possible by guaranteeing a monopoly in a particular occupation to

[151] *Vāṣiṣṭa Dharmasūtra, Sacred Laws of the Āryas*, tr. by George Buhler, S.B.E., Vol. XIV, p. 94; *Baudhāyana Dharmasūtra*, ibid., pp. 197–8. See V.N. Jha for a detailed analysis of the theory of the *varṇasaṃkara* ('Varṇasaṃkara in the Dharmasūtras: Theory and Practice', *J.E.S.H.O.*, Vol. XIII, Pt. III, 1970, pp. 273–88.)

[152] N.K. Bose, *Culture and Society*, p. 207.

[153] It is evident from the *Aggañña Sutta* of the *Dīgha Nikāya* that the *suddas* who were the lowest *vaṇṇa* of the social system were tribal groups living mainly by hunting and fishing (*D.N.*, III, p. 74).

each caste within a given region.[154] The process of absorbing tribals at the lower level of the hierarchy was made possible because Hindu society gave them a minimum economic security which could not be attained under the tribal system, particularly after the tribes had been affected by encroachment on the more fertile portions of their lands.[155] They then became not only a part of the larger economic unit but also part of the larger cultural unit represented by the caste system. This process of tribal absorption was conceptualized in the theory of *varṇasaṃkara.*

The importance of kinship ties

The process of political and economic expansion could have affected kinship ties adversely, breaking them down in the emerging social system of the sixth century B.C. However, in reality the kinship structure adapted itself to the changing situation and became one of the principles of caste (*jāti*) organization. The expanding economy had created a new demand for specialization and a proliferation of occupations, but this development was tied to the kinship factor since specific occupations became the monopoly of certain categories in society. The emergence of hereditary specialization meant that one was born not only into a family (*kula*) but also into an occupation which was the hereditary preserve of that *kula*. This has led one historian to suggest that Buddhist society was kinship-based rather than caste-based.[156] There is little doubt about the importance of kinship ties in this period when it appears to have played a greater role than in later times.[157] The Buddha himself recognized the strength of kinship bonds and treated them as a valid reason for providing exceptions to a large number of *vinaya* rules. *Bhikkhus* were allowed to maintain contacts with members of their families,[158] visiting them even in the *vassāvāsa*, if necessary, when travel was normally forbidden. Similarly, *bhikkhus* who were strictly prohibited from watching army parades or visiting the battlefront were allowed to meet kinsfolk who were seriously ill or dying on the battle front. Further women were permitted to enter the *saṅgha* only after women of the Buddha's kin-group had repeatedly pleaded with him, and through the subse-

[154] N.K. Bose, *Culture and Society*, p. 209. [155] Ibid., p. 210.
[156] N.N. Wagle, *Society at the Time of the Buddha*, pp. 157–8.
[157] Ibid., p. 157. [158] *Mahāvagga*, p. 154.

quent intervention of another kinsman, Ānanda, in their favour.[159] The loss of kin is described as the greatest loss that could affect a man and was rated much higher than the loss of wealth.[160] The cutting off of ties with kinsmen was the greatest sorrow to be faced by a family which was being renounced by the imminent *bhikkhu*. Even the Buddha recognized this fact of family life when he ruled that various categories of people had to obtain permission from their kinsmen before being ordained into the *saṅgha*. In addition, the Buddha realized that since kinship ties were so strong in the wider society, the *saṅgha* must provide alternative ties to the *bhikkhus* to substitute for the lost ones. This probably explains the use of kinship terminology to characterize the new fraternity of the *bhikkhus*. Every *bhikkhu* who joined the *saṅgha* now had a new relationship with the founder as well as with other *bhikkhus*. All were referred to as the *Sākyaputta samaṇas*, as distinct from other *samaṇas* and *paribājjakas*, who did not share the same bond as sons of the Buddha. Their new bond tied them in a relationship of brotherhood among themselves. Significantly only the Buddhists displayed this feature which appears to have been a Buddhist innovation in the *samaṇa* world. Sects like the Ājīvikas or Jainas did not develop similar attitudes to kin groups. It is possible that the influence of kinship bonds on the Buddhist *saṅgha* can be attributed to the stronger basis of kinship in the *gaṇa-saṅghas* of which the Buddha had been a member before he renounced the world.

Women in the Buddhist literature

Patriarchal values in relation to women are also reflected in early Buddhist literature. Such an assertion may appear to be a contradiction since the period as a whole is supposed to have been characterized by a higher status for women than in the past[161] for dissident sects allowed women to join their respective sects. The *samaṇa* culture no doubt recognized that regardless of caste, class, or sex, everyone had the potential for salvation. But, apart from conceding this principle the attitude of society was generally against women. The narrative describing the entry of *bhikkhunīs* into the *saṅgha* illustrates this bias. The Buddha did not want *bhikkhunīs* in the *saṅgha*. If permission was finally (and grudgingly) granted it was en-

[159] *Cullavagga*, p. 374. [160] *A.N.*, II, p. 401.
[161] I.B. Horner, *Women Under Primitive Buddhism*, p. 2.

tirely because Ānanda made the Buddha concede that women were as capable of salvation as men,[162] which in itself was a recognized principle of the *samaṇa* culture. In fact, in the entire early Buddhist literature only Ānanda seems to have genuinely believed in the principles of equality between men and women, and he systematically championed their cause.[163] After Buddha's death the *saṅgha* even criticized him for espousing the cause of women on two occasions: first for pleading Mahapājāpatī Gotamī's case on the question of the entry of women into the *saṅgha*; and second, for his gesture of sympathy to the weeping Mallā women who wanted a glimpse of the Buddha's last remains.[164] This was treated as defiling the Buddha's sacred body. Whatever Ānanda's compatriots may have thought, Ananda's gesture was born out of his genuine humanity which recognized women as equal human beings. Ānanda in fact appears to be the only figure in Buddhist literature who was concerned about the evidently unequal relationship between men and women. On one occasion he sought an explanation from the Buddha as to why women did not sit in court, or conduct business.[165] Ānanda obviously felt that they should have been participating in all such activities.

Apart from Ānanda's espousal of their cause, the general tone of Buddhist literature is antagonistic to women. Once they were grudgingly admitted into the *saṅgha* they were firmly (and unfairly) placed under the authority of *bhikkhus*. This was one of the preconditions that Mahāpajāpatī Gotamī had to accept before women were permitted into the *saṅgha*.[166] Subsequently, this grand old lady seems to have resented a particularly offensive rule which demanded that no matter how old or senior a *bhikkhunī* was, she must rise and salute even the junior-most *bhikkhu*.[167] Gotamī made a valiant attempt to have the rule rescinded, and again it was Ānanda who pleaded on her behalf. However, the Buddha was firm in his refusal. He argued that since the *añña titthiyas* did not grant this privilege to women the Buddhists could not permit such a concession.[168]

[162] *Cullavagga*, p. 374.

[163] I.B. Horner, *Women Under Primitive Buddhism*, pp. 295ff.

[164] *Cullavagga*, p. 411. [165] *A.N.*, II, p. 87.

[166] *Cullavagga*, pp. 374–77.

[167] This is particularly offensive in a society where age and seniority is normally respected irrespective of sex.

[168] *Cullavagga*, p. 378. Incidentally the argument indicates how far Buddhism was

There is both dignity and pathos in this episode with the aged but spirited Gotamī being denied her justifiable rights by the Buddha, whom she had nurtured as her own son and it speaks volumes for the discrimination against women.

Considerable distrust of women is displayed in the Buddhist texts. They are likened to black snakes, treated as evil smelling and adulterous; they are accused of ensnaring men,[169] and are labelled as secretive and not open;[170] they are full of passion, easily angered, stupid and envious and have no place in public assemblies. They are incapable of carrying out any business or earning a living by any profession because they are uncontrolled, envious, greedy and stupid.[171] A wide range of restrictions were placed on *bhikkhunis*, who were even required to offer their alms to the monks if they ran into them.[172] No similar obligation was placed on *bhikkhus*. In some cases the *bhikkhunis* receive severer punishments than *bhikkhus* for similar offences.[173]

A woman's existence is described as centring round men, adornment, her son, and being without a rival.[174] Women were expected ideally to be like slaves and be obedient to their husbands.[175] They were under the control of various bodies like the king, the *saṅgha*, the *seṇi* (guild) or *pūga* (company). Women who led their lives as daughters, wives, and mothers were therefore quite clearly subjected to the authority of men and this attitude was projected even into the asocial world of the *saṅgha* as we have noted above. However, there were occasional glimpses of greater understanding of the position of women in relation to men. Among her five special disadvantages, three were biological but two others refer to a woman having to leave her relatives at a tender age and going to her husband's home, and having to wait upon men all her life (*pāricariyam upeti*).[176] Unfortunately, such insights are few and the over-

---

willing to go in its view of change. While they may have been more progressive than the *brāhmaṇas*, the Buddhists certainly did not want to deviate from the norms established by the wider *samaṇa* culture. No innovation was considered apart from the general traditions of the *samaṇas*.

[169] *A.N.*, II, p. 498; *G.S.*, III, p. 191.

[170] *A.N.*, I, p. 263; *G.S.*, I, p. 261

[171] *A.N.*, II, p. 87; *G.S.*, II, p. 93.

[172] *Cullavagga*, p. 388.

[173] I.B. Horner, *Book of Discipline*, Vol. III, p. xxxix.

[174] *A.N.*, II, p. 76. [175] *A.N.*, III, pp. 224, 361–7.

[176] *S.N.*, III, pp. 212–13.

whelming tone of the Buddhist texts merely reflected the existing attitude to women. According to the Buddha, it is inconceivable that a woman can be either a *tathāgata* or a *cakkavatti*.[177] In other words, they could not be heads of the social or the asocial world.

Despite the general discrimination against women, which is reflected most sharply in their lower status *vis-à-vis* the *bhikkhu* within the asocial world of the *saṅgha*, women did join the organization in noticeable numbers. More women came into it from the *gaṇa-saṅghas* drawn probably by kinship ties with other entrants, but many also came in order to escape what may be termed the misery of the 'pestle and mortar'. This becomes very clear from the sentiments expressed in the *Therīgāthā*.[178] The fact that a woman had to wait on a man all her life, sometimes without the slightest recognition, was resented by some women for whom the *saṅgha* represented a measure of freedom. Others seem to have turned to it for succour in times of distress. In fact, the basic tenets of Buddhism: that the world is transitory and full of sorrow, clearly struck a more responsive chord in women who, by their very nature, felt deeply the pain of illness and of death. This is beautifully illustrated in the story of Kisā Gotamī, who lost all her loved ones in a succession of tragedies and finally lost her only child. Wild with grief and desperately seeking her child's revival she turned to the Buddha, who brought home to her the inevitability of death.[179]

One of the features of the period is the fact that the courtesan did not suffer from social ostracism or a low status. The Buddha accepted Ambapāli's invitation to a meal and received the gift of the *Ambavana* from her.[180] Nevertheless, the most valued principle for a woman remained that in which she was the dutiful wife and mother, a matriarch who ruled over her vast family consisting of numerous children and grandchildren, as exemplified in the person of Visākha Migāramātā.[181] It is significant that Visākhā with her mother image, supporting the *saṅgha* from outside and leading a lay existence, is the most important woman in the Pāli texts and not Mahāpajāpatī Gotamī who had renounced the world in search of liberation.

[177] *A.N.*, I, p. 29. [178] C.A.F. Rhys Davids, *Psalms of the Sisters*, pp. 15, 25.

[179] The *Therīgāthā* contains some verses depicting her agony (*Psalms of the Sisters*, pp. 108–11).

[180] *D.N.*, II, p. 78.

[181] Visākhā Migāramātā was considered auspicious for these very qualities.

It may be argued that the early Buddhist want of sympathy for women is not a unique phenomenon, but rather one that was typical of monastic sentiment all over the world.[182] It is also typical of the sixth century B.C. social environment, not withstanding the presence of an exceptional progressive like Ānanda. Like-minded men and women must have existed along with Ānanda, but not in sufficient numbers to have made any real impact on the discrimination against women.

We have depicted in the sections above a broad outline of the political, economic and social environment of early Buddhism. The process of political consolidation, the expansion of the economy in general and of agriculture in particular, was a crucial factor of society at the time. The importance of agriculture was reflected also in the appearance of new social and economic categories associated with this phenomenon. We focus more sharply upon the problems of economy and society in the following chapters. But, before doing so it is necessary to turn to an important and vital aspect of the environment of the sixth century B.C., the religious milieu of Buddhism.

Section III: The Religious Milieu

Philosophical speculation in the sixth century B.C.

The religious milieu in which Buddhism was founded was distinguished by the proliferation of sects in the Ganga Valley. This was a unique feature of the period, unmatched in later years for its sheer dimensions, which spanned a wide range of ideas from annihilationism (*ucchedvāda*) to eternalism (*sāsvatvāda*), and from the fatalism of the Ājīvikas to the materialism of the Cārvākas. The Buddhist texts make frequent references to other sects (*añña titthiyas*) and the *Brahmajāla Sutta* of the *Dīgha Nikāya* mentions 62 such sects.[183] Jaina sources also corroborate the existence of numerous sects.[184] Of these, special status has been given to six contemporary 'non-conformist' mendicant philosophers in the Pāli canon,[185] which indicates the eminence and influence which early Buddhist tradition

[182] A.K. Coomaraswamy, *Buddha and the Gospel of Buddhism*, p. 154.

[183] *D.N.*, I, p. 34.

[184] *Sūtrakritānga*, tr. by Hermann Jacobi, *Jaina Sūtras*, S.B.E., Vol. XIV, pp 315–19.

[185] A.L. Basham, *History and Doctrine of the Ājīvikas*, p. 10.

attributed to these six dissident teachers.[186] Significantly, there is a curious reference to the same six sects and their leaders in the *Milindapañha*, a Pāli text attributed to the first century B.C.,[187] which might indicate the continuing importance of the dissident tradition even into later years.

Renunciation: The samaṇa *tradition*

India had been familiar with hermits, thinkers, and philosophical speculation generally from very early times but, as Rhys Davids has argued, the intellectual movement before the rise of Buddhism (as it has come down to us) was largely a lay movement, not a priestly one.[188] What distinguished the period in which Buddhism arose was the appearance of the *paribbājaka* or the *samaṇa*. The characteristic feature of the *paribbājakas* was their state of 'houselessness'. In Pāli texts they are described as going forth from the home into homelessness (*agārasmā anāgāriyum*). They wandered from one place to another with the chief object of meeting distinguished teachers and philosophers, and entering into discussions with them. Dutt has treated the *parivrājaka* tradition as the seed-bed which gave rise to all the wandering groups, whatever their sects, denominations and ideals may have been.

The roots of the *parivrājaka* tradition itself have been traced to pre-Āryan times. Scattered evidence from the Indus Valley civilization and Vedic texts has been pieced together by scholars to argue that the ascetic tradition was derived from the pre-Āryans. The *Keśi Śukta* of the *Ṛg Veda*[189] indicates the awe which the figure of the *muni* evoked in the Ṛg Vedic mind, and indicates that the figure of the *muni* was alien to Ṛg Vedic culture. It is also argued that asceticism was directly opposed to the entire *weltanschauung* of the *Ṛg Veda*.[190] Similarly, Dutt has suggested the possible connection between śramanism and the imperfectly Aryanized communities of the east.[191] According to Kalupahana, although the ascetic tradition of the non-Āryans was relegated to the background by the more

[186] *D.N.*, I, pp. 41–4.

[187] *Milindapañha*, tr. by I.B. Horner, *Questions of King Milinda*, Vol. I, p. 6.

[188] T.W. Rhys Davids, *Buddhist India*, p. 69.

[189] *Ṛg Veda*, X, 136.

[190] G.C. Pande, *Studies in the Origins of Buddhism*, p. 258.

[191] S. Dutt, *Early Buddhist Monachism*, p. 56. See also D.R. Bhandarkar, *Some Aspects of Ancient Indian Culture*, p. 53.

mundane Āryan tradition, it could not be completely wiped out. After remaining dormant for a while it seems to have re-emerged with fresh vigour and vitality at the time of the Buddha. Kalupahana observes that the history of Indian philosophy may be described as a story of the struggle for supremacy between these two traditions.[192] It seems fairly clear that the sixth century B.C. was heir to a tradition which existed from the earliest times and became a unique feature of Indian civilization; one that has even survived into contemporary times.

What united the *paribbājakas* was their opposition to the established tradition of the *brāhmaṇas* based on the cultus of the sacrifice, which was central to their ideology. They were also opposed to the claims of the *brāhmaṇas* to pre-eminence in society. It was in regard to these two features that dissent was expressed most sharply by the various non-conformist sects. At the time of the Buddha the *brāhmaṇas* were strongly identified with the ritual of sacrifice, and this was a major area of disagreement between them and the *titthiyas*. By the medieval period the *brāhmaṇas* did not have a homogeneous set of beliefs with which they could be identified. Nevertheless, non-conformist groups of the future, such as the Lingayats, continued to express their dissent to the *brāhmaṇa's* claim to pre-eminence. In the sixth century B.C. the *paribbājakas* were both anti-Vedic and anti-Brahmanic in their attitude,[193] opposed in particular to the *brāhmaṇa's* claim to a special knowledge of the revealed teaching hereditary in their caste.[194] The Pāli canon bears ample testimony to both these features. The *samaṇa* shunned all tokens of Vedic culture such as the sacred thread (*upavīta*) or the symbolic tuft of hair on the head (*śikhā*), and he did not perform *yagña*. The rituals relating to renunciation make this quite clear. The renouncer was to stretch his limbs symbolically over the sacred utensils, thereby signifying his renunciation of them. He was to throw the wooden utensils into fire, the earthen into water, and give the metal ones to his teacher.[196] The *Mahāvagga* gives a similar account of the symbolic

[192] David J. Kalupahana, *Buddhist Philosophy: A Historical Analysis*, pp. 3–4.

[193] B.M. Barua, *Pre-Buddhist Indian Philosophy*, p. 189.

[194] A.K. Warder, 'On the Relationship between Buddhism and other Contemporary Systems', *B.S.O.A.S.*, Vol. XVIII, 1956, p. 51.

[195] S. Dutt, *Buddhist Monks and Monasteries of India*, p. 38.

[196] Paul Deussen, *The Philosophy of the Upanishads*, p. 376.

gesture made by the *jaṭila* Uruvela Kassapa and his followers, who shaved their heads and threw away their matted hair along with their implements of fire worship into the nearby river, before they approached the Buddha for ordination (*upasampada*).[197]

Renouncers and householders

The *samaṇa* or the *paribbājaka* broke especially those rules that applied to the householder (*gahaṭṭha*). Unlike the Upanishadic seers, who often retreated into the woods accompanied by their wives, the *samaṇas* or *paribbājakas* renounced their homes, cutting off all ties with their kinsmen, and lived by collecting alms from the people. The *gahaṭṭha* and *paribbājakas* were therefore polar opposites. The *samaṇas* advocated lifelong renunciation since they believed in a complete division between the social and asocial worlds. Buddhist texts clearly reveal a complete separation of the social and asocial worlds. The world of the householder (*gihī*) and the world of the *bhikkhu* were clearly demarcated and irrevocably opposed to each other.[198] The opposition between the social and asocial worlds is strikingly demonstrated in the *Mahāvagga*, where the Buddha appears in the image of a destroyer and wrecker of homes in the eyes of the Magadhan people.[199] This opposition forms a constant and unifying theme of the Buddhist texts in general, and of the *Pātimokkha* rules of the *Vinaya Piṭaka* in particular. The *Pātimokkha* was a list of 227 rules of conduct to be observed by the *bhikkhu*. A section of the *Pātimokkha* called the *Sekhiya Dhamma*[200] consists of 75 rules of etiquette which were to be observed by *bhikkhus*, and almost all deal with the *bhikkhus*' interaction with the laity. The opposition between the *bhikkhu* and the *gihī* is repeatedly stated in this section of the rules, and, interestingly, the laity themselves expected the separation to be maintained. Their criticism of the *bhikkhus* is frequently stated thus: 'How can these recluses, sons of the Sākyans, dress with their inner robe hanging down . . . [or] sit down lolling about . . . [or] laugh a great laugh . . . just like

[197] *Mahāvagga*, p. 33.

[198] This is best demonstrated with the example of the *mahāporisa*. The *mahāporisa* has two clear alternatives: either to live the life of a householder and become a *cakkavatti* thus heading the social world; or to renounce the world and become a *tathāgata* thus heading the asocial world.

[199] *Mahāvagga*, p. 41.

[200] *Pācittiya*, pp. 245–78.

householders who enjoy the pleasures of the senses?[201] The division between the social and the asocial world and the opposition between *bhikkhu* and *gihī*, sometimes explicitly stated and at other times latent, runs like a thread through the Buddhist texts. It is a central feature of Buddhist ideology which should be borne in mind, since it helps explain many apparent contradictions in Buddhism.[202]

Samaṇas *and* brāhmaṇas

It is clear that the *samaṇas* or *paribbājakas* were opposed to the notion of progress by stages or the theory of *āśramas* which became a central feature of Hindu *dharma*. A well-drawn contrast is made between the *āśrama* ideal of Brahmanism advocated by the father, and the renunciation ideal espoused by the son, in the famous *pitāputra samvāda* in the *Śānti Parva* of the Mahābhārata.[203] While controversy on the question of the *āśrama* theory pre-dating the rise of Buddhism may be irrelevant here, certain points related to the term *śramaṇa* (Sanskrit for Pāli *samaṇa*) need to be noted. The word first appears in the *Bṛhadāraṇyaka Upaniṣad*[204] and is used for one engaged in a religious endeavour but significantly, in the later *Upaniṣads* and the *Dharmasūtras*, where the *āśrama* theory finds mention, the term is conspicuous by its absence. After the Buddha, it came to be monopolized by Buddhists and Jainas and was used as a generic term for the *titthiyas*. Similarly, the term *sannyāsin* for a renouncer became denominational in usage, confined only to the Brahmanical and semi-Brahmanical tradition, but never used by Buddhists and Jainas.[205] That *samaṇas* saw themselves in opposition to *brāhmaṇas* is evident from numerous references in Pāli literature. Buddhist monks were looked upon with disfavour by *brāhmaṇas* and criticized for having renounced social life and duties prematurely: the Buddha himself was once abused for this by a *brāhmaṇa* householder at Rājagaha.[206] Brahmanical literature in the form of the *Upani-*

[201] *Seyyathāpi gihī kāmabhogino* (*Pācittiya*, p. 245; *B.O.D.*, III, p. 120).

[202] See Chapters III, IV and V.

[203] *Mahābhārata*, ed. by V.S. Sukhtankar and S.K. Belvalkar, Vol. 15, pp. 961–9. See also D.R. Bhandarkar, *Some Aspects of Ancient Indian Culture*, p. 54.

[204] *Bṛhadāraṇyaka Upaniṣad*, tr. by F. Max Muller, S.B.E., Vol. XVI, p. 169.

[205] S. Dutt, *Buddhist Monks and Monasteries of India*, p. 42.

[206] *S.N.*, I, p. 161. See also Haripada Chakraborty, *Asceticism in Indian Culture*, p. 216.

sads and *Dharmasūtras* frequently refer to the *grihastha āśrama* as the best *āśrama*.[207] It is significant that in the Pāli canon even Māra, the evil one, takes the form of a *brāhmaṇa* when he advocates to the Buddha the giving up of *samaṇḍ*hood.[208] Later however, the *brāhmaṇa* came to champion some of the values of an ascetic and, according to Tambiah, this created a paradoxical situation in which *brāhmaṇas* became the repository of important *sannyāsin* values while remaining in the world.[209] At the time of the Buddha however, the *brāhmaṇa* was seen as a householder by the *brāhmaṇas* themselves as well as by others. The *Aṅguttara Nikāya* gives a clear instance of this in a statement of the *brāhmaṇa* Vassakara, an important official of Magadha. Vassakara declared that the *brāhmaṇas* proclaimed a man to be great if he possessed four qualities, one of which was skill in the business of being a householder.[210] Similarly, the *brāhmaṇa* Subha, who was on a business visit to Sāvatthi, tells the Buddha that the *brāhmaṇas* believed that only the householder could accomplish the right path and not the recluse (*gahaṭṭho ārādhako hoti, na pabbaja ārādhako hoti*).[211] The people similarly see the terms *gahaṭṭha* and *brāhmaṇa* as interchangeable categories.[212] It has been held that the root of the contradiction of renunciation as a social phenomenon was the negation of the social function of *grihastha* by the renouncer.[213] In this context the references to Uddalaka's two sons are worth noting: Svetaketu who became an ascetic and Nachiketas who was a supporter of Vedic religious rites and duties as a householder.[214] Clearly the two embody opposing principles and are symbolic of the new developments in the religious milieu of the time. The *Mahābhārata* also refers to some *brāhmaṇas* who, taking to asceticism immediately after *brahmacarya*, were denounced by Indra and made to marry.[215] There are also references in the

[207] S. Dutt, *Early Monastic Buddhism*, pp. 57–8; *Chāndogya Upanishad* 8.15; *Gautama Dharmasūtra*, tr. by F. Max Muller, S.B.E., Vol. II, p. 193; *Vāsishṭha Dharmasūtra*, tr. by George Buhler, S.B.E., Vol. XIV, p. 44.

[208] *S.N.*, I, pp. 116–17; For a similar idea in Jaina literature see *Sūtrakritāṇga*, tr. by F. Max Muller, S.B.E., Vol. XLV, p. 265.

[209] S.J. Tambiah, *Buddhism and the Spirit Cults of North-East Thailand*, p. 64.

[210] *A.N.*, II, p. 38.

[211] *M.N.*, II, p. 469.

[212] *Mahāvagga*, p. 43.

[213] R. Thapar, 'Renunciation: The Making of a Counter Culture?' in *Ancient Indian Social History*, p. 80.

[214] G.S. Ghurye, *Indian Sadhus*, p. 34.

[215] H. Chakraborty, *Asceticism in Indian Culture*, p. 52.

Atharva Veda and the *Aitereya Brāhmaṇa*[216] to Indra killing *yatis* (another term for ascetics), which suggests that *sannyāsa* or renunciation was originally only the theory of dissidents who revolted against the ritualism of the orthodox *brāhmaṇas*. It is of some significance that Buddhism provides the earliest references to the debate on the utility of renunciation. In the *Samaññaphala Sutta* of the *Dīgha Nikāya*[217] king Ajātasattu is depicted as having approached the leaders of the six dissident sects, who were the Buddha's contemporaries, with the same question: 'What is the fruit, visible in this very world, of the life of a recluse?' There is no indication of the same question being put to any *brāhmaṇa*. It is reasonably clear from the evidence available to us that the dissident sects were the first to advocate lifelong asceticism as the path to salvation. It is also in Pāli literature that the compound expression *samaṇa-brāhmaṇa* became a current one, denoting the two opposing systems of the *samaṇas* and the *brāhmaṇas*.[218] Significantly the grammarian Patañjali uses the example of *śramaṇa-brāhmaṇa* to illustrate an antagonistic compound (*samahāra dvanda*) and remarks that the opposition of the two was eternal (*yesham cha virodhah śāśvatikah*), like that of the snake and the mongoose.[219] The two categories were so important at the time of the Buddha that the period as a whole has been characterized by Barua as the 'Age of the Śramaṇas and the Brāhmaṇas'.[220]

The opposition between the *brāhmaṇas* on the one hand, and the *samaṇas* as typified by the Buddhist *bhikkhu* on the other, is a constant feature of the Pāli texts. There are numerous derogatory references to the *brāhmaṇas*, who are depicted in a variety of negative situations. Their vices include pride, deceit, avarice, and even crimes such as matricide and patricide, beside milder human failings such as gluttony. In the *Vessantara Jātaka* the well-known classic of the Buddhist tradition, which relates the deeds of a prince

216 Ibid., pp. 10–11, 52; *Atharva Veda*, II, 3; *Aitereya Brāhmaṇa*, VII, 28. I.

217 *D.N.*, I, p.45; *D.B.*, I, p. 6.

218 The expression also occurs in the Jaina texts (*Sūtrakritāṅga* tr. by Hermann Jacobi, *Jaina Sūtras*, S.B.E., pp. 237, 241, 245, 287, 339), and in the Aśokan inscriptions (E. Hultzsch, *Corpus Inscriptionum Indicarium*, Vol. I, pp. 4, 5, 14, 15, 18,), and in Greek writings (R.C. Majumdar, *Classical Accounts of India*, pp. 425–48).

219 *The Vyākaraṇa Mahābhāṣya of Patañjali*, ed. by F. Kielhorn, Vol. I, pp. 474, 476.

220 B.M. Barua, *Pre-Buddhist Indian Philosophy*, p. 191.

who practised perfect generosity (and whose legend is one of the most popular in the entire Buddhist world), the villain of the narrative is an old and greedy *brāhmaṇa*. This crotchety *brāhmaṇa* is married to a young beautiful woman who exhorts him to get all kinds of impossible things for her. Since the old *brāhmaṇa* dotes on his wife, he is willing to do anything for her, regardless of ethical considerations. He even asks for the gift of Vessantara's young children to slave for his spoilt wife.[221] The actual basis of the opposition was the fact that *brāhmaṇas* lived like other householders, acquiring wealth and possessions, and led a thoroughly mundane existence. They were an integral part of the social world which, according to the Buddhists was an obstruction to the 'higher life'.[222] This opposition is explicitly stated in the *Chavaka Jātaka* which gives an amplified version of a story leading to one of the *vinaya* rules, namely, that the *bhikkhu* should not occupy a seat which is lower than that of a person being taught the dhamma.[223] Both versions exhort the *brāhmaṇa* to 'go forth' and become a *paribbājaka*, and this focuses on the root of the opposition between the *bhikkhu* and the *brāhmaṇa*: the condition of homelessness.

Commenting on the Jātaka version, Alsdorf points to the 'anti-brahmanical' tenor of the verse which represents the *brahmaṇa* as a glutton who violates the sacred prescription that a teacher must not sit on a lower seat than his pupil in the case of a king who provides excellent food and an easy life.[224] The *brāhmaṇa* actually states his position thus: 'I eat pure food (consisting) of the best quality rice with meat sauce. Therefore, I do not practice that *dhamma* practiced by the rishis.'[225] According to the Buddhists, this greed for material possessions and comforts was the root cause of the *brāhmaṇa's* fall from the values and norms expected of him. In a graphic description in the *Sutta Nipāta*, the ritual of the sacrifice was itself related to the *brāhmaṇas'* drive for wealth. A group of wealthy but decrepit and old *brāhmaṇas* of Kosala came to see the Buddha and inquired of him whether *brāhmaṇas* of the day were engaged in the

[221] The *Jātakas*, ed. by V. Fausböll, Vol. VI, pp. 479–547.

[222] *D.N.*, I, pp. 208–9. See also *Uttarādhyayana, Jaina Sūtras*, tr. by Hermann Jacobi, S.B.E., Vol. XLV, p. 52.

[223] The *Jātakas*, ed. by V. Fausböll, Vol. III, pp. 27–30; *Pācittiya*, pp. 275–6.

[224] L. Alsdorf, 'The Impious Brahman and the Pious Candala' in L. Cousins et al. (eds.), *Buddhist Studies in Honour of I.B. Horner*, pp. 9–13.

[225] Ibid., p. 12.

brāhmaṇa-dhamma of ancient *brāhmaṇas*. This gave the Buddha an opportunity to vent his grievances on the faults of contemporary *brāhmaṇas*. According to him,[226] the *brāhmaṇas* of old were self-restrained and penitent, having abandoned the objects of the five senses. They owned no cattle, gold, or corn: but they had instead the best treasure, which was meditation. They collected as alms what was prepared for them and placed as food at the door, and they were revered by the people for their austerity. If householders they were moderate in their bodily desires, but the best were completely chaste. They collected rice, butter, and oil from the people justly and performed sacrifices with them, but they did not kill cows. Subsequently, however, there was a change among the *brāhmaṇas*, and this was attributed to their witnessing the prosperity of kings. The *brāhmaṇas* began to covet the wealth and beauty that they saw around them, and this led them to advocate sacrifices such as *assamedha*, *purisamedha*, and *vājapeya* to the king Okkāka. The king then offered these sacrifices and gave the *brāhmaṇas* wealth, including cows, beds, garments, adorned women, well-made chariots drawn by well-bred horses, and beautiful places filled with corn.[227] The entire narrative suggests that the *brāhmaṇas* were unable to resist the increasingly materialistic orientation of society. This resulted in a transformation of the simple sacrificial ritual into an elaborate and cruel one involving the slaughter of numerous animals as a means to gaining great wealth and possessions for themselves. The *brāhmaṇas* thus earned their image in Buddhist literature as exploiters.

The *brāhmaṇas'* firm entrenchment in the social world is very evident from the Pāli texts. They were a well-settled category of people who lived in villages, sometimes cultivating large tracts of land. There is no evidence of a taboo on the *brāhmaṇa's* participation in agriculture. In fact, the picture of the *brāhmaṇa* that emerges from the Pāli texts is one in which most *brāhmaṇas* were firmly entrenched in agriculture.[228] There is no indication of their living on

[226] *Sutta Nipāta, Khuddaka Nikāya*, Vol. I, pp. 311–14.

[227] Ibid., p. 313.

[228] See, for example, the *Kasībhāradvāja Sutta* of the *Sutta Nipāta* (*Khuddaka Nikāya*, Vol. I, p. 281). Similarly Dhananjani *brāhmaṇa* states that he has no time for practicing diligence (*appamato*) since he has to look after his wife and children, support his parents and work people and perform services for his kith and kin and his guests (*M.N.*, II, p. 450; *M.L.S.*, II, p. 373).

alms. Only a few *brāhmaṇas* appear to have been pursuing the task of teaching other young *brāhmaṇas*, but even many of these were well provided for. They were the major recipients of the *brahmadeya* lands in Kosala and Magadha and sometimes possessed additional property away from their homes. Jāṇussoṇī is a good example of the wealthy *brāhmaṇa*. Pāli texts mention his possessing a white chariot with silver fittings and white trappings drawn by four pure white mares. He drove about in this chariot dressed in white garments, a turban and sandals. His chariot was considered the finest in all Sāvatthi.[229]

Unlike the *paribbājakas* who wandered around meeting other thinkers and having discussions with them, the *brāhmaṇas* remained in their own settlements, except when they travelled in connection with their work, which was in the nature of business. If *bhikkhus* or the Buddha met some of these *brāhmaṇas* it was because the *bhikkhus* toured from one place to another. In contrast to those of the *samaṇas*, the discussions of the *brāhmaṇas* hardly ever centred on philosophical questions.[230] The stock questions that the *brāhmaṇas* took up with the Buddha related to the pre-eminence of the *brāhmanas* as a social group who deserved the best gifts because of their knowledge of the *Vedas*.[231] Occasionally they sought an explanation from the Buddha for his allegedly not respecting aged and well-established *brāhmaṇas*.[232] They also censured the Buddha for advocating a path for the *bhikkhus* which would yield gain, if any, for one individual only, whereas the system of sacrifice advocated and performed by them brought merit to many people.[233]

Brāhmaṇa *as a normative term*

However, not all the references to the *brāhmaṇas* in the Buddhist texts are negative. While there are numerous attacks on them for making unwarranted claims to social pre-eminence and their system of sacrifice which involved the slaughter of animals, there are also frequent positive references to them as possessors of spiritual-

[229] *S.N.*, IV, p. 6.

[230] *S.N.*, II, pp. 18–19, 21, *S.N.*, III, pp. 204, 223; *M.N.*, I, pp. 291, 126; *M.N.*, II, p. 173.

[231] *D.N.*, I, p. 80; *M.N.*, II, p. 404; *A.N.*, I, p. 153.

[232] *The Vinaya Piṭaka* opens with a passage of this kind (*Pārājika*, p. 3). See also *A.N.*, II, pp. 24, 487.

[233] *A.N.*, I, p. 155.

ity. The compound term *samaṇa-brāhmaṇa*, which we have earlier shown to represent two distinct and opposing categories, also possesses a unity in relation to the ordinary mass of people to whom they are jointly opposed. The term appears in this sense not only in the Pāli canon but also in Jaina literature, in Megasthenes' *Indica*, and in the Aśokan inscriptions. It refers to a respected group who were possessors of knowledge and merit that distinguished them from the common people. The Buddhist texts often refer to the laity's criticism of any moral lapses on the part of the *bhikkhus* which according to them is unlike the behaviour expected from a *samaṇa* or a *brāhmaṇa*. The *Pārājika*, for example, states that some *bhikkhus* suggested suicide to a lay follower whose wife complained that the *Sākyaputtas* were shameless and immoral. She says: 'There is no recluseship among these, no brahminhood among these . . . fallen from recluseship are these, fallen from brahminhood are these.' The people around were also angry and said: 'These have departed from brahminhood'.[234] There are numerous other examples of this kind in the texts and in all these situations the wider society is shown to treat *brāhmaṇas* and *samaṇas* ideally as possessors of spiritual merit for whom the norms are different from those for ordinary people. That the *brāhmaṇas* represented the traditional and established religious category in society was recognized not only by the people but also by the dissident sects. The *titthiyas* could not ignore the *brāhmaṇas* potential for a 'higher life', nor could they fail to notice the image of the *brāhmaṇas* in the existing Indian mind. This accounts for their special status in the Pāli and Jaina texts. Both use the same metaphor to express this idea. The God Sakka (Indra) comes in both traditions in the form of a *brāhmaṇa* to bless the respective sects in the presence of a wide audience.[235]

Significantly while the Buddha refused to accept that the *brāhmaṇas* had any inherent qualities that were superior to others he did not reject the term *brāhmaṇa* as a conceptual category. The Buddha used it instead in the sense of an ideal value to represent acquired spiritual merit which was open to everyone. It appears in the same sense in the Jaina literature too.[236] The Buddha even used the term

[234] *Pārājika*, p. 89; *B.O.D.*, Vol. I, p. 125.

[235] *Mahāvagga*, p. 37; *Uttarādhyayana*, tr. by Hermann Jacobi, *Jaina Sūtras*, S.B.E., Vol. XLV, p. 40.

[236] *Uttarādhyayana*, tr. by Hermann Jacobi, *Jaina Sūtras*, S.B.E., pp. 138–9.

as an epithet, for himself and a whole section of the *Dhammapada*[237] contains a compilation of verses in which the term is used to describe a person who has *acquired* a spiritual status. It appears sometimes as a synonym for *arahant*, or a person who has achieved the goal of the higher life. In this ideal sense there was no contradiction between the *brāhmaṇa* and the *samaṇa*, as both would then be part of a similar tradition of people striving to attain salvation through their own effort.

Other sects at the time of the Buddha

The Buddhists quite naturally had a sense of identity with the *añña titthiyas* as they were part of the wider *paribbājaka* culture in which the Buddhists had many of their roots. The *Majjhima Nikāya*[238] points to the similarities between the Buddhists and the *paribbājakas*, which indicates that it was sometimes difficult to tell the difference between the two, even through the discerning eyes of other *paribbājakas*. The word *bhikkhu*, which was adopted by the Buddhists, means receiver of alms.[239] This aspect of the *bhikkhus'* existence became the basic feature by which a recluse was defined. The *Dīgha Nikāya* treats the *samaṇa* as one who lived on food provided by others.[240] However the *bhikkhu* was distinguished from the ordinary beggar by the sacramental character of his begging, which was not merely a means of subsistence but the outward token of an inner state of a person who had renounced the world.[241] Men of this community were recognized by their begging bowls, the visible symbol of the mendicant's calling. The *samaṇa* or the *paribbājaka* was recognized as someone who had released himself from social ties and economic tasks in order to pursue certain goals. The wider society, by and large, endorsed these goals, although the phenomenon of renunciation did have its critics. In the *Kasībhāradvāja Sutta* for example, the non-economic life of the *bhikkhu* is questioned, significantly enough by a *brāhmaṇa*. The *brāhmaṇa* Kasībhāradvāja, who owned a large tract of land and was personally involved in its management, pointedly told the Buddha to work and sustain himself, instead of begging. He says, 'I plough and I

[237] *Dhammapada*, *Khuddaka Nikāya*, Vol. I, pp. 53–7.
[238] *M.N.*, I, p. 117.
[239] S. Dutt, *Buddhist Monks and Monasteries in India*, p. 36.
[240] *D.N.*, I, p. 7.
[241] S. Dutt, *Buddhist Monks and Monasteries in India*, p. 46.

sow and then I eat. You also plough and sow and then eat.' (*ahang kho samaṇa, kassāmi cha vapāmi cha; kasitva cha, vappitvā cha bhunjāmi; tvang pi, samaṇa, kassasu cha vappassu cha; kasitvā cha vappitvā cha bhunjassū*).[242] The Jaina texts also depict the humiliation which a monk had to face in his daily alms round.[243] Nevertheless the institution of the renouncer was already well established in the sixth century B.C. This is evident from the narrative describing the Buddha's first sortee outside the cloisters of the palace. Three of the disturbing sights that he encounters are: a sick man, an old man, and the corpse of a dead man. Finally he comes across a renouncer and this is a pointer to the way out of the cycle of misery. The fourth sign indicates that the act of renunciation by the Buddha was neither original nor without precedent. He had before him when he left the world the example of the world forsaker and mendicant.[244]

Some of these *paribbājakas* wandered alone, others had small bands of followers, but they seemed to share an active involvement in the tradition of debate. Some were still groping while others had worked out a broad philosophy, but all tried to comprehend each other's thinking. The Buddha himself went through various stages of association with other thinkers, two of whom he publicly acknowledged as having helped him to arrive upon final enlightenment.[245] The usual greeting between various *paribbājakas* would be to inquire about the particular *dhamma* and the teacher (*sattha*) that they followed. The *dhamma* was the inner sign of the almsman's calling, just as the begging bowl was its outer symbol.[246]

The tradition of debate was greatly facilitated by the existence of debating halls (*kūṭāgārasāla*) and special parks or orchards where the *samaṇas* could stay in the course of their travels. The Pāli texts give numerous instances of discussions in these meeting places.[247] The *Majjhima Nikāya* mentions *paribbājakas* collecting in a wanderer's park for the period of the rains. This generated a discussion on the eminence of each sect. All the *paribbājakas* referred to their respective leaders (*gaṇācariyo*) as *bhagava*, which was also used for the

242 *Sutta Nipāta*, Khuddaka Nikāya, Vol. I, p. 281.
243 *Sūtrakritāṇga*, tr. by Hermann Jacobi, *Jaina Sūtras*, S.B.E., Vol. XLV, p. 263.
244 S. Dutt, *Buddhist Monks and Monasteries in India*, p. 36.
245 *M.N.*, I, pp. 213–15.
246 S. Dutt, *Buddhist Monks and Monasteries in India*, p. 46.
247 *M.N.*, II, pp. 173, 224; *M.N.*, I, pp. 126, 291; *A.N.*, II, p. 32.

Buddha by his followers.[248] The frequent interaction in common meeting grounds not only encouraged a movement of ideas from one group to another but probably enabled the fostering of the basic culture which all the groups seem to have shared.

The *samaṇa* tradition as a whole was also affected in varying degrees by asceticism, which appears to have been a vital aspect of their culture. This is most striking in the case of the Cārvākas or the Lokāyatas, and even the Ājīvikas whose philosophies should logically have discounted the need for asceticism. Both sects have been characterized by Jayatilleke as Rationalist, as distinct from the Traditionalists and the Experientialists.[249] The Rationalists derived their knowledge from reasoning and speculation without any claims to extra-sensory perception. The Lokāyatas, in particular, rejected idealist metaphysics and treated the physical world as the only reality. The physical world functioned according to a set pattern which they called 'inherent nature' (*svabhāva*).[250] Human life was completely determined by this physical law, and psychic law was nothing but a by-product of the four great material elements (*mahābhūtas*), earth, water, fire, and air, and hence could not exert any influence on the physical personality or the outside world. Discourse on morality was meaningless since the destruction of the physical personality meant that man was completely cut off and annihilated after death. There was no after-life and no *karma* which affirmed continuity of action in the form of consequences. The Cārvāka leader is depicted as telling king Ajātasattu, 'There is no such thing as alms or sacrifice or offering. There is neither fruit nor result of good or evil deeds. There is no such thing as father nor mother. . . there are in this world no *samaṇas* or *brāhmaṇas* who have reached the highest point. A human being is built of four elements. When he dies the earth in him relapses to the earth, the fluid to water, the heat to fire, and wind to air, and his faculties pass into space. It is a doctrine of fools, this talk of gifts. Fools and wise alike are cut off and annihilated on the dissolution of the body.'[251] The Ājīvikas represented another form of natural determinism, but they combined materialism with a theory of natural evolution. The Ājīvikas believed in continuity and survival, but this took the form

[248] *M.N.*, II, p. 224.
[249] K.N. Jayatilleke, *Early Buddhist Theory of Knowledge*, p. 101.
[250] D.J. Kalupahana, *Buddhist Philosophy: A Historical Analysis*, p. 12.
[251] *D.N.*, I, p. 48; *D.B.I.*, pp. 73–4.

of evolutionary transmigration with a predetermined end. According to Basham, the Ājīvikas represent a thorough recognition of the orderliness of nature in the principle of *niyati* (impersonal cosmic principle) which was the only determining factor in the universe.[252] The principle of predetermination meant that human effort was ineffectual. In the *Dīgha Nikāya*, their philosophy is depicted as one where 'Existence is measured as with a bushel, with its joy and sorrow, and its appointed end. It can neither be lessened or increased, nor is there any excess or deficiency of it. Just as a ball of thread will, when thrown, unwind to its full length, so fool and wise alike will take their course and make an end of pain.'[253] Despite their avowed rejection of spiritual phenomena, adherents of the two schools have been included among the sects subscribing to the renunciation tradition, and this has been one of the puzzles of Indian philosophy. We suggest that their inclusion indicates their adherence to the broad *samaṇa* culture which was vital for any group wanting to propagate its philosophy. It was only in *samaṇa*[254] culture that the mendicant philosophers were mobile, met others like themselves and participated in philosophical debates. In the sixth century B.C. this was the only way in which a philosophy could be propagated. It was not so much asceticism that was important, but, rather, the wandering tradition; and since asceticism was an integral part of the wandering tradition it became an aspect of the culture of any philosophical group.

Buddhism and other sects

The common tradition of the *paribbājaka* in which Buddhism was embedded had considerable influence in shaping and conditioning Buddhism, and in settling the ethos and character upon which its own system of *vinaya* was gradually built.[255] The central ritual of the *bhikkhu* was the fortnightly assembly of monks called the *Pātimokkha*, and was introduced into Buddhism following the custom of the Jainas who gathered together on *uposatha* days (first and fifteenth days of the month).[256] The Jainas assembled and discussed

[252] A.L. Basham, *History and Doctrine of the Ājīvikas*, p. 6.

[253] *D.N.*, I, p. 47; *D.B.*, I, p. 73.

[254] The main features of the *samaṇa* culture apart from asceticism were anti-Vedism and the negation of the *grihastha* status.

[255] S. Dutt, *Buddhist Monks and Monasteries of India*, p. 24.

[256] *Mahāvagga*, p. 105.

the *dhamma* whereas the Buddhists transformed it into an occasion at which the *vinaya* rules were repeated. Similarly, the custom of observing a retreat during the rains (*vassā-vāsa*), whereby *bhikkhus* suspended their incessant tours during the period of the rains, grew out of similar rules followed by other wandering groups. The *Mahāvagga* gives a very interesting account of the Buddha sanctioning the *vassā-vāsa* for *bhikkhus*. The narration refers to the people being annoyed by the *bhikkhus*' wanderings during the rains which resulted in injury to the new crops being grown. They criticized the *bhikkhus*, saying, 'How can these *Sākyaputta samaṇas* walk on tour during the rains? Shall it be that those members of other sects . . . cling to and prepare a rains residence, shall it be that these birds having made nests in tree tops, cling to and prepare a rains-residence, while these *Sākyaputta samaṇas* walk on tour during the cold weather, the hot weather and the rains. . . .?[258] The implication is that all the other wandering groups, even birds, observed the rain-retreat and so should the Buddhists. There is clear evidence of the custom being observed by other wandering groups. The Jainas called it *pajjusana* and even *brāhmaṇa sannyāsis* were required to be of fixed residence (*dhruvaśila*) during the period.[259]

Like the relationship of Buddhists with *brāhmaṇas*, their relationship with the *añña titthiyas* was twofold. While they shared a common anti-Vedic and anti-Brahmanic culture which gave them a sense of unity, the *bhikkhu* was also opposed to the *añña-titthiyas* in a variety of ways. In fact there is evidence that the Buddha found the rival ascetic leaders and their monastic orders more subtle and dangerous opponents than the champions of the ancient faith.[260] The opposition to them was based essentially on doctrinal differences, but also flowed to some extent from their position on the question of asceticism.[261] The Buddha was distinguished from most of his rivals by his dissenting attitude towards self-mortification, in which the others saw the path to deliverance. It is evident that the *paribbājakas* were disturbed by his disparagement of extreme asceticism just as *brāhmaṇas* were bothered by the Bud-

[257] Ibid., p. 144.

[258] *B.O.D.*, IV, p. 183.

[259] S. Dutt, *Buddhist Monks and Monasteries of India*, p. 53.

[260] *A.N.*, I, pp. 33–5.

[261] The problem of asceticism was actually in a way part of the doctrinal differences with the *añña titthiyas*.

dha's apparent lack of respect for their seniority, and wisdom. In the *Kassapasīhanāda Sutta* of the *Dīgha Nikāya*, the *acelaka* (a type of ascetic) Kassapa asks if the Buddha disparaged all penance and all ascetics who lived a hard life.[262] The Buddha had to explain that he did not disapprove of all penances, but only of the more extreme practices of the *samaṇas*. He stated his position on the subject of asceticism thus: 'Monks, these two extremes should not be followed by one who has gone forth as a wanderer. . . devotion to the pleasures of the senses [which] is unworthy and unprofitable: and devotion to self mortification which is painful, unworthy and unprofitable.'[263]

However, the Buddha's moderation on the subject of self mortification made *bhikkhus* the object of numerous attacks by the *añña titthiyas*, who dismissed them contemptuously as '*muṇḍagahapati*', literally shaven householders, thereby denying their *samaṇa* status.[264] On one occasion the Ājīvikas sarcastically remarked that *bhikkhus* who were carrying sunshades looked like treasury officials (*gana mahāmatta*) and that they were not true *bhikkhus* (*bhikkhu na bhikkhu*).[265] Basham points out that Buddhists were particularly vulnerable as accusations of laxity in discipline were likely to affect the simple layfolk in whose eyes the sanctity of a religious order was estimated by the severity of its discipline and who bestowed alms accordingly.[266]

The idea that greater asceticism has more impact on the people was used by Devadatta in his manoeuvres to split the *saṅgha*, and gain the *bhikkhus'* support. This was his last move to capture the leadership of the Buddhist *saṅgha*, after having failed in a series of other attempts which included an attack on the life of the Buddha. Finally, he approached the Buddha with a proposal that the *saṅgha* should advocate stricter rules for its *bhikkhus*, which included compulsory forest dwelling; begging for alms and not accepting invitations to meals; clothing themselves in cast-off rags and not accepting the gift of robes; living under trees, and abstaining from eating fish. When the Buddha rejected the suggestion that these should be the minimum essential conditions for *bhikkhus*, Devadatta and his following seceded from the *saṅgha*. The significant points in this account are that Devadatta carried a section of the *bhikkhus*

[262] *D.N.*, I, 138. [263] *K.S.*, V, p. 356; *S.N.*, IV, p. 360.
[264] *Pācittiya*, p. 128. [265] *Cullavagga*, p. 220.
[266] A.L. Basham, *History and Doctrine of the Ājīvikas*, p. 137.

with him and that he had planned his strategy thus because he knew he would receive support. Subsequently, the departing *bhikkhus* had to be won back by loyal followers of the Buddha. Some lay people were also carried away by Devadatta's stand and accused the Buddha of living in luxury.[267] There are instances of kings expecting certain minimum standards of asceticism from the religious sects. Thus Udena expressed disapproval of Ānanda's acceptance of a gift of five hundred robes.[268] Similarly in the *Majjhima Nikāya* the king censures some *samaṇa-brāhmaṇas* for not upholding the ascetic tradition and for enjoying the pleasures of the senses instead.[269]

There were of course very important doctrinal and metaphysical differences between various sects too. Derogatory statements about the respective philosophies of the Buddhists and the Jainas were common, and occasionally it appears that the criticisms consciously or unconsciously misrepresented philosophical positions.[270] There was an undercurrent of tension among the sects for they competed not only for growth and advancement but also in receiving alms from the laity. The leaders of the sects attempted to prevent any erosion in their ranks as this meant loss of prestige. Nevertheless, there was considerable movement from one sect to another so that 'sects waxed and waned or coalesced and remained constantly in a fluctuating state in the community.[271] However even in this cross movement the *paribbājakas* seem to have evolved certain norms. It was thus considered ethical for a person leaving one sect to join another, to do so only after informing his original *gaṇācariya*. Sāriputta and Moggallāna were originally followers of Sanjaya Belaṭṭhiputta but later joined the Buddhist saṅgha and they represent the best examples of this tradition. Sanjaya sought to prevent this move by offering to share the leadership of the group with them but Sāriputta and Moggallāna declined the offer.[272] A similar obligation was placed upon the leader of a sect when he decided to join another religious sect. When the *jaṭila* Uruvela Kassapa informed his followers of his impending action he gave them the op-

[267] *Cullavagga*, pp. 297–9.

[268] Ibid., p. 413.

[269] *M.N.*, II, p. 367.

[270] *M.N.* II, p. 177; *M.N.*, III, p. 287; *Sūtrakritāṅga*, tr. by Hermann Jacobi, *Jaina Sūtras*, S.B.E., Vol. XIV, p. 411.

[271] S. Dutt, *Buddhist Monks and Monasteries in India*, p. 49.

[272] *Mahāvagga*, pp. 40–1.

tion of deciding whether to remain *jaṭilas* or join the Buddhist *saṅgha*.[273]

The widest doctrinal differences that the Buddhists exhibited against a particular sect were with regard to the Ājīvikas. The *Aṅguttara Nikāya* condemns Makkhali Gosāla as 'one who has perverted views and leads people astray, causing discomfort and sorrow to mankind'.[274] Basham argues that Makkhali Gosāla rather than Mahāvīra emerges as the Buddha's chief opponent and rival.[275] This appears somewhat strange in an era when there was such a wide range of doctrines to oppose, and the Ājīvikas by comparison seem to have advocated a philosophy that was hardly aggressive. But in spite of their seeming mildness the Ājīvikas formed a fairly popular sect which survived into medieval times. The Buddhists evidently grasped the fact that a fatalistic philosophy could have great appeal in a fast-changing world. Since Buddhists were ardent advocates of the doctrine of causality and the power of human effort in determining the future of individuals, they particularly singled out the Ājīvikas for an attack on philosophical grounds.[276] The philosophy of fatalism could also have a dangerous appeal. One of the six thinkers, Pūraṇa Kassapa, whose teachings became merged in Ājīvika thought,[277] believed that neither self-mastery, nor control of the senses, nor speaking the truth, nor alms-giving would result in an increase in merit. Similarly, no guilt would ensue from crimes such as murder, dacoity or adultery, or the oppression of others. The *Digha Nikāya* contains an account of the powerful language in which these ideas were expressed:

> To him who acts,. . . . or causes another to act, to him who mutilates or orders another to mutilate, to him who punishes or causes another to punish, to him who causes grief or torment, . . . to him who causes others to tremble, to him who kills a living creature, who breaks into houses, who commits dacoity, or robbery, or highway robbery, or adultery, or who speaks lies; to him thus acting there is no guilt. If a discus with a sharp edge like a razor should make all the living creatures on the earth one heap, one mass of flesh, there would be no guilt thence resulting, no increase of guilt would ensue. Were he to go along the south bank of the Ganga striking and slaying, mutilating and having men mutilated, oppressing and having

[273] *Mahāvagga*, p. 33. [274] *A.N.*, I, p. 34.
[275] A.L. Basham, *History and Doctrine of the Ājīvikas*, p. 55.
[276] *A.N.*, I, pp. 34, 367.
[277] A.L. Basham, *History and Doctrine of the Ājīvikas*, p. 24.

men oppressed, there would be no guilt thence resulting, no increase of guilt would ensue.[278]

In the light of these extreme views, the rationale of the Buddhist condemnation of the Ājīvikas becomes evident. In contrast, the *jaṭilas* were given a special place in the Buddhist system because their doctrines were more acceptable to Buddhists. The *jaṭilas* are described as being *kammavādin* and *kiriyavādin* (doctrines of action) in the Buddhist literature.[279]

Although Buddhism was influenced by the *paribbājaka* culture, it separated itself from the parent community gradually by its own modifications. Dutt states that the milieu of the wandering almsmen was the starting point from which Buddhism's evolution commenced; it subsequently went through several stages and 'varieties of being' before becoming established as a full-fledged and autonomous *saṅgha*[280] The creation of a monastic order with well-defined rules of governance seems to have emerged for the first time in the sixth century B.C. Earlier the *paribbājaka* culture had consisted largely of single or small bands of wanderers who were loosely held together around their *gaṇācariyas*. Warder has argued that there is no proof that organized schools based on an agreed canon of doctrine and discipline, existed before the time of the Buddha, Mahāvīra and Makkhali Gosāla. He also suggests that Makkhali Gosāla united all the freelance ascetics who thus far acknowledged no single authority and compiled a canon for them.[281] The evolution of the *saṅgha* became inevitable given the Buddha's decision that the new doctrine should receive the widest possible audience.[282] *Bhikkhus* were exhorted to go forth with his message, touring constantly in order to reach the *dhamma* to the people. By their *raison d' etre* the Buddhists had to function differently, and isolation from society could not be the object of monastic life.[283] Nāgasena makes this quite clear to Milinda in the *Milindapañha*.[284]

278 *D.B.*, I, pp. 69–70; *D.N.*, I, p. 46.

279 *Mahāvagga*, p. 76; *B.O.D.*, IV, p. 89.

280 S. Dutt, *Buddhist Monks and Monasteries of India*, p. 24.

281 A.K. Warder, 'On the Relationship between Buddhism and other Contemporary Systems', *B.S.O.A.S.*, Vol. XVIII (1956), p. 44.

282 The decision is depicted as being a difficult one which took some hard thinking on the part of the Buddha to arrive upon (*Mahāvagga*, p. 6).

283 S. Dutt, *Buddhist Monks and Monasteries of India*, p. 26.

284 *Milindapañha*, ed. by V. Trenckner, p. 212.

He argues that though monks could have lived in the forest, it was necessary for them to live in monasteries for only then would they be easily accessible to the people. There was also a recognition that *bhikkhus* owed a debt to society in return for the essentials of life provided to them by the people. This debt could be discharged only through the teaching of the *dhamma* to them. The idea was actually made explicit in the *bhikkhunī* Kundala Kesi's statement: 'I am living on the alms of the people but I owe no debt for I preach the *dhamma* to the people in return'.[285]

The saṅgha

The Buddhists are unique in that they alone have left a detailed account of their rules in the form of the *Vinaya Piṭaka*. Buddhism is the earliest surviving religion to have organized itself and to have created a confederate institution in the process. The use of the term *saṅgha* for the federal organization of *bhikkhus* and the analogy with the Lichchhavis, which the Buddha used for the *bhikkhu-saṅgha*,[286] has been noticed by scholars[287] who argue that the political system of the *gaṇa-saṅghas* was the model for the *bhikkhu-saṅgha*. To some extent this feature may have been shared by all the *titthiya* sects whose leaders were called *saṅghino*, *gaṇino*, *gaṇācariyo*. However the Buddha's organizing ability enabled this system to be translated into one which could work for an expanding group like the Buddhists. The *Vinaya Piṭaka* bears testimony to the wide range of rules embracing all aspects of a *bhikkhu's* existence. The *Vinaya Piṭaka* covered two vital aspects of the *bhikkhu's* life: (1) his relationship with members of the confraternity, and (2) his interaction with the lay public outside the *saṅgha*, with whom he came into contact in the course of his daily alms-round. The *Vinaya Piṭaka* was given a unique status in Buddhism. After the death of the Buddha, when the *saṅgha* attempted to compile a canon, it was the *Vinaya* which was enumerated and codified first and took precedence over the *Sutta Piṭaka*.[288] Horner states that the commentary to the *Vinaya Piṭaka* refers to it as *āyu*, the life or vitality of Buddhist dispensation, and this accounts for its being chanted first.[289]

285 *Paramattha Dīpani*, ed. F. Muller, Vol. V, pp. 101–2.
286 *D.N.*, II, pp. 61–2.
287 See, for example, K.P. Jayaswal, *Hindu Polity*, p. 86.
288 *Cullavagga*, p. 408.
289 *B.O.D.*, V, p. xvi.

The solid foundation on which the *saṅgha's* development was based in its early stages is one of the major reasons for the popularity of Buddhism. Even outsiders, like *brāhmaṇas* and King Pasenadi,[290] were impressed by the great concord that existed in the *saṅgha*. This atmosphere was fostered by the federal structure of the *saṅgha* and the elimination of leadership tussles. While it was clear that the Buddha was the undisputed leader of the *saṅgha* during his lifetime, there was to be no question of nominating a successor after his death.[291] Instead, the *vinaya* was to be the only guide of the *saṅgha*.[292] How successfully the system worked immediately after the death of the Buddha, when the leadership issue was likely to have been most live, is demonstrated in the *saṅgha's* censure of Ānanda. Despite Ānanda's seniority and closeness to the Buddha and apart from his wide popularity with the laity, he was censured for various faults. Ānand's humble acceptance of the *saṅgha's* indictment is remarkable particularly as he did not consider himself at fault. However, never for a moment did Ananda dispute the authority of the *saṅgha* to censure him.[293]

In addition to the *vinaya* rules which guided the moral and ethical behaviour of the *bhikkhus*, the growing *saṅgha* necessitated the development of norms regarding the minimum material needs of the *saṅgha*. Initially *bhikkhus* lived by the stricter rules which they shared with the wider *samaṇa* culture. But, as the *saṅgha* expanded the institution of the *vassā-vāsa* became the basis for developing permanent residential settlements for *bhikkhus*. Associated with this development was the acceptance by the *saṅgha* of land, which came into the exclusive possession and control of the Buddhist *saṅgha*. From the evidence available in the Pāli canon it appears that in pre-Buddhist days there were common areas of residence for all *samaṇas*, either in open parks[294] or in common halls. These were provided by members of the royal family, as, for example, the Ekasālā park donated by queen Mallikā,[295] or by the resident community as a whole as in the case of the Lichcchavis and the Vesāliyan *kūṭāgārasālā*.

[290] *M.N.*, II, p. 368; *S.N.*, I. p. 73.

[291] This cannot be traced to the lack of existing talent. There were at the time of Buddha's *nibbāna* a number of senior monks like Upāli, Mahā Kassapa, and Ānanda, who could very well have stepped into the Buddha's place.

[292] *D.N.*, II, p. 118. [293] *Cullavagga*, p. 411. [294] *D.N.*, I, p. 150.

[295] *M.N.*, I, pp. 126, 291; *M.N.*, II, pp. 173, 224.

The first gift of property exclusively to the *saṅgha* was made by a king. This introduced a new feature in the development of religious organizations, for other individual sects were thus far given *ārāmas* where they could reside or use as halting places from time to time. The *Mahāvagga* gives the following account:

> Sitting near him the Magadhan King Seniya Bimbisāra thought: 'Where may I find a place for the Blessed One to live in, not too far from the town and not too near, suitable for going and coming, easily accessible for people [who want to see him], by day not too crowded, at night not too exposed to much noise. . . clean of the smell of people, hidden from men, well fitted for retired life?'
>
> And the Magadha King Seniya Bimbisāra thought 'There is Veḷuvana, my pleasure garden, which is not too far from the town and not too near. . . . What if I were to make an offering of the Veḷuvana pleasure garden to the fraternity of *bhikkhus* with the venerable Buddha at its head'.[296]

The Buddha accepted the Veḷuvana *ārāma* as the first gift of property to the *saṅgha*. That this was a new phenomenon for the *samaṇa* culture is indicated by the Buddha's statement to the *saṅgha*, immediately after receiving the gift: 'I allow you Bhikkhus, to receive the donation of an *ārāma*.'[297]

The probable precedent for this development could have been the tradition of gifting *brahmadeya* lands to *brāhmaṇas* by the kings of Kosala and Magadha. However, there were very important differences between the gift of *brahmadeya* lands to *brāhmaṇas*, and the *dāna* of *ārāmas* to the Buddhists. The *brahmadeya* lands were granted to individual *brāhmaṇas*, who then used them for agricultural purposes. Sometimes he used the income from these lands to perform large sacrifices.[298] This income was the personal property of the individual *brahmadeya* holders. The *dāna* to the Buddhists on the other hand was always made to the *saṅgha* as a collectivity. The recurrent formula when a gift to the Buddhists was being made was that it was a gift dedicated (*patiṭṭhapeti*) or established to the *saṅgha* of the four quarters (*catudissā saṅgha*)[209] of the present and the future. It was used entirely for residential purposes, and, according to Dutt, it was maintained by the original donor.[300]

296 *Mahāvagga*, p. 38; *B.O.D.*, IV, p. 51.
297 Ibid. 298 *D.N.*, I, p. 109.
299 The *Vinaya* defines *vatthu* or property as consisting of an *ārāma* or a *vihāra*. Both served as residences for the *bhikkhus* (*Pārājika*, p. 60).
300 S. Dutt, *Buddhist Monks and Monasteries of India*, p. 58.

The gift of an *ārāma* was followed by the special sanctioning of the institution of the *vihāra*, which the *Cullavagga* reports. *Vihāras* were permanent structures, distinct from the temporary rain shelters (*āvāsas*) which the *samaṇas* had probably erected themselves in the common parks in the past. The *Vinaya* account of the various objects that the Buddha is reported to have sanctioned[301] gives a graphic account of the development of the *saṅgha* from the original position, where all that *bhikkhus* collected from the people was alms-food. For the rest, they either depended on nature or on cast off objects from the people. Their robes, for example, were originally pieced together from rags collected by the *bhikkhus*.[302]

The bhikkhus *and the laity*

The growing needs of the *bhikkhu saṅgha* naturally resulted in the establishment of permanent ties between the *saṅgha* and the laity. So long as *bhikkhus* toured incessantly no *continuing* relationship between the *saṅgha* and the people was likely to emerge. The original relationship had existed in the basic gift of alms in exchange for which the *bhikkhu* taught *dhamma* to the giver and then moved on. With the development of permanent residences or *vihāras* a constant relationship was built up between *bhikkhus* and some sections of the people who became *upāsakas* and *upāsikās*, supporting the *saṅgha* for its minimum needs and accepting the Buddha's basic teachings at the same time.

The transformation of the *saṅgha* from an association of eremitical *bhikkhus* to a settled monastic organization made *dāna* one of the central concepts of Buddhism, particularly in relation to the lay supporters of the religion. *Dāna* was described as the most important means available to the layman of accumulating merit.[303] The relationship between *dāna* and *puñña* for the layman is stated in the *Cullavagga* by the *seṭṭhi* of Rājagaha, who had sixty dwelling places built in a day: 'Lord, I had these sixty dwelling-places built because I need merit, because I need heaven' ('*ete me, bhante, saṭṭhi vihāra puññyathikena saggathikena kārāpita*').[304] Further on, the Buddha states that among all gifts the *dāna* of a *vihāra* is considered the chief gift to the *saṅgha* (*vihāra dānang saṅghassa aggang buddhena vannitang*).[305] The *Mahāvagga* observes that the people were over-

[301] *Cullavagga*, pp. 239, 282, 336. [302] *A.N.*, II, p. 29.
[303] *A.N.*, II, p. 69. [304] *Cullavagga*, p: 240. [305] Ibid.

joyed when first permitted to gift robes to *bhikkhus*. They ran about happily saying 'now we will give *dāna*, now we will gain *puññya*.'[306] Sīha the Lichchhavi general once asked the Buddha if the visible results of *dāna* could be demonstrated. The Buddha affirmed that this could be done and proceeded to enumerate the concrete results of *dāna*, which include fame, confidence, and rebirth in heaven after death.[307] Similarly the Buddha tells a *mahāmatta* (great official) that a gift of food results in much merit accruing to the giver and ensures heaven for him.[308] Suppavāsā, the Koliyan *upāsikā* who once gave food to the Buddha, was told that the person who gave food gave life, beauty, happiness and strength but in doing so one also became a receiver of the same benefits.[309] The best path open to the householder (*gihī sāmici paṭipada*) was to provide the *saṅgha* with essentials. The Buddha tells Anāthapiṇḍika: '*Gahapati*, possessed of four things, the *ariyasāvaka* enters the householder's path of duty, a path which brings good repute and leads to the heaven world . . . the *ariyasāvaka* waits upon the *saṅgha* with the offer of a robe, alms-food, lodgings, and medicines for use in sickness.'[310] The ideal *ariyasāvaka* was one who believed in the *dhamma* and gave *dāna* to the *saṅgha*.[311] Various items are listed as objects of *dāna*. They include food, drink, robes, vehicles, wreaths, perfumes, bedding, dwellings, and lights.[312] The giver surpasses the non-giver in five ways: in lifespan, beauty, happiness, honour, and fame, and the god Sakka (Indra) himself exhorts the *yajamāna* to give *dāna* to the *saṅgha*.[313] *Dāna* also ensures rebirth in a higher status, whereas the effect of non-giving meant downward mobility in the next life.[314] In a rare early Buddhist use of the word *caṇḍāla* the term is used to describe a person who looks for a gift-worthy person outside the *saṅgha* and offers service there.[315]

Dāna *versus* yañña

In giving primary importance to *dāna* as a means of gaining merit the Buddha was shifting the focus away from *yañña*. It must however be made clear that the Buddha did not completely substi-

[306] *Mahāvagga*, p. 298. [307] *A.N.*, II, pp. 304–5.
[308] *Mahāvagga*, p. 239. [309] *A.N.*, II, p. 66.
[310] *G.S.*, II, p. 73; *A.N.*, II, p. 68.
[311] *A.N.*, IV, p. 47. [312] *A.N.*, II, p. 217.
[313] *A.N.*, II, pp.299–300; *G.S*, III, p. 24.
[314] *A.N.*, II, p. 217; *S.N.*, I, p. 32. [315] *A.N.*, II, p. 452.

tute *dāna* for *yañña*, but rather moved *dāna* to a central position for the layman and edged *yañña* to the periphery. A stock passage in the Pāli canon indicates this very clearly: those who did not believe in *dāna* or *yañña*, nor the results of action, are criticized for their barren and perverse philosophy.[316] Sacrifice was not completely eliminated, only animal sacrifice was rejected, but *yañña* was now to take a secondary place in the Buddhist scheme of things. *Yañña* for the welfare of the family is redefined as a perpetual *dāna*.[317] The *Kūṭadanta Sutta* makes this very explicit. When the *brāhmaṇa* Kūṭadanta wished to perform a large *yañña* he consulted the Buddha on the subject. The Buddha told him the story of King Mahāvijita who had wished to perform a great animal sacrifice but was persuaded by his wise *purohita* to distribute gifts instead. After the gifts had been distributed to all the deserving, the king performed a sacrifice which did not include the massacre of animals. The sacrifice was entirely voluntary with only those who wished to work helping in its organization. The sacrifice was performed using only ghee, oil, butter, milk, and honey. The Buddha identifies himself with the wise chaplain of the past and tells Kūṭadanta that, better than performing sacrifices, is the giving of perpetual gifts to virtuous recluses. Even better is to put up *vihāras* for the *saṅgha*, and at the top of the scale comes the observance of the *pañcasīlas*,[318] which, of course, relates to the cultivation of the mind and therefore to the moral uplift of the individual rather than the means of gaining merit.

While the principle of *dāna* was exhorted in general the Buddhists also made it clear that the maximum merit would accrue when the donor made a gift to a worthwhile donee. The Buddha did not advocate the termination of gifts to other religious sects even though he was unfairly accused of this occasionally.[319] Nevertheless, he did indicate that his own *saṅgha* was the best recipient of *dāna* and often described the Buddhist *saṅgha* as the 'peerless field of merit.'[320] The description of Sīha's acceptance of Buddhism is a good example of the Buddha's position on *dāna*. Sīha, a Lichchhavi, was originally a follower of the Jainas but, on expressing his desire to switch allegiance to Buddhism he was asked to continue giving

[316] *M.N.*, III, pp. 84, 115, 135. [317] *A.N.*, II, p. 44.
[318] *D.N.*, I, pp. 115ff. [319] *A.N.*, I, p. 148.
[320] *M.N.*, II, p. 402; *A.N.*, II, p. 195.

alms to the Jainas.[321] This may have been a result of the Buddha's recognition of the general need for support through alms, in the *samaṇa* way of life. Given this, it might have seemed unethical to advocate a complete severance of all relations with other religious sects, merely because the teachings of one particular sect were more appealing to a layfollower.

It might be of some significance to point out that the *yañña* appears to have been specially associated with *brāhmaṇas* and kings in the Pāli canon.[322] It is only they who are depicted as making arrangements for the performance of *yaññas*. According to the *brāhmaṇa* Sundarika Bhāradvāja the categories of people who made oblations to the Gods were *isis*, *brāhmaṇas*, and *khattiyas*.[323] The absence of the *gahapati* is striking since in every way he *should* have been an ideal sacrificer—he was eminent, wealthy, and learned (see Chapter III). In this context it might also be useful to point out that according to the Pāli canon the system of sacrifice, especially the large animal sacrifice, did not have the support of the common people. The *dāsa-kammakaras* who were required to help in making the preparations are described as being forced into doing so. They are pushed around, with tears on their faces, and 'hectored' about by blows in the process.[324] The importance given to *dāna* on the other hand brought the large majority of the people into the orbit of religious experience. Everyone from the king and the *gahapati* downwards, including the more humble sections,[325] could make a small gift to the *saṅgha* by feeding a few of the *bhikkhus*. *Dāna* thereby replaced *dakkhiṇā* (*dakṣiṇā*) as the major link between the religious categories on the one hand and the people on the other.

In the shift of focus away from *yañña*, *dāna* never came to occupy the central role of *yañña* in the Brahmannical system, however. *Yañña* had been the core of the Brahmannical religion, so vital in its potency that almost everything including, the seasons, creation, and the world itself were founded on the sacrifice. *Dāna*, on the other hand despite its tremendous significance for the layman, was

321 *A.N.*, III, p. 298; *B.O.D.*, IV, p. 323.

322 *M.N.*, I, p. 114; *A.N.*, II, p. 221.

323 *Sutta Nipāta, Khuddaka Nikāya*, Vol. I, p. 335.

324 *S.N.*, I, p. 94; *A.N.*, II, p. 221.

325 There is an example of a poor *kammakara* who took an advance on his wages from his master in order to feed some *bhikkhus* (*Pācittiya*, p. 108). The typical alms giver however is the *gahapati*.

only a means of gaining merit available to people leading a lay life. Anāthapiṇḍika, who was famous for his generous *dāna* to the *saṅgha*, was once asked not to be satisfied with *dāna* alone but to undertake further training.[326] By itself *dāna* would not achieve even as much as the observance of the five *sīlas* by the *upāsaka*, and it was certainly not a means to the ultimate goal of *nibbāna*.

The laity's influence on the saṅgha

The relationship between the *bhikkhu-saṅgha* and the laity, through the medium of *dāna*, brought the laity more sharply into focus in the Buddhist world. Since the laity provided for the *saṅgha*, they were an important constituent of Buddhist society and often exercised their influence upon the *saṅgha*. Many instances of this shall be given in Chapter V but here attention should be drawn to the fact that the renouncer could not really function 'above and beyond the conventional laws' as held by Thapar.[327] On the other hand, the conduct of the *bhikkhu* was ultimately shaped and moulded by the very society he had opted out of. This is clear from the many rules laid down for *bhikkhus* that had emanated from criticism by the laity. Sometimes the laity asserted itself in relation to the *saṅgha*, as indicated by the *upāsaka* Udena's complaint that his request to establish a *vihāra* for the *saṅgha* during the *vassā-vāsa* should not have been turned down, since he was a benefactor, a builder, and supporter of the *saṅgha*. His complaint led to a relaxation of the original rules.[328]

A notable feature of the relationship between the *saṅgha* and the laity was the *bhikkhu's* lack of control over his lay-followers. If there was occasion for discord between the two the only way open to the *bhikkhu* to express disapproval was to turn his alms-bowl upside down in a symbolic refusal of the proferred alms,[329] thereby depriving the lay-follower of merit. The relationship between *bhikkhu* and layman could easily become tenuous (as seems to have happened after a while in India) in a situation where the *bhikkhus* and *upāsakas* were not firmly bound together, apart from their relationship through *dāna*. This was bound to make a difference once

[326] *A.N.*, II, p. 452.
[327] R. Thapar, 'Renunciation: The Making of a Counter Culture', *Ancient Indian Social History*, p. 89.
[328] *Mahāvagga*, p. 145. [329] *Cullavagga*, p. 214.

monasteries became firmly established through the patronage of selected sections of society, reducing the need for the daily alms-round. The layman would not then normally meet the *bhikkhus* unless specifically seeking them out by inviting them to his home for special meals. There were no common rituals at which the *bhikkhus* and the *upāsakas* could meet. The major Buddhist rituals like the *pātimokkha* ceremony were exclusively for *bhikkhus*, so that the laity remained only very loosely tied to the *saṅgha*. There were also large areas of an *upāsaka's* life upon which Buddhism does not seem to have had an impact, at least in the Indian situation. For example, the domestic rituals based on the life cycle or *saṃskāras* continued to be performed according to the existing tradition, probably because they were already deep-rooted and Buddhism did not attempt to substitute different rituals. This led Udayanacarya to remark that there was no sect in India which had given up the performance of domestic rituals: 'There does not exist a religious system, the followers of which do not perform the Vedic rites beginning with the *garbhadhāna* and ending with the funeral rites, even though they regard them as *saṃvrita*, that is, having but a relative or tentative truth.'[330]

Although Buddhism did not seem to take any stand on the issue of domestic rituals, it endorsed some other traditions such as the *uposatha* which acquired a significant place in Buddhism. All the *cakkavattis* are depicted as observing it as a prelude to the appearance of the *dhammacakka* (wheel of *dhamma*) in the sky.[331] The *Aṅguttara Nikāya* approves of its observance by laymen.[332] The *uposatha* was also significant for the *añña titthiya's*.[333] It was on the *uposatha* day that the ritual of the *pātimokkha* was held for the *bhikkhu saṅgha*. *Uposatha* appears to have been one of the popular existing traditions which Buddhism adopted. In addition, the Buddhists exhibited a certain sympathy with the popular cult of venerating *caityas* or the local shrines—a particularly marked feature of worship in the *gaṇa-saṅghas*. The Lichchhavis had seven such spots just outside Vesāli, of which Buddha spoke admiringly.[334] One of the seven conditions that he outlined for the prosperity of the Lich-

[330] R.G. Bhandarkar, 'A Peep into the Early History of India', *J.B.B.R.A.S.*, Vol. XX, 1897–1899, p. 363.

[331] *D.N.*, II, p. 132; *D.N.*, III, p. 48

[332] *A.N.*, I, p. 197; *A.N.*, III, p. 355; *A.N.*, IV, pp. 164–7.

[333] *Mahāvagga*, p. 105.

[334] *D.N.*, II, p. 92.

chhavis was their continued veneration of *caityas* in the region.[335] This tradition appears to have been especially associated with the *gaṇa-saṅghas* which the Buddha adopted.

The new society and the phenomenon of renunciation

Before concluding our review of the main features of the religious world of the sixth century B.C., we must attempt to account for the large-scale appearance of the phenomenon of renunciation. The first part of this chapter has indicated the major changes that the period experienced in the system of production, the growth of cities and the emergence of considerable prosperity all around. The comparatively simple communal existence of the past had given way to a more complex economic and social order. The early Buddhists, as also other *samaṇas*, who witnessed these changes were emphatic that salvation was possible only for those who renounced the householder status and the social world. Their opposition to the *brāhmaṇa* (whose primary function they considered to be religious) was precisely because the *brāhmaṇas* as a group had not done so. In fact there is ample evidence in early Pāli texts to show that Buddhists thought the *brāhmaṇas* had deviated from the ideal of the seers of old by falling prey to the increasingly materialistic tendencies of society—to wealth, land, possession, honour, and fame.

It has been suggested that Buddhism had a dialectical relationship with the new system of production and the new society emerging in the sixth century B.C., demonstrating simultaneously both an opposition to and unity with it.[336] The Buddhists can be said to have a similar relationship with the religious society of the time, between the existing Brahmanical tradition and the opposing *samaṇa* culture. The structure of significant categories in the religious ethos of Buddhism were the *brāhmaṇas*, the *samaṇas* and the *bhikkhus*, and the interaction between these three created the dynamic religious system of the age of the Buddha.

[335] Ibid., p. 60.

[336] D.D. Kosambi, *The Culture and Civilization of Ancient India*, p. 100; D.P. Chattopadhyaya, *Lokāyata*, p. 468.

CHAPTER III

The *Gahapati*

Changing connotation of the term gahapati

The term *gahapati* is of crucial significance to the understanding of society at the time of the Buddha. Although it appears frequently in Buddhist literature, it does so in a variety of situations and does not appear to have a fixed or constant meaning. This has led to confusion in the term's interpretation. Like some other terms appearing in Buddhist literature, the word *gahapati* is given a special connotation by Buddhists, even though it had been in existence from very early times. This in itself is an important reason for analysing the term. In an attempt to unravel the total meaning of *gahapati*, we shall examine the wide range of possibilities that the word denotes in early Buddhist literature.[1] We shall bear in mind the context of the times, without which the full implications of the term cannot be understood.

Gahapati is the Pālī equivalent of the Sanskrit word *grihapati* (*griha*+*pati*). Grihapati appears from the *Ṛg Veda*[2] onwards and is used for the householder as master of the house.[3] Similarly, the mistress of the house is called *grihapatnī*. Later, the word features in Pāṇini's *Aṣṭādhyāyī* in the sense of master of the house, a householder.[4] While early Buddhist texts occasionally use the word in this sense, more often this connotation is overshadowed by other implications of the term. The householder aspect of *gahapati* is sup-

[1] We have already pointed to the value of textual studies in our analysis of the term *gahapati* in the Introduction. It was possible to understand the term only by taking the entire passage in which it occurred as semantically relevant. The precise meaning of the word could then be elucidated concretely by means of verbal description, resulting in a contextual definition of the term (see T. Izutzu, *The Structure of Ethical Terms in the Koran: A Study in Semantics*, p. 33).

[2] *Ṛg Veda*, XI, 53, 2; *Atharva Veda*, XIV, 1, 51; XIX, 31, 13; '*Śatapatha Brāhmaṇa*, IV, 6, 8, 5; VIII, 6, 1, 11; quoted in Macdonell and Keith, *Vedic Index of Names and Subjects*, p. 231.

[3] Ibid., p. 231.

[4] Pāṇini, *Aṣṭādhyāyī*, ed. and tr. by S.C. Vasu, Vol. I, pp. 833–4.

ported by the old commentary of the *Pātimokkha* which was incorporated in the *Vinaya* texts, where the term is explained as, 'he who lives in a house'.[5] While the term *gahapati* in the sense of householder or one who lives in a house or possesses a house is equivalent to other words implying the same—such as *gihi*, *gahaṭṭha* and *ajjhāvasati*—these terms do not imply the range of characteristics that *gahapati* carries with it. Clearly, therefore, there is a distinction between *gahapati* and the other terms and this indicates that the definition of *gahapati* as householder is insufficient.

The domains of power, religion and economy

A more comprehensive explanation of *gahapati* is given at another point in the *Vinaya* texts which states that except a king or one who is in the service of a king, and the *brāhmaṇa*, he who remains is a *gahapati*.[6] It is immediately apparent that this explanation of *gahapati* has a wider application than the preceding one of the *gahapati* as householder. This wider definition is extremely significant in determining the full implications of the term and is the most inclusive definition that has been given in the Pāli texts. It reflects a division of society by the Buddhists into three categories: the *khattiya*, the *brāhmaṇa*, and the *gahapati*, and this scheme itself implies a conceptual categorization of society into the domain of power, represented by the king and his officials or the *khattiyas*; the domain of religion, represented by the *brāhmaṇa*; and the domain of the economy, represented by the *gahapati*.[7] This implicit division is made more explicit in the *Aṅguttara Nikāya*, which states the aims of the three categories: *khattiya*, *brāhmaṇa*, and *gahapati*. While all three groups have wealth and wisdom as a common part of their quest, other factors reiterate the division of power, religion, and the eco-

[5] *gahapati nāma yo koci agārang ajjhāvasati* (*Pārājika*, pp. 307, 312; *B.O.D.*, II, pp. 47, 55).

[6] *gahapati ko nāmo*: *ṭhapetva rājānang rājabhogang, brāhmaṇang avaseso gahapati ko nāmo* (*Pārājika*, p. 319).

[7] The definition of the *gahapati* cited above also gives us a definition of the other two categories: of the king and his officials, and the *brāhmaṇas*. According to this definition the king is one who rules, the king's officials are those who are in the employment of the king, and the *brāhmaṇas* are those who are born as *brāhmaṇas* (*rājanāma yo koci rajjang karoti*; *rājabhoggang nāma yo koci rañño bhattavetanāhāro*; *brāhmaṇo nāma jātiyo brāhmaṇo*, *Pārājika*, p. 319). It is interesting to note that while the domain of power is represented by people who are actually wielding power, the domain of religion is represented by people who are born as *brāhmaṇas*.

nomy. The passage depicts the *khattiya* as aspiring for power and territory with dominion as his ideal; the *brāhmaṇa* wants *mantras* and *yañña* and has *brahmaloka* as his ideal; and the *gahapati* wants *kamma* (work) and *sippa* (craft), and has the completion of work (or the fruit of work) as his ideal.[8]

Khattiya, brāhmaṇa *and* gahapati

This categorization is an extremely frequent occurrence in early Pāli literature and is unique to the Buddhists. This theme will be examined in detail elsewhere; here we shall restrict ourselves to an examination of the use of this scheme of classification in a variety of situations. Early Pāli literature frequently refers to a division of the world into various constituents, and the most common scheme is one in which there is mention of *khattiya*, *brāhmaṇa*, *gahapati*, and *samaṇa*.[9] There is here an implicit division of the world into the social and asocial, with the *khattiya*, *brāhmaṇa*, and *gahapati* representing categories in the social world, and the *samaṇa* or recluse representing the asocial world. Within the social world the triumvirate of the *khattiya*, *brāhmaṇa*, and *gahapati* signify a division of their functions in the fields of power, religion, and economy. The triumvirate of power, religion, and economy is sometimes strikingly apparent, as, for instance, in the description of the Buddha's beginnings as preacher of a new philosophy. Soon after the Buddha made his first converts, Bimbisara, the king of Magadha, who features very prominently in Buddhist literature, is depicted as approaching the Buddha surrounded by 'twelve myriad *brāhmaṇas* and *gahapatis* of Magadha'. Later many of the *brāhmaṇas* and *gahapatis* along with the king are said to have become lay followers of the Buddha, so that the Buddha then had supporters from all the three divisions of the social world.[10]

We would like to argue that the *gahapati* represents the economy as far as the Buddhists are concerned and this broad classification includes within it all the facets of the *gahapati*. We shall now proceed to examine each of these facets.

The gahapati *as an element of the king's sovereignty*

One of the most significant features of the *gahapati* is that he is

[8] *A.N.*, III, pp. 75–6.
[9] *M.N.*, I, p. 103; *A.N.*, II, pp. 305, 491; *S.N.*, II, p. 246; *M.N.*, II, p. 199.
[10] *Mahāvagga*, pp. 35–7.

enumerated as one of the seven treasures of the *cakkavatti* or the ideal ruler of the world. The *Dīgha Nikāya* states that when the righteous ruler makes an appearance on the earth he is accompanied by seven treasures: the wheel, an elephant, horse, gem, woman, *gahapati*, and councillor.[11] This reference to the seven treasures possessed by the *cakkavatti* is frequently repeated elsewhere in the texts. In the *Aṅguttara Nikāya* only five treasures are mentioned instead of the usual seven and these are said to appear very rarely, but even here the *gahapati* is included.[12] The seven treasures of the *cakkavatti* appear to be symbols of sovereignty which implies that the *gahapati* was regarded as being intrinsic to kingship (see Chapter VI). He was obviously a prized and valued possession representing the economy without which sovereignty would be meaningless.

The *Mahāsudassana Sutta* of the *Dīgha Nikāya* gives a more detailed account of the seven treasures of the *cakkavatti* and here the association of the *gahapati* with the ability to raise wealth is strikingly apparent.[13] The symbolic narrative of the king and the *gahapati* getting treasure from the river makes it clear that it is the *gahapati* who locates the treasure and provides wealth to the king. The king cannot get it except through the effort and direct participation of the *gahapati*. In the course of this long *sutta* there is ample evidence of the *gahapati* being a major asset to the king, along with the king's other priceless possessions.

Apart from the fact that the *gahapati* features among the king's royal treasures and is intrinsic to his sovereignty[14] the *gahapati* was one of the components of society with whom the king had a close relationship. There are numerous references to the king dealing righteously with the *brāhmaṇas* and *gahapatis* of his territory. Just as a father is dear to his sons, the king is loved by the *brāhmaṇas* and *gahapatis* and is popular with them. The *brāhmaṇas* and *gahapatis* ask for the righteous ruler to pass by them slowly so that they can look at him for a long time. The king in turn asks for the carriage to be driven slowly so that he can similarly gaze at them.[15] The *Lakkhana Sutta* of the *Dīgha Nikāya* lists the various signs that signify a *cakkavatti* and it depicts the possession of a large number of *gahapatis* as an extremely valuable asset. The text states: 'It is a matter of good

[11] *D.N.*, I, p. 77. [12] *A.N.*, II, p. 419.

[13] The *gahapati* tells the *cakkavatti*, '*ahang te dhanena dhana karaṇiyang karissāmi ti*' (*D.N.*, II, p. 135).

[14] *D.N.*, III, p. 46. [15] *D.N.*, II, p. 136.

fortune if the *gahapatis* are well disposed towards the king, if he is popular with them, if he can gain their loyalty, if they conform to his wishes, if he can command their attention and if they are not divided against themselves.'[16] Right through the *sutta*, which enumerates the thirty-two signs of a *mahāporisa* (great man) and which symbolizes that the possessor would either become a great emperor or a great renouncer, various signs indicate that the *gahapati* is the most important social group in relation to the king.[17]

The gahapati *as controller of property*

It is evident from the early Pāli texts that the possession of property was an essential aspect of the *gahapati*. There are specific references to the management and control of property by the *gahapati*.[18] In the *Potaliya Sutta* of the *Majjhima Nikāya* the *gahapati* Potaliya is depicted as being offended by the Buddha's reference to him as a *gahapati* since he considered himself to have retired from that position. Potaliya specifically points to the fact that he had relinquished his control over property (*vohāra samuchhedam*) when remarking that he had handed over to his sons all his wealth and substance, all his gold and coins of silver, and that he no longer issued orders with respect to these things.[19] *Gahapatis* are also frequently shown travelling in order to transact business connected with the management and control of their property.[20] In a more general sense, the evidence for the *gahapati* being associated with the possession of large assets consisting of land, orchards, corn, cattle, slaves, gold and silver are too numerous to recount in detail. It is important to note that it was the possession of these assets that enabled the *gahapati* to become the donors of the *saṅgha* par excellence. The *gahapatis'* management and control of property is reinforced by the fact that the largest category of donors to the *saṅgha*, apart from the king, were *gahapatis* whose gifts included land in the form of *ārāmas* and the erection of *vihāras* for the use of *bhikkhus*.[21]

[16] *D.B.*, III, p. 141; *D.N.*, III, p. 114. [17] *D.N.*, III, pp. 110–38.

[18] *M.N.*, II, p. 15; *Pācittiya*, p. 216; *Cullavagga*, p. 32.

[19] *M.L.S.*, II, p. 26 (*idhame bho Gotama, yan ahosi dhanang va dhaññang va rajatang va jātarupa va sabbang tan puttānang dāyajang niyyātang, tathāyang anovādi anupavādi ghaschādan-paramo viharāmi, M.N.*, II, pp. 27–8).

[20] *S.N.*, III, p. 252; *Pācittiya*, p. 216.

[21] *Cullavagga*, pp. 240, 253; *A.N.*, I, p. 255.

The gahapati *as tax payer*

Since the *gahapati* was associated with property as owner and controller, he was actually the pivot of the economy and therefore the major tax payer. Apart from the implicit representation of the *gahapati* as the base of the king's treasury and the actual locator of the treasure in the mythical account of King Mahāsudassana referred to earlier, there is also an explicit reference to the *gahapati* as tax payer in the *Dīgha Nikāya*. The *gahapati* is described as someone who 'pays taxes and thus increases the king's wealth'.[22]

The gahapati *as associated with agriculture*

While it is established that the *gahapati* represents the economy and was its pivot, it is necessary to demarcate his exact function within the economy. Here again the term seems to appear with various facets. The *Samaññaphala Sutta* of the *Dīgha Nikāya* states that the *gahapati* is a 'free man, one who cultivates his land, one who pays taxes, and thus increases the king's wealth'.[23] The *Sumaṅgala Vilāsinī*, a commentary on the *Dīgha Nikāya* written by Buddhaghosha, also refers to the *gahapati* as 'one who cultivates'[24] and definitely associates him with the land as a cultivator. The *Aṅguttara Nikāya* also provides similar references to the *gahapati's* association with land and cultivation.[25] He is depicted as carrying on various agricultural activities such as ploughing and harrowing his field, sowing at the proper season and irrigating his lands. He is depicted as performing all these functions in rapid succession which is obviously the proper thing to do. The *Saṁyutta Nikāya* too associates the *gahapati* with agriculture[26] and it is significant that the *Milindapañha*, a Pāli work attributed to the first century A.D., and therefore considerably later than the earliest strata of Buddhist texts, continues to identify the *gahapati* with agriculture. While using a simile to explain a point to king Milinda the venerable Nāgasena says, 'As, sire, an agriculturist, a *gahapati*, when he had ploughed and sown, would fill his granary. . . .'[27] The association of the *gahapati*

[22] *D.B.*, I, p. 77 (*gahapati ko, kārakārako, rāisvaḍḍhako*; *D.N.*, I, p. 53).

[23] *D.B.*, I, p. 77 (*kassako, gahapati ko . . . . D.N.*, I, p. 53).

[24] *Kassati ti kassako* (Buddhaghosha, *Sumaṅgala Vilāsinī Dīgha Nikāya Aṭṭhakatha*, ed. by Mahesh Tiwari, p. 191).

[25] *A.N.*, I, p. 222. [26] *K.S.*, IV, p. 221.

[27] *Milindapañha*, ed. by V. Trenckner, p. 41; tr. by I.B. Horner, as *Questions of King Milinda*, Vol. I, p. 57.

with agriculture in the *Milindapañha* is important as later Pāli and Sanskrit Buddhist texts tend to lose the clarity of the early Pāli texts, particularly in the use of terms to specify economic categories.

Mendaka, a prominent *gahapati* in Buddhist literature, is definitely located in agriculture. In the *Mahāvagga* of the *Vinaya Piṭaka* he is said to possess certain psychic powers along with other members of his household. The important point, however, is that all the references to the psychic powers relate to the requirements of a land-based agricultural family. According to the text:

> Mendaka came to have this kind of eminence in psychic power. Having washed his head, having had the granary swept, he sat down just opposite the door, and a shower of grain having fallen down through the air, filled the granary. His wife came to have this kind of eminence in psychic power. Having sat down beside only one bowl and one helping of curry and condiments she served food to slaves, workmen and servants. His son came to have this kind of eminence in psychic power; having taken hold of only one purse containing a thousand (*kahāpana*) he gave six months wages to each slave, workman, and servant. His daughter-in-law came to have this kind of eminence in psychic power, she gave six months food to each slave, workman, and servant. When Meṇḍaka's slave ploughed with one ploughshare, seven furrows came from it.[28]

Mendaka's grand-daughter Visakhā was given ploughs, ploughshares and other farm implements along with cattle at her marriage to Puṇṇavadhana, the son of Migāra, a *gahapati* of Sāvatthi.[29] Anāthapiṇḍika *gahapati* is depicted as having some work in a village in the Kāsī country where he had an inmate of the village (*antevāsi*) as overseer or supervisor, possibly to handle his lands in the village since he himself lived at Sāvatthi.[30] Another prominent lay-follower, Citta *gahapati*, was a resident of a village called Macchikāsaṇḍa. He had a mango grove (*ambāṭaka ārāma*) in his village where a number of *bhikkhus* are said to have stayed for a while.[31] In the *Saṁyutta Nikāya* he is described as arriving in Migapathaka on some business.[32] The commentary describes Migapathaka as his tributary village and[33] the picture that emerges suggests that Citta was in possession of substantial tracts of land.

[28] *B.O.D.*, IV, p. 329; *ekena nangalena kassantassa satta sitāyo gacchanti ti* (*Mahāvagga*, p. 255).

[29] *D.P.P.N*, Vol. 2, p. 901.

[30] *Pācittiya*, p. 216.

[31] *S.N.*, III, pp. 252–7.

[32] Ibid., p. 252.

[33] *D.P.P.N.*, Vol. 1, p. 866.

The brāhmaṇa-gahapati

The image of the *gahapati* as a landed and agriculture based category that appears from these descriptions is reinforced by the compound term *brāhmaṇa-gahapati*.[34] The word *gahapati* is rarely suffixed to another category in early Pāli literature, the only exceptions being those of the *brāhmaṇa* and the *seṭṭhi*. Wagle has pointed out that one never comes across the expression *khattiya-gahapati*,[35] but it should be pointed out that similarly one never comes across the term *sudda-gahapati*. This has some significance for analysing the category of *gahapati* which we shall consider later. A striking feature of the term *brāhmaṇa-gahapati* is that it invariably occurs in the context of *brāhmaṇa-gāmas*, mostly in the kingdoms of Magadha and Kosala. For instance, it is stated in the *Majjhima Nikāya* that in the course of his travels the Buddha arrived in a *brāhmaṇa-gāma* of Kosala called Sāla and the *brāhmaṇa-gahapatis* of the village heard of his arrival and came to see him.[36] The same description is repeated for the *brāhmaṇa-gāmas* of Verañjā, Nagaravinda, Pañcasālā and Veḷudvāra.[37]

In some passages certain villages are not only described as *brāhmaṇa-gāmas* but, as we have pointed out in Chapter II, there is mention of a particular *brāhmaṇa* living in it and enjoying special privileges on the land in the form of a *brahmadeya* grant. The relationship between the individual *brahmadeya* holder and the *brāhmaṇa-gahapatis* is not explicitly stated anywhere in the texts. We have however suggested one possible connection in our earlier discussion of *brahmadeya* land. Apart from the contextual connection between the *brahmadeya* grantee holding land in a *brāhmaṇa-gāma* which was populated by numerous *brāhmaṇa-gahapatis*, the only other clue that we can use is the mode of address used for the *brāhmaṇa-gahapatis*.

An important aspect of the term *brāhmaṇa-gahapati* is that it is invariably used to describe a collective category, never individuals. Thus, the general inhabitants of all the *brāhmaṇa-gāmas* are collectively referred to as *brāhmaṇa-gahapatis*, and when addressed directly by the Buddha, as *gahapatayo*.[38] Kūṭadanta and Caṇkī, both

[34] This term also appears to be unique to Buddhist literature.

[35] N.N. Wagle, *Society at the time of the Buddha*, p. 152.

[36] *M.N.*, I, p. 349.

[37] *M.N.*, I, p. 356; *M.N.*, III, p. 395; *S.N.*, I, p. 113; *S.N.*, IV, p. 300.

[38] *M.N.*, III, pp. 394–7; *M.N.*, I, pp. 349–55; *M.N.*, I, pp. 356–9.

brahmadeya holders on the other hand, are always referred to and addressed as *brāhmaṇas*.[39] One explanation for this is that *brāhmaṇa-gahapati* is a descriptive term applying to *brāhmaṇas* based on the land, who nonetheless continued to be identified with the larger body of *brāhmaṇas* with priestly rather than economic functions. The *brāhmaṇas* were one of the distinct groups that had emerged by this time and possessed a cohesiveness which was probably different from that of other categories in society. In this context, the *Vinaya* definition of a *brāhmaṇa* as one who is born a *brāhmaṇa* may be recalled, even though this definition is contrary to the spirit of the Buddhist system of ideas. A further point to notice is that, while *brāhmaṇa* inhabitants of the *brāhmaṇa-gāma* of Opasāda are called *brāhmaṇa-gahapatis*, 500 other *brāhmaṇas* who were visiting it were not described as *brāhmaṇa-gahapatis* but simply as *brāhmaṇas*.[40] In the light of the evidence cited it may thus be reasonably established that the term *brāhmaṇa-gahapati* refers to *brāhmaṇas* based on land in villages which were probably inhabited almost entirely by *brāhmaṇas*. The *brāhmaṇa-gahapati* functioned in these villages as a substitute for the *gahapati* in non-*brāhmaṇa-gāmas*, and involved himself directly in agriculture, at least as a manager of agricultural operations. In this capacity he paid taxes to the king as is evident from the *Mahāsudassana Sutta* of the *Dīgha Nikāya* where *brahmaṇas* and *gahapatis* are described as tax payers.[41]

Gahapati, seṭṭhi *and* seṭṭhi-gahapati

While the definitions available in early Pāli literature clearly point to the *gahapati's* relationship with agriculture, there are many indications that at least some sections of the *gahapatis* were occupied with other economic functions. The Pāli texts refer to *seṭṭhis* and, significantly, there is also the appearance of the compound expression *seṭṭhi-gahapati*. It is important to note at this point that the three terms *seṭṭhi*, *seṭṭhi-gahapati* and *gahapati* are never used interchangeably in the *Vinaya* and *Sutta Piṭakas*, which suggests that the three terms represented different conceptual categories in early Buddhist society. This distinction is blurred in later Pāli texts and in the commentaries on the *Sutta* and *Vinaya Piṭakas* which were written con-

[39] For the mode of address of various categories see N.N. Wagle, *Society at the Time of the Buddha*, pp. 192, 199–200.

[40] *M.N.*, II, p. 428. [41] *D.N.*, II, pp. 137–8.

siderably later (about the fifth century A.D.). A prominent example is the case of Anāthapiṇḍika a well-known supporter of Buddhism, who is described as a *seṭṭhi* of Sāvatthi in the *Jātakas* and the commentaries. However, in the entire *Sutta* and *Vinaya Piṭakas* Anāthapiṇḍika is consistently described as a *gahapati* and never as a *seṭṭhi*. In contrast, his brother-in-law, through whom Anāthapiṇḍika first met the Buddha, is consistently referred to as the *seṭṭhi* of Rājagaha and this distinction is systematically maintained right through the passage in question.[42] The confusion in the use of terms in the Pāli literature has resulted in some serious misconceptions regarding a number of prominent figures associated with early Buddhism. Following the later texts, historians have indiscriminately used the term *seṭṭhi*, a merchant or banker, for many of the *gahapatis*. The case of Meṇḍaka is particularly striking. As we have already shown, he and his family are quite clearly based on the land. However both Meṇḍaka and his son Dhanañjaya are referred to in later Pāli sources as *seṭṭhis*.[43]

The first point to note is that both the terms *seṭṭhi* and *seṭṭhi-gahapati* are found most frequently in the *Vinaya Piṭaka*. This fact is of some significance because the *Vinaya Piṭaka* is considered to have been compiled a little later than some of the earliest texts, such as the *Sutta Nipāta* or the *Dīgha Nikāya*, where these terms do not occur at all. Also, the term *seṭṭhi*, or its Sanskrit equivalent *śreṣṭhin*, does not appear in the *Aṣṭādhyāyī* of Pāṇini whose work is generally regarded as falling between the period 500 to 300 B.C. The absence may be explained by the suggestion that the terms *seṭṭhi* and *seṭṭhi-gahapati* were new and represented an emerging phenomenon of a specific region. Broadly, this region is likely to have been north-eastern India and the NBP ware culture sites.

It is significant that *seṭṭhis* and *seṭṭhi-gahapatis* are most frequently located in the big urban centres of Varanasi and Rājagaha, followed by Campa and Sāketa. All references to the two terms suggest that they represented great wealth. For instance, Yasa, one of the Buddha's earliest converts, was a *seṭṭhi-putta* and is depicted as having three palaces for the different seasons: one for the winter, one for the summer, and one for the rains. The entire description relating

[42] *Cullavagga*, pp. 249–50.

[43] *Dhammapada Aṭṭhakatha*, tr. by E.W. Burlingame as *Buddhist Legends*, Vol. III, p. 130.

to Yasa is similar to that of a king or wealthy nobleman, for even his footwear consisted of golden sandals. Apart from three palaces, he had people to wait on him and amuse him constantly, watching every movement of his.[44] Soṇa Koḷivisa, another *seṭṭhi-putta*, is described as being so delicately nurtured that down grew on the soles of his feet. He was so unused to walking on his bare feet that after he joined the *saṅgha* his feet bled severely. At this point he reconsidered his decision to be a *bhikkhu*, particularly because he had 'much wealth' that he could enjoy.[45] Subsequently, the Buddha permitted *bhikkhus* to wear shoes. The *Saṁyutta Nikāya* also refers to a *seṭṭhi-gahapati* who died intestate and left behind immense property in gold and silver.[46]

A number of references to *seṭṭhis* and *seṭṭhi-gahapatis* are made in the *Jivaka Vatthu* of the *Mahāvagga*, which indicate their wealth and power. Jivaka Komārabhacca was a well-known physician of the Buddha's time who was reputed to have cured many important patients. Of the incidents recorded in the *Jivaka Vatthu*, all invariably refer to *seṭṭhis*, *seṭṭhi-gahapatis*, and kings. They include the treatment and cure of a *seṭṭhi-putta* of Vārānasi, the wife of the *seṭṭhi* of Sāketa, and a *seṭṭhi-gahapati* of Rājagaha, as well as King Bimbisāra of Magadha and King Pajjota of Avānti.[47] The ability of the *seṭṭhi* and *seṭṭhi-gahapati* to pay large sums to the famous physician is also evident. The wife of the *seṭṭhi* of Sāketa when finally cured after years of suffering from a head ailment is said to have given 4,000 *kahāpaṇas* to Jivaka Komārabhacca. Her son, daughter-in-law and husband also paid 4,000 *kahāpaṇas* each, and her husband additionally gave a horse, a chariot, a slave and a slave woman to Jivaka.[48]

The prominence of *seṭṭhis* and *seṭṭhi-gahapatis* and their links with power are reiterated in other references. The *seṭṭhi-gahapati* of Rājagaha who was treated by Jivaka is described in the texts as being important to the *negama* (urban council) and the king. The *negama* then approached King Bimbisāra and requested him to command Jivaka to attend the ailing *seṭṭhi-gahapati*. When cured the *seṭṭhi-gahapati* gave 100,000 *kahāpaṇas* to Jivaka and another 100,000 to the king. That the *seṭṭhis* had easy access to the king is evident from the fact that the *seṭṭhi* of Vārānasi approached Bimbisāra and sought

[44] *Mahāvagga*, p. 20. [45] *Mahāvagga*, p. 203. [46] *S.N.*, I, pp. 88–9.
[47] *Mahāvagga*, pp. 288–94. [48] *Mahāvagga*, pp. 289–90.

his permission to use the services of Jivaka for the treatment of his son.[49] The entire *Jivaka-Vatthu* demonstrates the links between the *seṭṭhi's* wealth and, through it, with power. Another passage in the *Cullavagga* also demonstrates the links between the *seṭṭhi* and the king. The *seṭṭhi* of Rājagaha, a brother-in-law of Anāthapiṇḍika, is depicted as being pre-occupied with preparations for a big feast when Anāthapiṇḍika visited him. This led Anāthapiṇḍika to wonder whether the *seṭṭhi's* involvement with the arrangements was because the king and his retinue were coming to the feast.[50] The narration clearly suggests that the *seṭṭhi* and *seṭṭhi-gahapati* not only had access to the king but close links with him.

Although the literature has helped to construct a general picture of the *seṭṭhi* and *seṭṭhi-gahapati* it does not clearly indicate the precise functions of the two categories. The Pāli dictionary also reflects a general picture in its explanation of the *seṭṭhi* as foreman of a guild, treasurer, banker, 'city man', and wealthy merchant.[51] This definition is not completely satisfactory for our purposes since it is based on a variety of texts, very disparate in time. In our sources it is apparent that the terms were just beginning to gain currency and there is nothing definite in them to suggest the broad range of characteristics mentioned in the dictionary. The contribution of Fiser[52] is very valuable, in this context, even though he has relied mainly on the *Jātakas*, which are later than our sources. Nevertheless, Fiser's conclusions are of some relevance in understanding the functions of the *seṭṭhi* as reflected in early Buddhist literature.

Fiser has ruled out the identification of the *seṭṭhi* as the foreman of a guild. He also argues that the association of the *seṭṭhi* with trade is not automatically warranted. It is notable that the term *seṭṭhi* is always used independently of the term *vāṇijja* and these two terms are never substituted for or confounded with each other.[53] The conception of the *seṭṭhi* as a banker is also not a very happy one, according to Fiser, because this would be only a loose way of defining the *seṭṭhi's* functions. However the possession of large liquid assets by a *seṭṭhi* and his city base suggest the possibility of business connections with trade, as lenders of money to traders, and, poss-

[49] Ibid, pp. 291–3. [50] *Cullavagga*, p. 249.

[51] T.W. Rhys Davids and W. Stede, *The Pāli-English Dictionary*, p. 722.

[52] I. Fiser, 'The Problem of the *Seṭṭhi* in the Buddhist *Jātakas*', *Archiv Orientalni*, Vol. XXIV, Praha, 1954, pp. 238–66.

[53] Ibid., p. 244

ibly, even as direct investors in it. However, there is no evidence, even in later Buddhist texts, of the *seṭṭhi* actually being involved in the buying and selling of merchandise. Fiser concludes, 'the *seṭṭhi* lent money, and . . . lent considerable sums . . . to people living by trade; the *seṭṭhi* was a man who had (considerable) wealth and therefore was a valuable connection for all those people who wished to make their living by trade and who needed some initial capital, or may be had run into debt and sought a way out by changing their way of living.'[54] Fiser quotes a *Jātaka* story of a *seṭṭhi* enforcing debts very rigorously and adds, 'here the *seṭṭhi* appears in a new function, in the role of a real usurer. We can now call him "treasurer" and with certain reservations a "banker" because the terms are convenient enough to denote a man of his wealth, position, and influence in society.'[55]

Having established somewhat generally the possible functions of the *seṭṭhi* let us now return to the earlier problem of distinguishing between the terms *seṭṭhi* and *seṭṭhi-gahapati*, and in turn distinguishing these from the term *gahapati*. Significantly the mode of address for all these categories was *gahapati*. The *seṭṭhi* of Rājagaha is described as a *seṭṭhi* but addressed as *gahapati*.[56] Similarly, Yasa's father was described as a *seṭṭhi* but addressed as *gahapati*.[57] If the mode of address is common to all three terms, what is the difference between them?

The common mode of address for all three categories probably reflects their broad classification as representatives of the economy where they are part of the scheme of categories: *khattiya*, *brāhmaṇa*, and *gahapati*, or the political, religious and economic groups mentioned earlier. The description of the various people, as distinct from the mode of address points to their specific functions within the larger framework of the economy. We suggest that the *gahapati* in the narrower sense, as a term of description, stands for someone who was primarily based on the land, whereas the term *seṭṭhi-gahapati* represents a person who combined in himself the functions of agriculture and accumulated capital, possibly through profits from it, which he then invested in business. There are more references to *seṭṭhi-gahapatis* than to *seṭṭhis* in the *Vinaya* literature and this might suggest that most money lenders combined the management of agriculture with usury, and that even when they were city-

[54] Ibid., p. 263. [55] Ibid. [56] *Cullavagga*, p. 249. [57] *Mahāvagga*, p. 21.

based they retained their association with land. This connection is also suggested by Fiser who remarks: 'It seems probable that the *seṭṭhis* invested in their transaction a certain part of the profits gained in agriculture.'[58] We have an example of the likely process by which the *gahapati* became a *seṭṭhi-gahapati* in the *Aṅguttara Nikāya*, where a *gahapati* is described as offering a loan on payment of interest to a shopkeeper (*pāpaṇika*) to expand his business.[59] Beginning as petty usurers, they probably built their capital over a period of time and came to possess substantial liquid assets.

We are now left to identify the term *seṭṭhi* to which, as we have stated earlier, there are only a few references in the early Pāli canon. An important point about these references is that they are invariably related to a specific place. All the references not only to *seṭṭhis*, but also to *seṭṭhi-gahapatis*, are made to unnamed individuals. It is as if the *seṭṭhi* or *seṭṭhi-gahapati* of a particular place was identification enough and no further details were necessary. For example, references to the *seṭṭhi* of Rājagaha,[60] or to the *seṭṭhi* of Vārānasi[61] suggest that there was a close relationship between the *seṭṭhi* and the place mentioned. While all *seṭṭhi-gahapatis* appear to be wealthy, the *seṭṭhi* of Rājagaha seems to be not only wealthy but extremely important too. According to the *Cullavagga*, he had a very valuable piece of sandalwood from which a bowl was made and suspended from a height. He then held a competition saying, 'If any *samaṇa* or *brāhmaṇa* be an *arahant* and possessed of *iddhi* [psychic power] let him get down the bowl and it is a gift to him.'[62] The leaders of the *añña titthiyas* all attempted to get the bowl down but failed. Only Piṇḍola Bhāradvāja, a Buddhist monk with psychic powers, succeeded in getting the bowl down. Contrasting Buddhists and the *añña titthiyas* is a device normally associated with the powerful and prestigious person of the king in Buddhist literature. Here it is associated with the *seṭṭhi* of Rājagaha. Apart from the king, the *seṭṭhi* was probably the most prominent figure in society.

On the basis of *Jātaka* evidence Fiser has suggested that the king could have appointed some *seṭṭhis* to his own services. He speaks of the occurrence of the term *seṭṭhi-thanam*, or the position of the *seṭṭhi*, in the context of towns and cities, probably held by the *seṭṭhi* until

[58] I. Fiser, 'The Problem of the *Seṭṭhi* in the Buddhist *Jātakas*', *Archiv Orientalni*, Vol. XXIV, Praha, 1954, p. 244.

[59] *A.N.*, I, p. 107. [60] *Cullavagga*, p. 249. [61] *Mahāvagga*, p. 293.

[62] *Cullavagga*, pp. 199–200; *B.O.D.*, V, p. 149.

his death. There is the possibility also of this position being hereditary. On the question of the *seṭṭhi* of a particular place, like the *Bārānasi seṭṭhi*, Fiser suggests that it could include in itself a distinct function or privileged position, and that the term meant the *seṭṭhi* working for the king of the region.[63]

Although based on the admittedly later sources of the *Jātakas*, Fiser's conclusions could explain the term *seṭṭhi* as it appears in the *Vinaya* literature. When it appears without the qualifying *gahapati* attached to it, and when associated invariably in the context of a particular place, the term *seṭṭhi* signifies a very prestigious semi-official position which the more common *seṭṭhi-gahapati* did not have, although he may have been wealthy enough in his own right.[64] We may now return to the specific category of the *gahapati*.

Gahapati *as employer of labour*

The image of the *gahapati* as an independent owner of the means of production is reinforced by frequent references to his employing labour. Although *gahapatis* as a category were generally owner-cultivators who were themselves involved in the process of cultivation, some differentiation had already come into existence within their ranks. The larger operators of land needed to employ labour, as is evident from early Pāli sources. The existence of the *dāsa*, *kammakara* and *porisa* are well known but it is notable that they frequently appear with *gahapatis* as their masters. A typical example is that of *gahapati* Meṇḍaka who employed a large number of *dāsas*, *kammakaras*, and *porisas,* whom the family fed and paid wages, both in cash and in kind. His ploughman was a slave called Puṇṇa who possessed psychic powers like the rest of the family.[65] Similarly, the Buddha exhorted the *gahapati-putta* Sigāla to treat his slaves and workmen well, by assigning them work according to their strength, by supplying them with food and wages, by tending them in sickness and giving them leave from time to time.[66] *Seṭṭhis* and *seṭṭhi-gahapatis* who were part of the wider *gahapati* category are also depicted as employing slaves and others in their service.[67] In fact, from a passage in the *Saṁyutta Nikāya* which depicts him as recruiting people into his service the typical employer appears to be

[63] I. Fiser, 'The Problem of the *Seṭṭhi* in the Buddhist *Jātakas*', *Archiv Orientalni*, Vol. XXIV, Praha, 1954, pp. 250–1.

[64] Ibid. [65] *Mahāvagga*, p. 255. [66] *D.N.*, III, p. 147. [67] *Cullavagga*, p. 249.

the *gahapati*.[68] The need to employ *kammakaras* or workmen would exist in the larger holdings of land.[69] These *gahapatis* were also likely to have been producing for the market, which explains the frequent need to travel that is often associated with *gahapatis* in the Buddhist texts.[70] Such activities would also have resulted in the gradual accumulation of capital, which ultimately transformed some *gahapatis* into *seṭṭhi-gahapatis*, and then to *seṭṭhis* investing in various business enterprises.

Gahapati *as a status term*

An important aspect of the term *gahapati* is its frequent occurrence as a status term. It is apparent that, while the term can be used in a generic sense to apply to a category, it also appears in a specific sense where it 'almost assumes the function of a title'.[71] A point to note is that there could be only one *gahapati* in each family and it was he who wielded actual authority in it. According to Rhys Davids, he was distinct from the subordinate members of the family who did not have the control and management of the common property.[72] This is further substantiated by the existence of the term *gahapati-putta*, which probably referred to the son of a *gahapati* as one who would eventually succeed to the status of a *gahapati*. Interestingly, the expression *gahapati-putta* is not matched by similar expressions like *brāhmaṇa-putta*, *khattiya-putta* or *sudda-putta*. The word *gahapati-putta* had a specific connotation, similar to the term *seṭṭhi-putta*, which also represents status and an eventual succession to the position of a *seṭṭhi*. In both cases the crucial factor is that they denote economic functions in which the management and control of assets is *indivisibly vested in one authority*. Buddaghosha definitely points to this view in describing the *gahapati* as *gehassapati*, *ekageha-*

[68] *S.N.*, III, pp. 334–5.

[69] This dimension of the *gahapati* was much sharper in the seventh century A.D. by which time the *gahapati* was invariably an employer of labour. The *Tantra-Vartika* of Kumarila states that the *gahapati* does not labour on his land, the *kammakaras* work on it for him (*Tantra-Vartika of Kumarila*, Poona, 1910, p. 3185).

[70] *S.N.*, III, p. 252; *M.N.*, II, p. 15.

[71] T.W. Rhys Davids and W. Stede, *Pāli-English Dictionary*, p. 248. The Jaina texts also indicate a similar use of the term *gahavai* which is their equivalent of the word *gahapati*. It appears as a status term and the same association with land, cattle, and ploughs is present (J.C. Jain, *Life in Ancient India as Depicted in the Jain Canon*, p. 143).

[72] T.W. Rhys Davids, *Buddhist Suttas*, S.B.E., Vol. XI, pp. 257–8n.

matte jeṭṭhako[73] or the head and oldest member of a house. The conception is similar to that of the *karta* in Bengal, who is the head of a house and in whom the management and control of the family property is vested. This view is supported by Wagle's conclusions on the mode of address adopted by the Buddha for *gahapatis*. The Buddha invariably addressed them as *gahapatis*, not by their names. However the *gahapati-puttas* were never addressed by anything but their names. Wagle makes a distinction between the use of terms as terms of reference and as terms of address. In certain situations the terms of reference are also those of address, but in others the terms of reference do not coincide with the mode of address. In the context of the *gahapati* the coincidence or otherwise between the term of reference and that of address focuses on the actual status of the individuals concerned.[74]

The general impression conveyed by the early Pāli texts is that, as a category, *gahapatis* had a prominent place in the social structure of early Buddhist society. They invariably featured along with *khattiyas* and *brāhmaṇas* as people of high status in relation to the rest of society. It was common to refer to *khattiyas*, *brāhmaṇas*, and *gahapatis* in idealized terms, which stressed their high social status. For instance, in his discourses dealing with the great pleasure given by visible forms to a viewer, the Buddha used the analogy of an ideal woman: 'A maiden of the *khattiya*, *brāhmaṇa*, or *gahapati* family, between fifteen and sixteen years of age, not too tall, not too short, not too plump, not too thin, not too dark, not too pale, is she then in her full flower of charms and beauty?'[75] Similarly, some *bhikkhus* considered people born in *khattiya*, *brāhmaṇa*, and *gahapati* families as deserving the highest privileges within the *saṅgha*.[76] These three groups were also generally associated with authority, wealth, and eminence. Stressing the inevitability of death the Buddha told King Pasenadi, 'Even they who are eminent *khattiyas*, eminent *brāhmaṇas*, or eminent *gahapatis*, men of authority owning great treasure, great wealth, immense hoards of gold and silver, immense aids to enjoyment, immense supplies of goods and corn, even they being born cannot live without decay and death.'[77] The same association is repeated by King Pasenadi to the Buddha when he complains

[73] Buddhaghosha, *Sumaṅgala Vilāsinī*, p. 191.
[74] N.N. Wagle, *Society at the Time of the Buddha*, p. 53.
[75] *M.N.*, I, p. 122; *M.L.S.*, I, p. 116.
[76] *Cullavagga*, p. 255. [77] *S.N.*, I, p. 70; *K.S.*, I, p. 97.

that, 'eminent *khattiyas*, eminent *brāhmaṇas*, and eminent *gahapatis*, men of authority. . . who [are] nevertheless found deliberately telling lies while seated in the judgement hall.'[78]

These groups were not only associated with authority, wealth, and eminence but also with learning and wisdom. Reacting to a charge levelled by the *paribbājaka* Magandiya the Buddha says, 'mind what you say Māgandiya . . . for many learned *khattiyas*, learned *brāhmaṇas*, learned *gahapatis* and learned *samaṇas* have great faith in this Gotama'.[79] It is apparent from the passage that the devotion of these categories was considered prestigious by the Buddhists. The three categories were also important enough to have assemblies (*parisas*) of their own and entering them required a degree of confidence. Talking to Sīha the Lichchhavi on the merits of alms giving, the Buddha pointed out that whichever *parisa* the alms-giver entered, whether of the *khattiyas*, *brāhmaṇas*, or *gahapatis* he 'enters untroubled and with confidence'.[80]

The three groups also feature together in the context of rebirth into families of high status. The *Majjhima Nikāya* states that a *bhikkhu* who possessed certain powers could, if he so desired, be reborn as a wealthy *khattiya*, a wealthy *brāhmaṇa* or a wealthy *gahapati*.[81] The status of a *gahapati* was obviously worth aspiring to. Conversely, it was possible to fall from the high status of a *khattiya*, *brāhmaṇa*, or *gahapati* in this life into that of a family of low status in the future.[82] It may be relevant to point out in this context that the *gahapati* Citta, a prominent lay follower of the Buddha, and one who was described as an ideal layman (*upāsaka*), is singled out for a unique honour in the Buddhist literature. On his deathbed the *devas* and kinsmen of Citta exhorted him to aspire to be reborn as a *cakkavatti*.[83] The *cakkavatti* was the counterpart of the Buddha in the social world and was therefore the highest position that any layman, who was already of high status, could aspire to. And further it was considered a potential possibility for the *gahapati* Citta.

The gahapati's *association with wealth*

Gahapatis are associated with wealth, prestige, and importance not only along with *khattiyas* and *brāhmaṇas*, but also on their own.

[78] *S.N.*, I, p. 73; *K.S.*, I, p. 100.
[79] *M.N.*, II, p. 199; *M.L.S.*, II, p. 182.
[80] *A.N.*, II, p. 305; *G.S.*, III, p. 31.
[81] *M.N.*, III, p. 162. [82] *A.N.*, II, p. 90. [83] *S.N.*, III, p. 268.

Gahapatis and *gahapati-puttas* are frequently mentioned in the texts along with people of inferior status and in opposition to them, thus seeming to represent a category of superior status in relation to them.[84] This image of the *gahapati* as a well-to-do and highly respectable person is strengthened by the great disapproval shown in Pāli texts of any attack upon them. They appear to be a category specially vulnerable to slander and physical harm and required strong bodyguards.[85] The royal police are depicted as seizing one such offender, binding his arms behind him with a stout rope, shaving his head and parading him round to the beat of a harsh-sounding drum. Taken from street to street, and from crossroad to crossroad he was then led to the south of the town and beheaded for the offence of 'spoiling the fortunes of some *gahapati* or *gahapati-putta* by resorting to falsehood'.[86] Since the offence related only to falsehood and not to something really criminal, the punishment seems unduly harsh: the *gahapatis* must certainly have been very powerful to have exacted such severe punishment for offences against them.

A special association is reflected in Buddhist literature between the *gahapati* and the pursuit of pleasure. The only other category that is similarly depicted is the king. The *bhikkhu* is frequently depicted as being tempted to give up his *bhikkhu* status as he happens to sight 'a *gahapati* or *gahapati-putta* indulging in the five sense pleasures. Then he thinks: I too when living at home indulged in . . . the five sense pleasures. Moreover since wealth exists in my family I could enjoy it and do good work with it'.[87] Similarly, in the *Māgandiya Sutta* of the *Majjhima Nikāya*, the Buddha repeats the association between the *gahapati* and pleasure when stating, 'A *gahapati* or *gahapati-putta*, rich or of great wealth, of many possessions who, endowed with the five strands of sense pleasures, might revel in them'.[88] The *Aṅguttara Nikaya* provides a vivid picture of the *gahapati*. 'A *gahapati* or *gahapati-putta* has a house with a gabled roof, plastered inside and outside with well-fitting doors and casements. Therein a couch is spread with a costly skin of antelope, having a canopy overhead and a scarlet cushion at each end. Here is

[84] *A.N.*, II, p. 222; *M.N.*, I, p. 229; *D.N.*, I, p. 55.
[85] *S.N.*, II, p. 334. [86] *K.S.*, III, p. 96.
[87] *A.N.*, II, p. 131; *G.S.*, II, p. 129.
[88] *M.L.S.*, II, p. 184; *M.N.*, II, p. 202.

a lamp burning and four wives to wait upon him with all their charms . . .'[89]

The gahapatis *as extenders of popular support to Buddhism*

Curiously enough, many prominent *gahapatis* appear in Buddhist texts in the unique position of having followers of their own. This is unusual, since the only other people usually referred to with followers of their own were the leaders of the other sects. The *gahapati* Anāthapindika, probably the largest donor of the *saṅgha*, is described in the *Aṅguttara Nikāya* as coming to see the Buddha surrounded by 500 lay disciples of his own.[90] Elsewhere, the *gahapati* Dhammadinna is similarly described as having 500 lay followers,[91] and the commentary to the *Saṁyutta Nikāya* states that six other *gahapatis* and Visākhā the woman lay disciple also had a following of 500 disciples each.[92] These disciples may have then become followers of the Buddha through their own *gahapati*, which suggests that the *gahapatis* played an important role in the extension of popular support to Buddhism.

The gahapati's *special relationship with the* saṅgha

Another important aspect of the *gahapati* was the special relationship some had with the *saṅgha*. It is customary in the texts to depict *bhikkhus* who were ill or on their deathbeds as being visited by the Buddha and given succour in their afflictions. The custom seems to have been largely restricted to *bhikkhus* apart from some very rare exceptions in the context of prominent lay disciples. All these exceptions invariably relate to *gahapatis*. Thus, the *gahapati* Nakulapīta was visited by the Buddha when he was ailing.[93] Similarly, Anāthapiṇḍika asked for Ānanda when he was ill and was visited and reassured by him.[94] The *gahapatis* Sirivaḍḍha and Manadinna also called for Ānanda when they were ill and specially inquired about their respective futures after death.[95] Their possession of wealth and high social status, along with their position as the largest donors of the *saṅgha*, gave them privileges which were normally restricted only to the *bhikkhus*. *Gahapatis* were clearly the most important category among the lay disciples of the *saṅgha*.

[89] *G.S.*, I, p. 120; *A.N.*, I, p. 127. [90] *A.N.*, II, pp. 452, 457.
[91] *S.N.*, IV, p. 348. [92] *K.S.*, V, p. 347n.
[93] *A.N.*, III, p. 19. [94] *S.N.*, IV, p. 329. [95] *S.N.*, IV, pp. 152, 153.

Gahapati *and* gāmanī

Another relationship which we need to explore is that between the *gahapati* and *gāmanī*. The term *gāmanī* has been translated by the Pāli-English dictionary as the head of a company, a chief, and a village headman. The *gāmaṇī* appears to have held an official position.[96] The *Mahāvagga* speaks of King Bimbisāra giving instructions to 80,000 *gāmikās*[97] on worldly or political matters, which points both to their political status as well as their numerical significance. While the *gāmaṇī* appears to have some relationship with the *gahapati*, there is nothing explicit in the Pāli texts to indicate the actual nature of the relationship. It is possible that the *gāmaṇī* was recruited from amongst the *gahapatis* and was the administrative head of the village. It is evident from a passage in the *Saṁyutta Nikāya* that the *gāmaṇī* was familiar with the nature of the soil and with agricultural operations generally, including the specific choices to be made in relation to them.[98] The *gāmaṇī* also appears to be fully conversant with the official machinery, including the system of laws and justice. They were well established, since one of them possessed a comfortable resthouse which was used by *samaṇa-brāhmaṇas* on their sojourns and sometimes by leaders of the different sects.[99] We suggest that the *gāmaṇī* represented the 'political' wing of the *gahapati* category. While the *gahapati's* function pertained to the economy, the *gāmaṇī* combined economic and political functions as the official head of the village. This explains the greater assurance of the *gāmaṇī* (in a *Saṁyutta Nikāya* account) when he defended Buddhist monks against various charges in the king's court.[100] In another incident, he also displayed a degree of self possession in the presence of the Buddha whom he accused of being no different from a magician.[101] The *gāmaṇī* may possibly have been the political arm of the *gahapati* category, wielding power within the village and providing a link for *gahapatis* with the power structure outside the village at the same time.

Gahapati: *from householder to agriculturist*

Before concluding our analysis of the term *gahapati* we must try to

[96] Rhys Davids and Stede, *Pāli-English Dictionary*, p. 249.

[97] *Gāmika* could be the official term for the *gāmaṇī* (*Mahāvagga*, p. 199).

[98] *S.N.*, III, p. 279. [99] Ibid., pp. 302–5.

[100] *S.N.*, III, p. 288. [101] Ibid., p. 299.

account for an important aspect of the term: its shift in meaning from a word that signified a householder, or head of the family unit, to one that signified an economic category and, more specifically, that of an agriculturist. The shift in the term *gahapati*, from denoting a householder to denoting an agriculturist, took place because there was an underlying relationship between the two senses of the term. This relationship was also intimately connected with the economy and society of the period in which the shift in meaning was actually taking place.

On the basis of early Pāli texts the image of the *gahapati* that we have already outlined is of a category of people who were the owners and controllers of the primary means of production in the form of land. They were the backbone of the economy and were responsible for agricultural production. Very often the *gahapati* laboured on the land himself, along with his family, producing both for his family and for the market through which he gradually built up a certain amount of capital. It was the *gahapati* who played a crucial role in the extension, and consolidation of the agricultural economy. *Gahapatis* were heads of family units that operated the land and it was primarily through the family unit that the system of production was organized. Wagle has briefly alluded to the *gahapati* as the head of the household as an economic unit. More specifically, the *gahapati* was the head of the household as a producing unit. This aspect of the term is important when we consider the near absence of the *gahapati* in the *gaṇa-saṅghas* and concentration in the kingdoms of Magadha and Kosala instead.[102] This feature is related not only to the existence of different political systems in the *gaṇa-saṅghas* and the monarchies, which we have already outlined in Chapter II, but also to the different social and economic systems in the two types of states.[103] It appears that the oligarchic political systems of the *gaṇa-*

[102] Chanana also remarks on the absence of categories other than the *dāsa-kammakaras* in the 'oligarchies' in contrast to the regions controlled by the kings (D.R. Chanana, *Slavery in Ancient India*, p. 158, n. 38).

[103] While there are numerous works on the political system of the *gaṇa-saṅghas* which show that they were markedly different from the monarchies (see Chapter II), no major work exists on the social organization of the *gaṇa-saṅghas* partly because of the paucity of material. We have tried to piece together stray references from the Buddhist texts as a whole and draw inferences from them. We have also had to rely on evidence from later Pāli texts which we have normally avoided in our work for reasons outlined in the Introduction. Since our sources give us information only for the eastern *gaṇa-saṅghas* we shall confine our analysis to them. General observations

saṅghas rested upon their lineage based social and economic organizations, which were marked by the absence of private property in the land. In contrast, the *gahapatis* spread out in the kingdoms of Kosala and Magadha were directly associated with the possession of private property in land. Let us now consider some of the facts that are available.

The social organization of the gaṇa-saṅghas

The existence of a large concentration of *khattiyas* in the *gaṇa-saṅghas* has also been pointed out in Chapter II. These areas reveal a comparatively simple social organization consisting preponderantly of one or more *khattiya* clans and their slaves and workmen. Some artisans are mentioned such as the barber and the metalsmith, but apart from these there are hardly any references to other social groups, and even those to *brāhmaṇas* are not very numerous. The early Pāli texts refer to only one *brāhmaṇa* village located in the Sākyan territory and also gives us the additional information that the *brāhmaṇa-gahapatis* of this village had their own assembly.[104] Apart from this reference, *brāhmaṇas* are rarely mentioned and only appear in their ritual function as the chaplains (*purohitas*) of the kings.

Landholding in the gaṇa-saṅghas

The conclusion that *khattiyas* in the *gaṇa-saṅghas* did not involve themselves with agriculture, except for performing managerial functions, is clear from a passage in the *Vinaya-Piṭaka*. Mahānāma the Sākyan describes agricultural functions to his brother Anuruddha thus: 'It is necessary to *get* the land tilled, and then *have* it irrigated . . . Once the crop is ready it is necessary to *get* it harvested and *get* the grain winnowed from the chaff' [italics mine].[105] Chanana has pointed out that these instructions are in the causative and therefore represent the *khattiyas* as supervising work done by others.[106]

---

available in the *Mahābhārata* and the *Arthaśāstra* have also been of some use in reaching conclusions. The discussion in Chapter II on the political organization of the *gaṇa-saṅghas* should also be borne in mind.

[104] *S.N.*, I, p. 183. This reference might indicate the spread of the trend, already well established in the monarchies, of the *brāhmaṇas* being settled on the land and creating their own villages.

[105] *Cullavagga*, p. 279; *B.O.D.*, Vol. V, pp. 253–4.

[106] D.R. Chanana, *Slavery in Ancient India*, p. 43.

Even the supervision was done by some members only, while others seemed to enjoy the benefit of communal ownership. Anuruddha, for instance was obviously unaware of even the managerial aspects of agriculture since his brother had to explain the unending nature of the agricultural cycle to him. This is reiterated in a story which describes the ignorance of three young Sākyans who did not even know where rice came from.[107]

The suggestion that land in the *gaṇa-saṅghas* was communally owned by the entire clan is supported by the reference to a dispute between the *dāsa-kammakaras* of the Sākyas and the Koliyas. The Sākyas and the Koliyas were neighbouring clans whose lands were separated by the Rohini river.[108] In the months of May and June when the water from the river would be at its lowest, the sharing of the river water to irrigate the fields of the Sākyas and Koliyas sparked off a quarrel between their respective *dāsa-kammakaras*, who are described as being employed by the residents of both territories. The *dāsa-kammakaras* in turn had to take up the dispute with ministers of both clans who had charge of the work.[109] The Sākyans and the Koliyans then came to the rescue of their own *dāsa-kammakaras*. The whole narration suggests the collective ownership of land by the clan.[110]

Another story narrates the king's role among the Sākyas in the annual ploughing festival called *vappa maṅgala*. According to the *Nidāna Katha*, the king wielding a golden plough and 107 of his councillors wielding silver ploughs participated in a ritual ploughing while their *dāsa-kammakaras* enjoyed the festival, wearing new clothes and garlands.[111] It is possible to infer from this description of the festival that the king and clan elders were jointly demonstrating their communal ownership of the land, which was normally worked by the *dāsa-kammakaras*.

The existence of the notion of common property among the *gaṇa-saṅghas* is more definitely stated in a *Vinaya* passage regarding

[107] E.W. Burlingame, *Buddhist Legends*, Vol. I, p. 232.

[108] Originally the Sākyas and Koliyas were related to each other since they are said to have had a common ancestor (see G.P. Malalasekhara, *D.P.P.N.*, Vol. I, pp. 689–90).

[109] E.W. Burlingame, *Buddhist Legends*, Vol. III, pp. 70–1.

[110] *The Jātakas*, ed. by V. Fausboll, Vol. V, p. 413.

[111] *Nidāna Katha*, tr. by T.W. Rhys Davids as *Buddhist Birth Stories*, pp. 163–4.

the *bhikkhu* Sudinna Kalandaka, who was a *seṭṭhi-putta* before his entry into the *saṅgha*. His family is described as possessing immense wealth, which led Sudinna's mother to plead with him to provide the family an heir so that the entire property would not pass to the Lichchhavis, who were treated as a collective entity.[112]

Tension within the gaṇa-saṅghas

According to Radhakrishna Chowdhary, Kauṭilya's reference to *vairājagaṇas* indicates societies where notions of mine and thine were not observed.[113] This would however apply only to *khattiya* clan members in relation to each other, who collectively exercised power. The equality of all clan members would also be possible in such a situation. The *Mahābhārata* states this quite clearly when it treats all members of a *gaṇa-saṅgha* as equal to one another in their birth and family status.[114] The only major difference that existed was between the *khattiya* clan members who jointly held the land, and the *dāsa-kammakaras* who jointly worked the land. The incident of the slaves of the Sākyans attacking the Sākyan womenfolk has already been cited as an example of the social tensions that existed in society (see Chapter II). It indicates also the inner tension that existed within the *gaṇa-saṅghas*. While there are numerous references to the *dāsa-kammakaras* in the Pāli texts, this is the only example we have of their having resorted to violence against their masters. We suggest that this attack on the Sākyans is itself an indication of the group consciousness of the *dāsa-kammakaras* in relation to their Sākyan masters. Since the *dāsa-kammakaras* worked *as a group* on the land for their masters *as a group*, they took collective action against their joint masters. The group consciousness itself was possible not only because the *dāsa-kammakaras* shared the same material interests but because it was possible to translate this into a 'we feeling' in a situation in which they and their masters both represented collective units in relation to each other. This example of inner tension within the *gaṇa-saṅgha* also provides the clue to the *Arthaśāstra's* injunction that, in order to create dissension within a republic, the king who wishes to destroy them should foster in-

[112] *Pārājika*, p. 22.

[113] Radhakrishna Chowdhary, 'Ownership of Land in Ancient India', *J.B.R.S.*, Vol. LIII, 1967, p. 35.

[114] *Mahābhārata*, Vol. 13, p. 509.

dignation amongst its inhabitants by highlighting economic disparity.[115]

Two types of saṅghas

The *Arthaśāstra* deals with two different types of *saṅghas*: one in which the *kṣatriya* inhabitants live by *vārtā* and *śastra*, and another in which they live by the title *rāja*.[116] The first type refers to such people as the Kāmbojas and Surasenas, and the second to the Lichchhavis, Mallās etc. Ruben[117] describes the two separate types as being derived from differences based on property in the soil. The first type he considers as vesting in the *saṅgha* as a group, in areas with barren soil and under poor conditions, as existed in the desert of Saurashtra and in the steppes of the north-west. Those who lived by *vārtā* were therefore *saṅghas* in which the inhabitants jointly performed both economic functions (agriculture and cattle-keeping), and military functions themselves. In the second type he believes that the *kṣatriyas* (all or some of them) were proprietors of their landed estates, which he implies were separate. However, we suggest that the differences in the two types of *saṅghas* were not based on communal holding in one and landed estates in the other, but on whether the *kṣatriyas* themselves worked the land, as in the case of the Kāmbojas and Suraṣṭras, or whether they had the land worked through others such as the *dāsa-kammakaras*, as outlined above.

Some implications of clan ownership of land

Another point of some significance in the context of the ownership of land in the *gaṇa-saṅghas* is that, although the Buddha had many individual followers in them, almost all the gifts of *ārāmas* and *vihāras* to the *saṅgha* mentioned in the early Pāli texts were made in the non-*gaṇa-saṅgha* regions. While in Rājagaha, Sāvatthi, Sāketa and Kosambī the Buddha is described as staying in various *ārāmas* which had been gifted to the *saṅgha*, no similar arrangements existed in the *gaṇa-saṅghas*. Instead, the Buddha is often depicted as residing in a common hall (*kūṭāgārasāla*) in Vesāli.[118] On his last *vassa* spent near Vesāli, Buddha's request to the *bhikkhus* to go and stay

[115] *Arthaśāstra of Kauṭilya*, ed. by R.P. Kangle, Vol. I, p. 245.
[116] Ibid., p. 244.
[117] Walter Ruben, 'Some Problems of the Ancient Indian Republics' in *K.M. Ashraf*, ed. by Horst Kruger, pp. 23–4.
[118] *D.N.*, II, p. 93; *D.N.*, I, p. 128.

around Vesāli with friends and acquaintances,[119] suggests that Buddhists had no *ārāma* with permanent structures of their own in Vesāli. Similarly, at least on one occasion, even among his own Sākyans, the Buddha had nowhere to stay in Kapilavatthu, although Mahānāma searched throughout the town.[120]

The only notable exceptions that we get of a gift of an *ārāma* in a *gaṇa-saṅgha* is the example of the courtesan Ambapāli's gift of an *ambavana* (mango grove) to the *saṅgha*, on the Buddha's last visit to the Lichchhavis. However, Ambapāli's position among the Lichchhavis is itself interesting. According to Buddhist tradition available in the Tibetan *Dulva*,[121] the Lichchhavis had a custom according to which a beautiful woman who was perfect in every way was not allowed to marry since that would make her the property of just one individual. She was reserved for the pleasures of the people as a whole and established as a courtesan so that everyone had equal access to her. The custom itself reflects the deeply embedded notion of common property among the Lichchhavis. The possession of the *ambavana* by Ambapāli might even be attributed to the Lichchhavis' having jointly bestowed this property on her in order to demonstrate their common claims on her. A gift of land to the *saṅgha* in the Vajjian territory would have been difficult in normal circumstances, since all the Lichchhavis would have had to agree on such a gift and this would not have been easy in a clan where many members were supporters of other sects, particularly of the Nigaṇṭhas.

Clan ownership of land, khattiyas, *and the* gaṇa-saṅghas

We have earlier pointed out that the compound expression *khattiya-gahapati* never occurs in the Buddhist texts and also to the fact that the *khattiyas* were specially associated with the *gaṇa-saṅghas*. These facts and the near absence of the *gahapati* from the *gaṇa-saṅghas*[122]

119 *D.N.*, II, p. 79. 120 *A.N.*, I, p. 258.

121 W.W. Rockhill, *The Life of the Buddha*, p. 64.

122 Two *gahapatis* are mentioned in the Vajjian territory and one in the Bhagga territory. The presence of these three may indicate the beginnings of a process of the breakdown of the social organization of the *gaṇa-saṅghas* which was bound to happen sooner or later, surrounded as they were by the monarchies where a different social organization had come into existence. It may also be pointed out that the Vajjian confederacy was a larger and less homogenous *gaṇa-saṅgha* than the Sākyans were. The Bhaggas on the other hand appear to have already become an appendage of the kingdom of Vatsa since the prince Bodhirāja Kumara had a palace in Suṃsumāragiri,

can be related to the absence of private property, at least in agricultural land, held by individual families in these areas. The oligarchic political system of the *gaṇa-saṅghas* can be better explained by such a social organization[123] since *collective political functioning would be facilitated by collective holding of the land itself.* On the other hand, the emergence of the *gahapati* elsewhere is related to the emergence of landed property held by individual families. This fact is of some significance in our attempt to understand the changing meaning of the term *gahapati*.

The gahapati, *the family, agriculture, and the private control of land*

It can be argued that the existence of the family is important in the new system of social and economic organization, since land or the individual holding must be passed on from one generation to another. The genesis myth of the Buddhists also points to the relationship between the family and private property because both appear at almost the same time in the narration.[124] The relationship between the family and agriculture is also attested to by the use of the same term for both the householder and the agriculturist in pre-Buddhist and Buddhist texts. This association has actually survived into contemporary times in the region in which the term itself was changing its connotation in early Buddhist times. Field observation in eastern Uttar Pradesh and Bihar have revealed the compound expression *kheti-grihasti* (agriculture-household functions), which is commonly used to describe agriculture. Sometimes *grihasti* alone is used to describe the occupation of agriculture and it appears that the words are synonymous and interchangeable. The term *grihast* is also widely prevalent to describe an owner-cultivator whether of a large or small holding.[125] The *grihast* may or may not work on his

the capital of the Bhaggas. These areas are likely to have therefore experienced changes in the social organization before the smaller and more homogenous *gaṇa-saṅghas* did.

[123] This view is supported by Jayamal Rai (*The Rural-Urban Economy of Ancient India*, pp. 20, 31, 38). He suggests that there was an intimate connection between property rights and the form of government.

[124] *D.N.*, III, pp. 69–71.

[125] That the term continued to carry the same connotation down the years is evident from mid-eighteenth century records of British administrators. The *grihast's* association with agriculture led a section of the administrators to recommend a settlement with them rather than with the Zamindars (R. Guha, *A Rule of Property for Bengal*, pp. 54–5).

own lands, but he never hires out his own labour to others.[126] This is exactly the image of the *gahapati* in the Pāli texts. An identical category also exists in Sri Lanka in the form of the *goyigāma*, which will be discussed in Chapter IV.

The special relationship between agriculture and the family has been explained by the anthropologist Meillasoux.[127] He argues that with the emergence of agriculture, continuity became an essential feature of social organization because of the special needs of the agricultural cycle. Members of an agricultural team are linked together, at least till the time of cropping, so that every member can benefit from the joint labour. Further, the problem of feeding the cultivator during the non-productive period of labour, between clearing the ground and harvest time, cannot be solved unless enough of the previous crop is available for the purpose. The members of an agricultural party are thus linked together not only to each other during the non-productive period of work, but also to the working party that produced the food in the previous cycle. As time goes on this amounts to a change of generation and, according to Meillasoux, provides the basis for the emergence of the family as a cohesive producing unit.

As already noted the Pāli texts furnish the example of the *gahapati* Meṇḍaka's family being jointly involved with operations on land and functioning as a cohesive producing unit. The example demonstrates the intimate relationship between the family and agriculture. The family was essential not only from the point of view of the inheritance of land from one generation to another, but, more importantly, to reproduce the labour to work the land itself. The shift in the meaning of the term *gahapati* reflects a very notable change in the social organization of north-eastern India: the emergence of the family as the basic producing unit in agriculture, along with the emergence of private control over land.

126 Personal communication from Dr A. Chakravarti on the basis of intensive fieldwork in North Bihar, and Dr Lal Bahadur Verma of Gorakhpur University.

127 Claude Meillasoux, 'From Reproduction to Production', *Economy and Society*, Vol. I, no. 1, 1972, p. 99.

CHAPTER IV

Social Stratification as Reflected in the Buddhist Texts

The problem

The problem of the stratification of society as reflected in early Buddhist texts has been a major concern of many historians and sociologists. Almost every serious writer on Buddhism has expressed some opinion on the Buddhist attitude to caste and the existing inequality in society. The fact that questions about caste and the claims of the *brāhmaṇas* to superiority appear so frequently in Buddhist texts suggests that this was a major preoccupation of the early Buddhists themselves. This explains, at least to some extent, why the subject has generated such interest amongst modern scholars.

Some of the major ways in which societies may be stratified are according to the principles of caste, class, and power. However, only caste has received the attention of scholars in the study of ancient Indian society, largely because of the emphasis on the Brahmanical viewpoint, either as the focus of study, or as the point of reference for a study of stratification. We shall attempt to analyse the problem of social stratification by taking the Buddhist texts as our main focus and try to unravel the system of ideas reflecting the Buddhist point of view. We shall also try to locate the empirical basis of these ideas. The Brahmanical system cannot be ignored and will feature wherever relevant. Since ideas about caste and class are both present in Buddhist literature it is necessary to indicate the sense in which we are using the terms. 'Caste' is used in the sense of an ascribed status group which is a component in a hierarchical arrangement of groups. 'Class', on the other hand, represents the relative importance of a group controlling the means of production.

Buddhism and caste

Two differing positions have been taken on the problem of the

Buddhist attitude to caste, which was by then already emerging as the major system of inequality in Indian society. Rhys Davids,[1] has argued that if one considers the position of the Buddha on the question of recruitment into the *saṅgha*—the only organ of society, over which he had complete control—advantages or disadvantages arising from birth, occupation, and social status were completely irrelevant. He gives numerous examples to support his argument: of Upāli, the expert on the *vinaya*, who had been a barber, of Sunita, who was a *pukkusā*;[2] of Sāti, who was a fisherman; of Puṇṇa and Puṇṇikā, who had been slave girls; and of Subhā, who was the daughter of a smith.[3] Rhys Davids argues further that on the subject of caste outside the *saṅgha* the Buddha tried to influence public opinion by a 'constant inculcation of reasonable views', as for example in the *Āmagandha Sutta* of the *Sutta Nipāta*, where he argued that defilement does not come from eating this or that, prepared and given by this or that person, but from evil deeds and words and thoughts.[4] In fact, Rhys Davids believed that, had the Buddha's views won the day, the evolution of social grades and distinctions would have developed differently and the caste system would never have been built up.[5] Rhys Davids has been the major proponent of the view that Buddhism was antagonistic to caste. This view has gained popular currency and the image of the Buddha as a social reformer led Ambedkar and the Mahars to adopt Buddhism when they rejected Hinduism as a system of institutionalized inequality.

Oldenberg, on the other hand, has pointed out that despite the fact that Buddhist theory acknowledged the equal right of all persons to be received into the *saṅgha*,[6] the actual composition of the *saṅgha* suggests that it was by no means in keeping with the 'theory of equality', and that a 'marked leaning to aristocracy seems to have lingered in ancient Buddhism.'[7] He also gives examples: of the

[1] T. W. Rhys Davids, *D.B.*, I, p. 102.

[2] The *pukkusās* are one of the five low groups frequently mentioned in the Buddhist texts. They were associated with sweeping flowers. Actually Sunita is described as a *pupphachaḍḍaka* in the *Theragāthā* (*Khuddaka Nikāya*, Vol. II, p. 330).

[3] *D.B.*, I, p. 102.

[4] *D.B.*, I, p. 104. See also *Sutta Nipāta*, *Khuddaka Nikāya*, Vol. I, pp. 304–7.

[5] *D.B.*, I, p. 107.

[6] H. Oldenberg, *The Buddha*, p. 154. He however points out that even this position was not unique to the Buddha, and long before his time there were religious orders who received members from all castes.

[7] Ibid., p. 155.

young *brāhmaṇas* Sāriputta, Moggallāna and Kaccāna; of *khattiyas* like Ānanda, Rāhula and Anuruddha; and of great 'merchants' like Yasa, who were 'men of the most respectable classes of society with an education in keeping with their social status'. People like them gathered round the teacher, who himself belonged to the Sākya nobility.[8] The problem of the social origins of early Buddhists recurs frequently in the debate on the Buddha's attitude to caste. These are actually two separate questions: one relates to practice, and the other to ideology, and we should guard against confusing the two. This chapter will attempt to deal with the question of ideology and the following chapter more with that of the practice.

On the subject of social inequalities outside the *saṅgha* Oldenberg is even more emphatic. According to him, there was nothing resembling a social upheaval in India. The inequality inherent in the caste system had no value for the Buddha and Oldenberg argues that it is historically untrue to treat the Buddha as a champion of the lower classes.[9] Similarly, Fick states that the development of caste was in no way broken or even retarded by Buddhism.[10] According to him the Buddha's doctrine did not aim at a transformation of social conditions and it was taken for granted that they were unchangeable.[11] Eliot also suggests that while Buddha attacked both the ritual and philosophy of the *brāhmaṇas*, so that after his time the sacrificial system never regained its earlier prestige, he was less effective as a social reformer.[12] Eliot argues that although the Buddha denied the superiority of the *brāhmaṇas* he did not preach against caste, partly because it existed only in rudimentary form at the time.[13]

The point that, while Buddhism was anti-Brahmanic it did not affect the caste system, has been elaborated by Bougle who states; 'Certainly Buddhism, more than any other sect, must have appeared formidable to the *brāhmaṇas*: it tended to make them superfluous by limiting . . . the place of rituals. It is clear that the Buddhist community worked to undermine the *brāhmaṇa's* clientele and the conflict of interests is undeniable.'[14] However, Bougle argues

[8] Ibid., p. 156. [9] *Ibid.*, p. 153.
[10] R. Fick, *The Social Organisation of North-East India in Buddha's Time*, p. 335.
[11] Ibid.
[12] Charles Eliot, *Hinduism and Buddhism*, Vol. I, p. xxii. [13] Ibid.
[14] Celestin Bougle, *Essays on the Caste System*, p. 73.

that Buddhists were far from 'reconstructing the edifice of Hindu society according to new plans: if they worked at replacing the roof, they never gave a thought to changing the foundations'.[15] In a similar vein Senart also writes that the conflict between the Buddhist and *brāhmaṇas* was primarily a struggle for influence, and that there was nothing in the Buddhist stand which aimed at changing the entire caste system.[16]

Weber's study of Buddhism pointed out that the membership of the *saṅgha* was predominantly recruited from the great noble families, the rich 'burghers', and the *brāhmaṇas* who were distinguished representatives of a 'cultured laity'. According to him, Buddhism had no tie with any social movememt and it ignored caste or the 'status order'. In his view, early Buddhism as a whole was the product not of the underprivileged but of a very clearly privileged strata.[17]

Both these attitudes to early Buddhism have been treated as historically unsatisfactory by Chattopadhyaya. Chattopadhyaya argues that while it is true that Buddhism was supported by monarchs, merchants and contemporary aristocrats, it would be superficial to see only this aspect of Buddhism. In Chattopadhyaya's opinion Buddhism was destined to become for various reasons the 'biggest socio-religious movement in Indian history'. He believes that the Buddha's attitude to injustices of the caste system and his attacks upon Brahmanic ritual were significant reasons for its appeal to the people. However, Chattopadhyaya also argues that the Buddha only created an illusion of liberty, equality, and fraternity by modelling his *saṅgha* on the tribal values, whereas in reality these values were being trampled upon in the world outside the *saṅgha*.[18] While Chattopadhyaya suggests a dialectical relationship between Buddhism and the new society emerging in the sixth century B.C., he does not explain or analyse the Buddhist attitude to social stratification, or the relationship between Buddhism and the actual social categories of the time; hence the earlier controversy has remained unresolved. The points of view here summarized are not based on a systematic analysis of the relevant Buddhist sources and it appears that the two contrasting positions discussed above do an injustice to the complex pattern of ideas on

[15] Ibid. [16] E. Senart, *Caste in India*, p. 205.

[17] Max Weber, *The Religion of India*, pp. 225–7.

[18] D.P. Chattopadhyaya, *Lokāyata*, pp. 466–7.

social stratification depicted in the early Pāli canon. It is important to first try and understand the Buddhist system of stratification, and then relate them to actual developments in Buddhism.

Two schemes of categorization in the Buddhist texts

A comprehensive reading of early Pāli texts reveals the use of two different schemes of categorization: one which reflects the existing Brahmanical divisions of society into *brāhmaṇas khattiyas*, *vessas*, and *suddas*; and a second, which we have already alluded to in Chapter III, as being unique to the Buddhists—that of the *khattiya*, *brāhmaṇa*, and *gahapati*.[19] While both schemes are evident throughout the texts without any clearly defined pattern being immediately apparent, the existing division of *brāhmaṇa*, *khattiya*, *vessa*, and *sudda*, is associated most often with situations in which the Buddha converses with a *brāhmaṇa*.[20] Occasionally the four-fold division also occurs in discussions with kings.[21] It is frequently mentioned while making the point that all divisions of people into these social groups are irrelevant in relation to their potential for salvation. It is never mentioned in discussions with the laity. The second scheme of classification is never used by the *brāhmaṇas*, nor by the Buddha while conversing with *brāhmaṇas*. It is used frequently in the context of wealth, learning, and eminence, in situations where Buddhist monks or the laity were present.[22]

Buddhist references to the four-fold division of society are not a replica of the Brahmanical system of differentiation. The Buddhists invariably place *khattiyas* first in the serial order of social groups being enumerated with *brāhmaṇas* following next.[23] This contrasts with the *brāhmaṇa's* enumeration of the four-fold scheme in the same texts.[24] The Brahmanical stand on the question of the superiority of *brāhmaṇas* as a social group over all others, including *khattiyas*, was emphatically denied by Buddhists.[25] Throughout the Buddhist texts a special tension is noticeable between the *khattiyas*

[19] Or sometimes the *khattiya*, *brāhmaṇa*, *gahapati* and *samaṇa*, as indicated in Chapter III.

[20] *D.N.*, I, pp. 80, 204; *M.N.*, II, pp. 404–13.

[21] *M.N.*, II, pp. 310–11; *M.N.*, I, p. 375.

[22] *A.N.*, II, p. 89; *M.N.*, I, p. 122; *M.N.*, II, p. 70; *Cullavagga*, p. 255.

[23] *D.N.*, III, p. 64; *D.N.*, I, pp. 80, 204; *M.N.*, II, pp. 311–12, 370.

[24] *M.N.*, II, p. 440.

[25] *D.N.*, I, p. 86; *D.N.*, III, p. 64; *D.N.*, II, pp. 442–8; *M.N.*, II, pp. 310–16.

and *brāhmaṇas*,[26] so that in any system of classification *khattiyas* were placed above *brāhmaṇas*.[27] If one looks at the *Aggañña Sutta*, the Buddhist genesis myth, the difference in the Brahmanic and Buddhist points of view is striking. It is the *khattiya* here who is first marked out from the mass of the people and represented as essential to the social order, not the *brāhmaṇa*.[28] In fact, in this myth the *brāhmaṇa* appears very similar to the *bhikkhu* who lives on the periphery of society, collecting alms from villages and towns and returning to the forest to meditate.[29] There is no evidence that the *brāhmaṇa* plays any role *in* society.

The Brahmanical arrangement of categories in a hierarchy of services in which the low automatically serve the high is rejected in Buddhism, even where the Buddhists mention the four-fold scheme. In the *Majjhima Nikāya*, the *brāhmaṇa* Esukārī states that *brāhmaṇas* have ordained three types of service: first where a *brāhmaṇa* may be served by another *brāhmaṇa*, or a *khattiya*, a *vessa* or a *sudda*; second, where a *khattiya* may be served by another *khattiya*, *vessa*, or *sudda*, and third where the *sudda* may be served by another *sudda* since 'who else could serve the *sudda*?'[30] The young *brāhmaṇa* Ambaṭṭha also refers to the three *vaṇṇas* of *khattiyas*, *vessas*, and *suddas* as serving the *brāhmaṇas*.[31] The Buddha refuted the Brahmanical division of society based on service and rejected *brāhmaṇa* attempts to force their opinions upon the people when the people did not accept them.[32] He however held that receiving services is not conditioned by one's position in a status hierarchy, but on one's ability to pay for service. In the *Madhurā Sutta* of the *Majjhima Nikāya* the *Buddha* pertinently refuted the *brāhmaṇa* claim to superiority based on the criteria of the lower *vaṇṇa* serving the higher. He pointed out that anyone including *suddas* who had wealth, corn, gold, and silver could have in their employment others who would rise earlier than the employer, rest later, carry out his pleasure, and speak

[26] R. Thapar, 'Social Mobility in Ancient India', *Ancient Indian Social History*, p. 131.

[27] Dumont has remarked on the relations between the *brāhmaṇas* and the *khattiyas*. He says. 'In theory power is ultimately subordinate to priesthood, whereas in fact priesthood submits to power' (L. Dumont, *Homo Hierarchicus*, p. 111). Buddhism reflects the actual situation when it places the *khattiyas* over the *brāhmaṇas*.

[28] *D.N.*, III, p. 72. [29] Ibid., p. 73.

[30] *M.N.*, II, p. 441; *M.L.S.*, II, p. 366.

[31] *D.N.*, I, p. 80. [32] *M.N.*, II, p. 441.

affably to him.[33] It is significant that in the *Aggañña Sutta* the *suddas* are associated not with the service of the higher *vaṇṇas* but with 'hunting and such like trifling pursuits'.[34] Their low level of culture accounts here for their status at the bottom of the social scheme. It is evident, therefore, that the idea of the *sudda* as one whose specific function was to serve the *brāhmaṇa*, *khattiya*, and *vessa*,[35] finds no parallel in Buddhist texts.

Terms of categorization

An important feature of the Pali texts is the use of a variety of terms to categorize people in society. Three terms are used frequently—*vaṇṇa*, *jāti*, and *kula*. In addition, a fourth categorization also appears which does not explicitly refer to *vaṇṇa*, *jāti*, or *kula*, but which is left unspecified. A comprehensive classification of the use of these terms (see Appendix A) leads to certain conclusions; first, that the four-fold scheme of *khattiya*, *brāhmaṇa*, *vessa*, and *sudda* appears most often under the Brahmanical *vaṇṇa* and *jāti* systems of classification. On the other hand, the Buddhist scheme of *khattiya*, *brāhmaṇa*, and *gahapati*, is never classified as either *vaṇṇa* or as *jāti*. It is used frequently in the context of *kula*. Alternatively, it is left unspecified. The second conclusion that emerges is the existence of the notion of high and low within all the systems of classification. It is pertinent that the Buddhists did not have a complex linear system of ranking. Instead, they had a simple two-tier system of stratification. The linear order of castes of the Brahmanical texts, where the four *vaṇṇas* are ranked one below the other, were reduced to two strata by the Buddhists in one passage of the *Majjhima Nikāya* where King Pasenadi asks the Buddha whether there could be any distinction between the four *vaṇṇas*.[36] The Buddha answers saying

[33] *M.N.*, II, pp. 311–12; *M.L.S.*, II, p. 274. The Buddhist texts also do not indicate the existence of judicial privileges based on caste. The Buddha argues that anyone committing a crime would be punished by the king, regardless of his *vaṇṇa* (*M.N.*, II, pp. 314–15).

[34] *D.N.*, III, p. 74; *D.B.*, III, p. 91.

[35] In fact the *Āpastamba Dharmasūtra* states that the higher the caste which is served by the *śūdra* the greater is the merit he gains (*The Sacred Laws of the Āryas*, S.B.E., Vol. II, p. 2). For references to *sūdras* serving the higher castes see *Gautama Dharmasūtra, The Sacred Laws of the Āryas*, S.B.E., Vol. II, p. 230; *Vashishta Dharmasūtra, The Sacred Laws of the Āryas*, S.B.E., Vol. XIV, p. 11; and *Baudhayana Dharmasūtra, The Sacred Laws of the Āryas*, S.B.E., Vol. XIV, p. 199.

[36] *M.N.*, II, pp. 375–6.

that among the four *vaṇṇas* the *khattiyas* and *brāhmaṇas* are pointed to as chief (*seṭṭho*) in the manner in which they are addressed, saluted, and served. The *vessa* and *sudda* are opposed to the *khattiya* and *brāhmaṇa* here in an implicit relationship of high and low. However, the *khattiya* and *brāhmaṇa* appear to stand in a relationship of equality *between* themselves. We shall refer to some situations where *khattiyas* are placed above *brāhmaṇas* by the Buddhists. However this invariably occurs in situations where the *brāhmaṇas* are claiming a pre-eminent position for themselves. The situations seem to be designed to humble the claims of *brāhmaṇas* to special privileges. In situations where *brāhmaṇas* were not present, *brāhmaṇas* and *khattiyas* were placed together, along with the *gahapati*.

High and low strata in Buddhist texts

A basic opposition between high and low appears in the context of *jāti*, *kula*, *kamma* (work), and *sippa* (craft); thus there are high *jatis* and low *jatis*; high *kulas* and low *kulas*; high *kamma* and low *kamma*; and high *sippas* and low *sippas*. The conception of high and low is quite explicit in the classifications of *jāti* and *kula*.[37] A long passage in the *Vinaya* texts represents *jāti*, *nāma*, *gotta*, *kamma*, and *sippa* as being of two kinds: *ukkaṭṭa* (high) and *hina* (low). While *nāma* and *gotta* refer to individuals, *jāti*, *kamma*, and *sippa* refer to groups. We shall confine ourselves to the groups being categorized as high and low. Thus *ukkaṭṭa jāti* is defined as *khattiya* and *brāhmaṇa*, while *hīna jāti* is defined as *caṇḍāla, veṇa, nesāda, ratthakāra,* and *pukkusā*.[38] The latter categories are conventionally translated as low casteman, bamboo worker or basket maker, hunter, cartwright, and flower sweeper or scavenger, by Buddhist scholars. The same division is repeated exactly in the same form further on in the *Vinaya Piṭaka*.[39]

In the *Aṅguttara Nikāya* we get an unusual scheme of *jātis*: the *khattiya*, *brāhmaṇa*, *vessa*, *sudda*, and the *caṇḍāla-pukkusā*, but they are not classified as high or low.[40] An important point to note in the above mentioned classifications of *jāti* is the absence of the *vessa* and *sudda* from the list of categories which is difficult to account for. Oldenberg has drawn our attention to the fact that the text gives

[37] *Pācittiya*, pp. 10–12; *B.O.D.*, II, pp. 173–6.

[38] Ibid., p. 10. These five *hina jātis* are frequently repeated as a group in the Buddhist texts. They are unique because this specific combination does not appear in the corresponding Brahmanical and Jaina texts.

[39] *Pācittiya*, p. 22. [40] *A.N.*, I, p. 149.

no indication of the possibilities of any other *jāti* being considered either high or low.[41] We shall return to this problem later in the chapter.

According to the Buddhist *kula* classification the *khattiyas*, *brāhmaṇas* and *gahapatis* are considered high whereas other *kulas* such as the *caṇḍāla*, *veṇa*, *nesāda*, *ratthakāra* and *pukkusā* are considered low.[42] In one reference the high *kulas* of *khattiya*, *brāhmaṇa* and *gahapati* are associated with white and the low *kulas* of *caṇḍāla*, *veṇa*, *nesāda*, *ratthakāra*, and *pukkusā* with black.[43] Further, the high *kulas* or the unit of *khattiya*, *brāhmaṇa*, and *gahapati* are invariably associated with attributes which are evaluated as high such as wealth, eminence, and learning.[44] In contrast the *caṇḍāla*, *veṇa*, *nesāda*, *ratthakāra*, and *pukkusā* are described as low and it is stated that fools will be born into such *kulas* in their next life.[45] It may be noted that there is a correspondence between the Buddhist enumeration of the *jāti* and the *kula* categories except for the marked inclusion of the *gahapati* among the high *kulas* which is missing in the high *jātis*. This is significant for our argument and will also be considered later in the chapter.

Regional dimension of stratification

The division of *kamma* (work) and *sippa* (craft) into low and high in the *Pācittiya* passage of the *Vinaya Piṭaka* already cited throws some light on the Buddhist view of stratification. Low *kamma* is defined as *koṭṭhaka kammam* (work of a storeroom keeper), and *pupphachaḍḍaka kaṁmam* (work of a flower sweeper), or 'what is disdained, disregarded, scorned, treated with contempt and despised in these districts'.[46] High work is defined as *kasī* (agriculture), *vāṇijja* (trade), and *gorakkhā* (cattle keeping), or 'what is not disdained . . . not despised' in the area.[47] It is evident from this passage that the Buddhists were reflecting an existing conception of high and low prevalent in the region where Buddhism was located. Similarly, in the case of the *sippas* too the division into high and low *sippas* is related to what was disdained and despised in the region and what was not. Thus, we have the *naḷakāra sippam* (craft of the basket-

[41] H. Oldenberg, 'On the History of the Indian Caste System', *Indian Antiquary*, 1920, Vol. XLIX, p. 225.

[42] *A.N.*, II, p. 89; *M.N.*, II, p. 447. [43] *A.N.*, III, pp. 94–5.

[44] *M.N.*, III, p. 248; *M.N.*, II, pp. 281, 287.

[45] *M.N.*, III, p. 240. [46] *Pācittiya*, p.11. [47] Ibid.

maker), *kumbhakāra sippam* (craft of the potter), *cammakāra sippam* (craft of the leatherworker), *nahāpita-sippam* (craft of the barber), and *pesakāra sippam* (craft of the weaver) rated as low; and *muddā* (reckoning on the fingers), *gaṇanā* (accounting) and *lekhā* (writing) were classified as high.[48] What is significant in the context of the *jāti* division into *hīna* (low) and *ukkaṭṭa* (high) is that the additional factor of what was disdained and despised does not appear. It can be argued that the notion of high and low in the case of *jāti* was not related to a specific area but was more widely prevalent, unlike the case of *kamma* and *sippa*, where regional differences were recognized. The regional criteria of ranking touched upon by Dumont[49] is already noticeable in the Buddhist texts, where *kamma* and *sippa* divisions of high and low were related to an area within which a similar system of ranking was prevalent.

The relationship of kula, kamma, *and* sippa

Some of the categories of the Buddhist texts can be classified under different heads. For instance, *kasī*, *vāṇijja* and *gorakkhā* are both *kamma* and *sippa*. In the *Majjhima Nikāya*, *kulaputtas* are associated with certain *sippas* such as *kasiya* (agriculture), *vāṇijjāya* (trade), *gorakhena* (cattle keeping), *issatthena* (bowmanship), *rājaporisena* (king's service), and with *muddāya* (reckoning on fingers), *gaṇanāya* (accounting) and *saṅkhānena* (computing).[50] However, regardless of the heads under which the classifications are made, groups are always consistently high or low. For instance, whatever the classification, *kasī*, *vāṇijja* and *gorakkhā* were invariably ranked as high. Thus *kulaputtas* or young men of good family who are always from *khattiya*, *brāhmaṇa* or *gahapati* families are associated with agriculture, trade, or cattle keeping,[51] or with computing, accounting, and writing, all of which are rated as high work or skills.[52] On the other hand, individual barbers and potters are described as being of low birth and the skills of the barber and the potter are identified as low.[53] One of the low *kulas*, the *pukkusā* is described as flower sweepers. This had a parallel in the low *kamma* of the *pupphachaḍḍaka* whose function is to sweep flowers.[54] Similarly the low *kula* of

[48] Ibid. [49] L. Dumont, *Homo Hierarchicus*, p. 82.
[50] *M.N.*, I, p. 119. [51] *A.N.*, III, pp. 375, 378.
[52] *M.N.*, I, p. 119.
[53] *Pacittiya*, p. 421; *M.N.*, II, p. 272.
[54] *Theragātha, Khuddaka Nikāya*, Vol. I, p. 300.

veṇa described as basket-weaver has a parallel among one of the low *sippas* in the craft of the *naḷakāra* or basket maker. It is thus possible to establish a correlation between *kula*, *kamma*, and *sippa* in the Buddhist literature especially in the context of categories that were ranked as high. Similarly one can also draw a correlation between low *kulas*, low *kamma*, and low *sippa*:

	Kula	*Kamma*	*Sippa*
High:	*khattiya, brāhmaṇa, gahapati*	*kasī, vāṇijja, gorakkhā*	*muddā, gananā, lekhā, rājaporisena, issathena*
Low:	*caṇḍāla, pukkusā, nesāda, veṇa, rathakāra*	*pupphachaḍḍaka, koṭṭhaka kamma*	*naḷakāra, nahāpita, kumbhakāra, pesakāra, cammakāra*

Empirical relevance of vaṇṇa, jāti *and* kula

One important feature of the term *vaṇṇa* is that it appears only in the context of abstract divisions of society into various social categories. We have no evidence of it being used in any concrete situation.[55] No one is ever described as belonging to the *brāhmaṇa vaṇṇa*, *khattiya vaṇṇa*, *vessa vaṇṇa* or *sudda vaṇṇa*. It seems to have remained a theoretical concept without any parallel in actual practice. On the other hand, the terms *jāti* and *kula* appear in concrete situations quite frequently. The Buddha refers to himself as of the Sākya *jāti*[56] and so do others. The young *brāhmaṇa* Ambaṭṭha repeatedly abuses the Buddha for being of the Sākya *jāti*[57] when he is sent by his teacher to meet the Buddha. Ambaṭṭha himself is referred to as a *dujjāto* (of low birth) by other *brāhmaṇas* when they discover that he is a descendant of a slave girl.[58] When he sees the Buddha for the first time Sundarika Bhāradvāja asks the Buddha to which *jāti* he belongs.[59] Similarly, King Bimbisāra, having sighted the Buddha approaching from a distance, is convinced from his appearance that the Buddha could only be of the *khattiya jāti*. When asked about his *jāti* the Buddha replies that his *gotta* affiliation is Ādicca, that he is of the Sākya *jāti*, and it is from that *kula* that he has 'gone forth'.[60] In another interesting reference, the Buddha asks the newly recruited *bhikkhus* Vāseṭṭha and Bhāradvāja whether,

[55] Except when it is used in the sense of colour or complexion.

[56] *Sutta Nipata, Khuddaka Nikāya*, Vol. I, p. 330.

[57] Ambaṭṭha is angry with the Sākyas for not having treated him properly on an earlier occasion (*D.N.*, I, p. 79).

[58] *D.N.*, I, p. 83. [59] *Sutta Nipāta, Khuddaka Nikāya*, Vol. I, p. 334.

[60] Ibid.

being *brāhmaṇas* by *jāti* and *kula*, they were reviled and abused by other *brāhmaṇas* for having joined the *saṅgha*.[61] In the *Majjhima Nikāya* the *brāhmaṇa* Caṇkī refers to the *Buddha* as being *sujāto* (of pure birth), as one who went forth from an *adina khattiya kula* (a leading *khattiya* family), and who is thereby worthy of being shown respect.[62]

From the references cited above some relationship between the terms *jāti* and *kula* is apparent. This is more noticeable in the *Sundarikabhāradvāja Sutta*. When the Buddha is asked about his *jāti* he replies that even the fact of having originated in a *nīca kula* (low family) is irrelevant in the case of a *muni*.[63] The two terms must have been closely linked for the Buddha to use *kula* in answer to a question on *jāti*. To sum up, it can be argued that the *vaṇṇa* divisions constituted a purely conceptual scheme which had no actual application, and that *jāti* was both a conceptual and actual scheme of categories based on ascribed status. However, what really seemed to matter to the Buddhists were the *kula* divisions. The *kula* categories were used more often than the *jāti* when the Buddhists themselves wished to indicate social stratification. Apart from the numerous references already cited we have instances of good behaviour and wisdom being rewarded with rebirth in the high *kulas* of *khattiyas*, *brāhmaṇas* and *gahapatis*;[64] the opposite characteristics on the other hand would result in rebirth in the low *kulas* of *caṇḍālas*, *nesādas*, *veṇas*, *ratthakāras*, and *pukkusās*.[65]

A further problem in the context of empirical verifiability is the absence of certain categories of the Brahmanical scheme of stratification. Only two of the social groups of the Brahmanical scheme are verifiable as existing categories in the Buddhist texts. These are the *khattiyas* and *brāhmaṇas*. On the other hand, the *vessa* and *sudda* categories are theoretical groups which are impossible to locate. Fick is sceptical about the real significance of these groups during the period for which the Pāli texts furnish an account. He points out that the expressions *vessa* and *sudda* occur only in passages where there is a theoretical discussion about caste, but there is nothing which points to their real existence.[66] Both terms occur occa-

[61] *D.N.*, III, p. 63. [62] *M.N.*, II, p. 430.

[63] *S.N.*, I, p. 167; *Sutta Nipāta*, *Khuddaka Nikāya*, Vol. I, pp. 334. 336.

[64] *M.N.*, III, p. 248. [65] Ibid., p. 240.

[66] R. Fick, *The Social Organization of North-East India in Buddha's Time*, p. 252. See also Wagle, *Society at the Time of the Buddha*, p. 133.

sionally in the *jāti* system of classification but they are associated more often with the *vaṇṇa* division of society. In the Brahmanical texts the *vessa* is associated with agriculture, cattle-keeping, and trade, and the *sudda* with service.[67] But nowhere in the Buddhist texts are people or groups occupied with agriculture, cattle-keeping or trade, referred to as *vessas*, or those associated with service referred to as *suddas*. Instead the Buddhist texts associate agriculture with the *gahapati*, the cattle keeper is described as a *gopaka*, and the term *vāṇijja* is used for the trader.[68] Another important category in the Buddhist literature was the *seṭṭhi* but none of these specific economic groups are in any way linked with the *vessas*. Similarly while there are no *suddas* there are innumerable references to *dāsas* and *kammakaras* who are associated not with service of the higher *vaṇṇas* but with providing labour for their masters who are almost invariably *gahapatis*.

The absence of certain categories which are empirically identifiable extends into the low status groups too. It is not just the *suddas* who are missing but the *hīna jātis* or *nīca kulas* of the Buddhist texts are also not discernible in real situations. Except for the lone example of Māṭanga, who was referred to as *caṇḍālaputto sopāko*,[69] *nesā-*

[67] *Vāśiṣṭha Dharmasūtra*, S.B.E., Vol. XIV, p. 11; *Baudhāyana Dharmasūtra*, S.B.E., Vol. XIV, p. 199; *Gautama Dharmasūtra*, S.B.E., Vol. II, pp. 232–3.

[68] *Mahāvagga*, pp. 5–6, 255; *Sutta Nipāta, Khuddaka Nikāya*, Vol. I, p. 270.

[69] *Sutta Nipāta, Khuddaka Nikāya*, Vol. I, p. 289. It may be pointed out that Māṭanga is a mythical character in the account where the reference occurs, and the reference to him as a *caṇḍālaputto* may be construed as being used in an abstract sense. (According to a personal communication from D. Devahuti it is used as a generic term for *śūdra* and occurs as such in Harṣa's time.) The term *caṇḍāla* was probably gaining currency in this period to connote the notion of low as a value in society. Similarly the *Dīgha Nikāya* describes a *sudda* stationing himself at a cross road and giving orders like a king (*D.N.*, I, p. 90). The whole situation in the narration is treated as ridiculous and, in our view, the example suggests that here also the *sudda* represents the notion of low in society, in opposition to what is high. Both *caṇḍāla* and *sudda* have been used in the Buddhist texts, in the situations described above to represent the value of low in an abstract sense. The early Buddhist period appears to be one in which the two poles of the system of inequality were being defined. The poles ultimately crystallized in the form of the *brāhmaṇa* at one end and the *caṇḍāla* at the other. If the *caṇḍālas* were a tribe who were originally on the margin of Āryan society, and represented a cultural contrast to the Āryans and were despised for this, over a period of time whether they actually survived as a distinct identifiable group or not, they became a symbol of the idea of low as a value. Subsequently with the crystallization of the caste system, tribe, race, occupation, and distinct cultural traits, were synthesized into a system with the *caṇḍāla* occupying the lowest status in socie-

das, *ratthakāras*, *veṇas* and *pukkusās* do not exist as real people. Instead, names were often associated with a profession which had *similarities* with one of these categories; but the terms themselves were never used. For example, the *bhikkhu* Sunīta is described as being of low origin and of having performed the work of a *pup-pachaḍḍaka*, but he is not called a *pukkusā*.[70] We also have the examples of *naḷakāras* (basket weavers) who are described as being in their own settlement,[71] and of a *bhikkhu* committing suicide after accidentally falling upon a *vilivakārang* (basket maker)[72] and killing him; but in neither situation is there any mention of the term *veṇa*. Similarly, there are references to specific hunting groups like the *sakuṇikā* (fowler), and *kevaṭṭa* (fisherman),[73] but there are no identifiable *nesādas*.

We may conclude on the basis of the evidence cited above that the significant factor in Buddhist society for purposes of identification, particularly for the service groups, were the occupational divisions among people.[74] The function actually performed by a person provided the basic identity of individuals. The Buddhist texts clearly indicate that the categories that can be located as having an existential reality were either the various occupational divisions like barber, metal smith worker, potter, etc., or the categories of *khattiya*, *brāhmaṇa*, and *gahapati*. It is not possible for us to list here the hundreds of examples that are available to us in the Buddhist texts (see Appendix III) but a few examples may be cited to substantiate the point. Thus Tapussa and Bhallika are referred to as *vāṇijjas*[75] (traders); Dhaniya as *gopaka*[76] (cattle-keeper); Cunda as a

ty. The Buddhists, as is usual with them, use the vocabulary of the *brāhmaṇas* which they infuse with their own meaning. *Caṇḍāla* is used by the Buddhists to express a moral value and not to indicate low birth. In a hard-hitting attack on the *brāhmaṇas* the Buddha turns the tables on them. He applies the term *brāhmaṇa caṇḍāla* for a *brāhmaṇa* who leads an immoral and depraved existence but claims at the same time that he can remain undefiled and pure, like the fire which burns unclean things but remains pure in spite of it (*A.N.*, II, p. 472).

[70] *Nīce kulamhi jāto aham daḷiddo appabhojano, hīnan kammam mamam asi, ahosim pupphachāḍḍako* (*Theragāthā*, *Khuddaka Nikāya*, Vol. II, p. 330).

[71] *M.N.*, II, pp. 478–9. [72] *Pārājika*, p. 101.

[73] *S.N.*, II, p. 212; *M.N.*, I, p. 315.

[74] In the *Vāseṭṭha Sutta* the Buddha states that *brāhmaṇas* who follow various occupations are agriculturists (*kassako*), traders (*vāṇijjo*), cattle keepers (*gorakkho*) etc. according to their respective work or occupation (*kamma*) (*Sutta Nipāta*, *Khuddaka Nikāya*, Vol. I, pp. 364–5).

[75] *Mahāvagga*, pp. 5–6 [76] *Sutta Nipāta*, *Khuddaka Nikāya*, Vol. I, p. 270.

kammāraputta[77] (son of a metal worker); a certain monk is referred to as having once been a *nahāpita*[78] (barber) and the *Dīgha Nikāya* refers to a *nahāpita* called Bhesika; [79] Ghaṭikāra and Dhaniya[80] are referred to as *kumbhakāras* (potters). This association with occupation is particularly true for those groups normally considered to be of low status in Buddhist society.

On the other hand, the status identification of groups which were ranked high in Buddhist literature correspond to the *kula* divisions of the *khattiyas*, *brāhmaṇas* and *gahapatis*. Apart from the instances cited where the Buddha is referred to as a *khattiya*, there are numerous examples of clans referring to themselves as *khattiyas*. In the *Mahāparinibbāna Sutta* various clans come forward and ask for a share of the Buddha's ashes saying '*mayam pi khattiya*'[81] (we too are *khattiyas*). The terms *brāhmaṇa* and *gahapati* appear too frequently as status terms to enumerate separately but it is important to note that the *brāhmaṇas* had most definitely emerged as a distinct social group who strongly asserted their Brahmanical identity as being based on ascribed status. This was the thrust of many of their discussions with the Buddha. But it is equally clear that the *brāhmaṇas* of Buddhist literature were not necessarily associated with the performance of ritual or with the pursuit of religious goals at all.

The Buddhist view of social stratification: the saṅgha

The evidence detailed above also provide an insight into the Buddhist attitude of stratification. The early Pāli texts are unambigious in their assertion that a person's *vaṇṇa*, *jāti* or *kula* are irrelevant in the context of the social world, as represented by the *saṅgha*. In their potential for salvation all are equal and neither the categories of the Brahmanical scheme nor the categories of the scheme used by the Buddhists have any bearing in the *saṅgha*. In the *Kannakaṭṭhala Sutta* of the *Majjhima Nikāya*, Buddha tells King Pasenadi that there is no distinction among people if they possess the proper qualities for striving and make the right effort, regardless of whether they are from *khattiya*, *brāhmaṇa*, *vessa* or *sudda vaṇṇa*.[82] Similarly, Mahākaccāna tells the king of Madhurā that a person from any of the four *vaṇṇas* was known simply as a *samaṇa* once he

[77] *D.N.*, II, p. 98. [78] *Mahāvagga*, p. 262. [79] *D.N.*, I, p. 191.
[80] *M.N.*, II, p. 272; *Pārājika*, p. 51 [81] *D.N.*, II, pp. 126–7.
[82] *M.N.*, II, p. 377; *M.L.S.*, II, p. 311.

renounced the world, and would be equally entitled to respect.[83] It is said that a man becomes without *vaṇṇa* (*vevaṇṇiyanti*) when he joins the *saṅgha*.[84] Describing his dreams, the Buddha says that he saw four birds of different *vaṇṇa* (colours) which came and fell at his feet and became entirely white. This is interpreted by him as symbolizing people belonging to the four *vaṇṇas* joining his *saṅgha* and being freed from their original distinctions.[85] It is considered unseemly in the texts to question a *samaṇa* about his *jāti*, and a *muni*, although he might be from a *nīca kula*, becomes noble by his good conduct.[86] People belonging to *brāhmaṇa*, *khattiya*, *vessa*, and *sudda kulas* are all equally capable of accomplishing the right path if they follow the discipline promulgated by the Buddha and go forth from the home into homelessness.[87] *Bhikkhus* belonging to *brāhmaṇa*, *khattiya*, or *gahapati kulas*, along with others, would all be equal in the *saṅgha* where the best dwelling places and alms would be allotted according to the seniority of the monks, regardless of their social origins.[88] Thus neither conceptual categories, nor empirical categories are relevant within the *saṅgha*.

Stratification outside the saṅgha

The problem of determining the Buddhist attitude to the *vaṇṇa*, *jāti*, and *kula* divisions in the context of the world outside the *saṅgha* is more complex, however. It is evident from the preceding sections that Buddhists had a system of stratification, although this was clearly different from the Brahmanical notion of hierarchy. The idea of high and low expressed itself in the context of *jāti*, *kula*, *kamma* and *sippa*. However, it is important to point out that the system of stratification as portrayed in the Pāli canon depicts a social phenomenon or an existential reality, without religious sanction, unlike the Brahmanical conception of hierarchy. The Buddhist texts were merely reflecting the situation prevailing in the region in which early Buddhism was located.

It appears that *vaṇṇa* divisions were unimportant to the Buddhists even within the social world.[89] This was probably because the

[83] *M.N.*, II, p. 316; *M.L.S.*, II, p. 277

[84] *A.N.*, IV, p. 210. [85] *A.N.*, II, p. 482.

[86] *Sutta Nipāta*, *Khuddaka Nikāya*, Vol. I, p. 336.

[87] *M.N.*, II, p. 445; *M.L.S.*, II, p. 370. [88] *Cullavagga*, pp. 255–6.

[89] We have already cited a passage where the Buddha regards the *vaṇṇas* as irrelevant in the matter of service to the higher *vaṇṇas* by the lower *vaṇṇas*.

vaṇṇas were a purely conceptual categorization of society. *Jāti*, on the other hand, seems to have been relevant in Buddhist society. A significant passage in the *Ambaṭṭha Sutta* states that *jātivādo* applies not in the context of 'wisdom and righteousness' (or the asocial world concerned with salvation) but in the context of marriage, where references are made to questions of *jāti* and *gotta*.[90] This idea is a fairly recurrent theme in early Buddhist literature and we often come across the idea of pure, unblemished birth (*jāti*) going back seven generations on the side of both mother and father.[91] Another striking example is the reference to degenerate *brāhmaṇas*, who are criticized for marrying non-*brāhmaṇas* in contemporary times. They are contrasted with the good *brāhmaṇas* of old who did not marry non-*brāhmaṇas*. Significantly, this is enumerated by the Buddha as the first of the offences of degenerate *brāhmaṇas*.[92]

Although the Buddha frequently denied the *brāhmaṇas* any special values based on ascribed status, the rationale for placing the *khattiyas* above the *brāhmaṇas* is precisely of the purity of birth of *khattiyas*. When the young *brāhmaṇa* Ambaṭṭha abused the Sākyas as 'base born',[93] the Buddha retorted not by dismissing the notion of low birth, but by arguing that his own descent was absolutely unsullied. The Buddha's major point of attack was that Ambaṭṭha himself was of impure descent and the Sākyas were originally his masters since he was a descendant of a union between a Sākya lord and one of their slave girls. In contrast, other Sākyas were so conscious of the purity of their blood that when exiled they intermarried with their own sisters for fear of spoiling their umblemished lineage. The Buddha reiterated his point by establishing that *brāhmaṇas* were more lax in their disapproval of mixed unions than *khattiyas*.[94] For instance, the child of a union between a *khattiya* and a *brāhmaṇa* was allowed to participate in all the activities of the *brāhmaṇas*. This would include participation in making offerings to the gods and having access to *brāhmaṇa* women.[95] However, *khat-*

[90] *D.B.*, I, p. 123; *D.N.*, I, pp. 86–7. The original reads as follows: *na kho Ambaṭṭha, anuttaraya vijjācharaṇa sampadaya jātivādōvā vucchati, gottavādo vā vucchati, māna vādo vā vucchati . . . yatha kho Ambaṭṭa avāho vā hoti, vivāho vā hoti . . . ethena vucchati jātivādo vā iti pi gottavādo vā iti māna vādo vā iti.*

[91] *M.N.*, II, p. 430; *D.B.*, I, pp. 146–7. It was the first in the list of honourable traits possessed by the Buddha himself.

[92] *A.N.*, II, p. 466. [93] *D.N.*, I, pp. 78–84.

[94] Ibid., pp. 84–6. [95] Ibid.

tiyas would not permit the child of such a union to participate in the *abhiseka* (consecration) ceremony of the *khattiyas*.[96] The Buddha argued from this that *khattiyas* were higher (*seṭṭha*) and the *brāhmaṇas* inferior (*hīna*) to them.[97]

The Pāli texts suggest that the Buddha's pure birth and an unblemished lineage were one of the attributes which led people to pay homage to him. A notable example of this was the statement of the *brāhmaṇa* Caṇkī to other *brāhmaṇas* trying to dissuade him from going to see the Buddha. 'Well then sirs', says Caṇkī, 'hear from me why it is right that we ourselves should go and see the honoured Gotama, and why it is right that the honoured Gotama should not himself come to see us. Indeed, sirs, the recluse Gotama is of pure birth on both sides, of pure descent from his mother and father, back through seven generations, unchallenged, irreproachable in respect of birth. And because the recluse Gotama is of pure birth on both sides . . . irreproachable in respect of birth, this is the reason why it is not right for the good Gotama to come and see us, while it is right that we ourselves should go and see the honourable Gotama'.[98]

Principles of stratification based on kula, kamma *and* sippa

It is clear that Buddhists acknowledged the importance of *jāti* in the context of marriage and birth. They recognized also a system of stratification for the social world where *kula*, *kamma* and *sippa* were either high or low. The kind of family one originated from and the nature of work one performed was an important index to the placement of a person in the social system as either high or low. This categorization of *kula*, *kamma* and *sippa* into high and low was based on certain principles. First, in the Buddhist system those who work for themselves as owners and producers are ranked high, whereas those who work for others are regarded as low. For instance, the *gahapati*, as we have established earlier, was consistently ranked high and represented the category of owner-producer ideally. In this Buddhism clearly displayed a different point of view from the existing Brahmanical notions. The Brahmanical system of ranking placed economic functions below religious and political

[96] *D.N.*, I, p. 86. There is no evidence of the *varṇasaṃkara* theory in early Buddhist texts. It would appear that in the Buddhist period children of mixed castes do not become part of a new caste, but are absorbed in the caste of one of the parents.

[97] Ibid., p. 86. [98] *M.L.S.*, II, pp. 356–7; *M.N.*, II, p. 430.

functions.[99] The Buddhists, however, attached tremendous significance to the economic function and considered it to be as important as religious and political functions. Brahmanical texts refer to the *vaiśyas* or the economic groups as an eminently exploitable category, to be oppressed at the will of the higher *vaṇṇas*.[100] The Buddhists, in contrast, always treated the *gahapati* as an eminently respectable category. Consistent with this, the occupations of agriculture, cattle-keeping and trade were rated high, whereas those who performed services for others such as storeroom-keepers (*koṭṭhaka kammakara*), and flower sweepers (*pupphachaḍḍaka*), were low. Secondly, among the *sippas* there is a division of high and low corresponding to non-manual and manual skills, since *muddā*, *gaṇanā* and *lekhā* (counting, accounting and writing) were ranked high, whereas basket making, pottery, leatherwork, weaving and the work of a barber was low. Thirdly, the Buddhists exhibited some notions of racial superiority since aboriginal groups like the *nīca kulas* or the *hīna jātis* (*caṇḍāla*, *pukkusā*, *veṇa*, *ratthakāra* and *nesāda*)[101] who were probably associated with low material culture were given a low rank.[102] Purity of blood and unblemished lineage was extremely important to the Buddhists.

There is also no indication in the Buddhist texts that social distinctions are irrelevant or escapable. In fact, the texts contain the idea of what can be called a 'package deal' where wealth, eminence, beauty and wisdom was associated with high *kulas*. Similarly, poverty, stupidity and ugliness were associated with low *kulas*. In the *Bālapaṇḍita Sutta*, the Buddha states 'if at some time or other that fool came to human status again, he would be born into those families that are low; a *caṇḍāla* family, or a *nesāda* family, or a *veṇa* family, or a *ratthakāra* family, or a *pukkusā* family; in such a family as is needy, without enough to eat and drink, where a covering for the back is obtained with difficulty. Moreover, he would be ill-favoured, ugly, dwarfish, sickly, blind, or deformed, or lame or paralysed; he would be unable to get food, drink, vehicles, garlands, scents, perfumes, bed, dwelling and lights.'[103] Conversely, if a wise man was reborn, 'He would be born into one of those fami-

[99] *Vaśiṣtha Dharmasūtra, The Sacred Laws of the Āryas*, S.B.E. Vol. XIV, p. 11.
[100] *Aitereya Brāhmaṇa*, XXXV.
[101] R. Fick, *The Social Organization of North-East India in Buddha's Time*, p. 324.
[102] *Pācittiya*, p. 11; *M.N.*, III, p. 240.
[103] *M.N.*, III, p. 240; *M.L.S.*, III, p. 215.

lies that are high: a rich *khattiya* family or a family of rich *brāhmaṇas*, or a family of rich *gahapatis*, in such a family as is well to do, of great possessions, of great resources, with abundant gold and silver, abundant means, abundant wealth in grains. Moreover, he would be lovely, good to look upon, charming, endowed with the greatest beauty of complexion; he would be able to get food, drink, clothes, vehicles, garlands, scents and perfumes, bed, dwelling and lights.'[104] The only possibility of escape from this system of stratification envisaged by the Buddhists is the idea that by leading a virtuous and generous life in this existence one can ensure rebirth with an improved social status in the next.[105] Alternatively, joining the *saṅgha* and renouncing the social world itself was necessary in order to escape from the system of stratification. Bougle has argued that by adopting the vows of mendicancy and chastity *bhikkhus* simultaneously turned away from the work of production (or economic effort) and reproduction (family life).[106] We have already demonstrated the existence of stratification in Buddhism, both in the context of marriage and occupation. In the social world everyone had necessarily to be involved both with production and with reproduction and therefore could not evade becoming part of the system of stratification. Only the *bhikkhu* could possibly escape from the system, for both the nature of occupation and endogamous marriage no longer had any relevance for him.[107]

We have earlier pointed out that Buddhist society does not display a complex system of ranking. The elaborate design of the Brahmanical system is missing. Instead, we have a simpler two-tier system of stratification with a conception of high and low working separately in the context of *jāti*, *kula*, *kamma* and *sippa*. The idea that all these strands can be woven into a comprehensive system with birth, race, occupation and service being accommodated in it clearly does not exist in the Buddhist texts. This was probably because at the time of the early Pāli canon caste was in an embryonic state. It was still in the process of being formulated and did not yet have all the features that it was to exhibit later.

Evidence of stratification from Ceylon

The principles of stratification relevant in Buddhism can be illus-

104 *M.N.*, III, p. 248; *M.L.S.*, III, p. 222.
105 *M.N.*, III, pp. 282–4; *S.N.*, I, pp. 92–6.
106 Celestin Bougle, *Essays on the Caste System*, p. 73.
107 Ibid.

trated meaningfully with the empirical evidence of caste in Sri Lanka. This is particularly relevant as Sri Lanka was the first region in which Buddhist principles of stratification were applied in their own unique form. The idea of stratification was carried there by Buddhists and could develop unhampered by existing traditions. In India, however, Buddhist principles had to contend with the existing system of stratification and its elaboration under *brāhmaṇa* influence in later times and thus the Buddhist principles themselves have become somewhat obscured.[108]

It has been established that the Sinhalese caste system is historically and conceptually related to the Indian system, although there are fewer castes in Sri Lanka. There is also less scope here for ritual pollution through the violation of caste tabus, partly because both the top and bottom strata of the Indian caste system are missing in Sri Lanka. Of the four Brahmanical social castes the Sinhalese lack the *brāhmaṇa* and *khattiyas.*[109] The fact that they do not exist as social groups in Sri Lanka is of some importance to our analysis. We have earlier pointed out (see Chapter II) that in the monarchical kingdoms mentioned in Buddhist texts, the *khattiyas* were restricted to the royal family, and were not numerically significant. This accounts for their non-existence in Sri Lanka, where the *khattiyas* were reduced to their representation in the person of the king. The absence of *brāhmaṇas* is also logical. In a society based entirely on Buddhist principles, the *brāhmaṇas* were redundant as their religions function was performed by the *bhikkhu.*[110]

The absence of the *brāhmaṇa* has been of utmost importance in determining the nature of caste in Sri Lanka. Ryan has argued that there is some basis for believing that Sinhalese caste, rather than being a pale expression of a classical, rigidly defined hierarchy of ancient times, is instead the modern expression of a primitive Indian system.

[108] Hutton suggests that Buddhist countries reflect an earlier form of caste before the systematization of the Hindu thinkers (J.H. Hutton, *Caste in India*, p. 148).

[109] Richard F. Gombrich, *Precept and Practice*, p. 296.

[110] Consequently there is no opposition between the *brāhmaṇa* pursuing religious goals and living in the social world, and the *bhikkhu* who pursues religious goals outside it as in Indian society (see Chapter II). Similarly in a purely Buddhist society the conflict between the *khattiya* and the *brāhmaṇa* has also been eliminated.

Ryan says:

> The accoutrements of caste developed, but without sacred systematization as in India and hence with the retention of the essentially secular hierarchy of early times. The period in which the historical groundwork of the Sinhalese civilization was laid was one in which caste, as a crescive institution, was in its incipient, and one might almost say, doctrinal stages. The caste system of Ceylon which first struck the European observer was no degenerate form but an automous growth, under Indian influence it is true, but which never knew the structuralizing power of the *brāhmaṇa*.[111]

With the elimination of two of the three high groups of the early Buddhist texts, only the *gahapati* has survived in the form of the *goyigāma* or rice agriculturist in Sri Lanka. They are the highest caste here and are known among themselves as the 'good men', as distinct from the lower castes.[112] The Sinhalese work, the *Cūḷavaṃsa* (A.D. 500–1500) also usually divides people into *kulīna* (people of family) and *hīna* (inferiors), and this corresponds to the distinction between the *goyigāma* and the low castes. Significantly, the Sinhalese hardly have anyone corresponding to the vast array of Hindu outcastes. Ryan remarks, 'Perhaps the most notable feature of Sinhalese stratification in its contrast with the Indian, is the absence of untouchables in the Hindu sense. In Buddhism no man is "unclean" in the sacred meaning of the concept. The absence of the Hindu concept has rendered the Sinhalese caste system mild and humanitarian when judged by Indian standards'.[113]

The hierarchical position of a caste in Sri Lanka corresponds to the numerical size. Thus, the highest caste of the *goyigāma* includes almost half the total population.[114] Although the dominant and wealthiest people in peasant village areas are usually *goyigāmas*, not all of them are well off in a material sense. It is often true, however, that among the abjectly poor the *goyigāma* are notably under-represented, and among the wealthy of the peasant village they are notably over-represented.[115] Apart from the traditional occupation

[111] Bryce Ryan, *Castes in Modern Ceylon*, pp. 7–8.

[112] Richard Gombrich, *Precept and Practice*, p. 296; A.M. Hocart (*Caste: A Comparative Study*, p. 3) also says 'The good people are opposed to the "low castes" who comprise fishermen, smiths, washermen etc.'.

[113] Bryce Ryan, *Castes in Modern Ceylon*, p. 15. [114] Ibid., p. 19.

[115] Ibid., p. 97.

of cultivation, Hocart has described the actual functions performed by the *goyigāma* in the Kandyan kingdom of Sri Lanka. They were village headmen and held all the other offices of state apart from the priestly ones; they fed the king and the temple, and received service from the lower castes.[116] The last function is an extremely important aspect of stratification in Sri Lanka. Villagers when asked 'what is caste?' replied that lower castes had to perform certain tasks for the cultivator, and this was how caste was generally understood. Illustrating what they could not easily define they said: 'The people of X are drummers. They are like servants. When called they must come for dancing, festivals and processions. The farmers give them food and also cash for their hard work'. Hocart concludes that what was uppermost in the minds of all his witnesses was the idea of service.[117] Ryan reiterates this point: 'Direct personal services to the *goyigāma* are preserved in the Kandyan provinces, particularly where economic power, usually in the form of rentable land, is in the hands of the highest caste or the *goyigāma*. Caste status must be approximately congruent with the type of service required'.[118] The *goyigāma* is ranked high in Sinhalese society and is superior to the low castes because he is an independent owner-producer who may or not work on his own land, but who commands service from others. His similarity with the *gahapati* of the Buddhist texts is striking.

Other notable features of the Sinhalese caste system relevant to our analysis include the absence of sub-castes and the idea that new castes arise from a breach of endogamous practices. The Brahmanic theory regarding the fissiparous origins of a multiplicity of caste divisions has no significance in Sri Lanka in legend or in fact.[119] We have earlier indicated that Buddhist texts do not reveal the conception of the *varṇasaṃkara* origins of various castes. The use of terms to indicate social groups in Sri Lanka also corresponds to our conclusions of early Buddhist society. The ordinary term for caste is *jāti*, which is associated with birth, and carries the connotation of a specie or a category. The more scholarly term *vaṇṇa* is never used.[120] The term *kula* may also signify caste. For instance, the

[116] A.M. Hocart, *Caste: A Comparative Study*, p. 5.

[117] Ibid., pp. 7–8.

[118] Bryce Ryan, *Castes in Modern Ceylon*, p. 192.

[119] Ibid., p. 14.

[120] Nur Yalman, *Under the Bo Tree: Studies in Caste, Kinship and Marriage in Interior Ceylon*, p. 61.

myth of caste origins is called *kula bedimak* and refers back to the mythological ancestor Mahā Sammata who, needing various kinds of services done for him, first divided people into castes.[121]

In the context of family and marriage also the Sinhalese evidence is valuable. Ryan remarks that concepts of family and marriage provide the most substantial bulwarks for the preservation of caste structure. The solidarity of kin as a unit of action and loyalty, the concepts of family honour and reputation, the injunctions and custom of marriage all lead to the maintenance of caste integrity and to some extent of caste hierarchy. He holds that an indispensable and fundamental characteristic of caste in Ceylon is its restriction upon marriage. The marriage system of the Sinhalese prevents marriage outside caste, and, together with concepts of family honour, is part of the very substance of caste, where family integrity is inevitably defined in terms of caste and birth status.[122]

It is evident from an analysis of the Buddhist texts and the empirical evidence of Sri Lanka, that Buddhists had certain central principles for the social organization of a Buddhist society. Ryan has observed that these principles were not merely the acceptance of a social system by a religious movement but, rather, an ideological integration with it, since through the principle of *kamma* it accepted an ideological justification for the existence of social hierarchy. However, Buddhism was not a driving force in building and elaborating social hierarchy as a sacred institution. It rationalized rather than promoted caste.[123] The existence of social hierarchy was far from being inconsistent with the ideology of Buddhism, and concepts evident in the early Pāli canon probably provided the concrete blueprint for the development of the social organization of Sri Lanka.

The example of Ceylon has been cited to demonstrate the relationship between the idea of social stratification reflected in early Buddhist literature and a concrete expression of these ideas in social reality. Except for the penetration of caste distinctions into the *saṅgha* itself, which certainly violated a fundamental tenet of Buddhism (see Chapter VI also), there was a significant converg-

[121] Ibid., p. 89. [122] Bryce Ryan, *Castes in Modern Ceylon*, p. 29.

[123] Ibid., pp. 36–7. See also the *Bālapaṇḍita Sutta* and the *Cūḷakammavibhanga Sutta* of the *Majjhima Nikāya* which state that wrong actions will result in re-birth in families which are poor and of low social status (*M.N.*, III, pp. 240, 283; *S.N.*, I, pp. 92–6).

ence between principle and practice in the context of Sinhalese social stratification. It should not surprise us if both caste and Buddhism went to Sri Lanka from India. One can argue from this that ideas on social stratification as revealed in early Buddhist literature show two features. On the one hand, they may be depicting contemporary notions of social stratification as they actually existed in the popular mind, as distinct from the ideas in the Brahmanical mind. On the other, these ideas may have been the specifically Buddhist conception of social stratification, and an intrinsic part of the Buddhist world view. Both features are likely to have been an integral part of Buddhist texts. While the classification of social categories into high and low was probably influenced by Buddhist values, the Buddhist point of view itself reflected the system of stratification as it existed at the time, and was related to the empirical categories that were widely recognized in society. Both points are best elucidated by the case of the *gahapati*.

The importance of the gahapati *in the Buddhist view of stratification*

The consistently high status that is accorded to the *gahapati* in the Buddhist texts is likely to have been, at least in part, the real status of the *gahapati* in society at the time of the Buddha. This is clear from the relationship that existed between the king as the head of state and the major economic representatives of the time. The high status of *gahapatis* in relation to the people is also evident from the term of address, *ayya putta*, sometimes used for them.[124] However, the Buddha's own recognition of the significance of the economic function as being *basic* to any society, despite his advocacy of renunciation as a means to salvation, clearly indicates his specific contribution to ideas on social status. Further by attributing the *khattiya*, *brāhmaṇa* and *gahapati* to high status he equated the functions of all three on the same scale. The *khattiya*, *brāhmaṇa* and *gahapati* were all equally important to the social system. There is absolutely no indication in the Pāli texts of a difference in status of the three *ucca kula* categories of *khattiya*, *brāhmaṇa* and *gahapati*, even though the serial order is always the same. The serial order of the low *kulas* is also always the same and, similarly, the Pāli texts give no indication of a hierarchy of status among them. The question of rebirth in an *ucca kula* is a good index of the equal status of the

[124] *S.N.*, III, p. 269.

three. Rebirth in a *ucca kula* is equally valued whether in a *khattiya kula, brāhmaṇa kula* or a *gahapati kula*. Similarly, *kulaputtas*, or young men of good families (which include *khattiyas, brāhmaṇas* and *gahapatis*), pursuing certain occupations such as cattle-keeping, agriculture and trade are placed along with occupations like accounting and joining the king's service. Significantly, the statement about *kulaputtas* following occupations such as agriculture, cattle keeping and trade is made to a *brāhmaṇa* and a *khattiya* and represents the Buddha's attitude to economic functions. One who produces is not less important than the person who wields power or who teaches and performs religious functions. All three categories contribute in equal measure and perform complementary functions in the social system. In this the Buddha is reversing radically the Brahmanical position wherein the role of the economy is clearly subservient to the role of ritual and power.

The arguments contained in the preceding sections brings us to a crucial aspect of the evidence examined by us: the marked absence of the *gahapati* from the Brahmanical *vaṇṇa* and *jāti* schemes both in the Brahmanical sources as well as in the references to the *vaṇṇa* and *jāti* schemes contained in the Buddhist and Jainā texts. In contrast the *gahapati* is an *inherent* part of the *kula* scheme depicted in the Buddhist literature. Since the *gahapatis* as a group were intrinsic to the economic domain, and more specifically were the owners and controllers of the primary means of production in the form of land, their inclusion in the Buddhist scheme is of particular importance. The *gahapatis* were not a caste or a group whose status was based on birth. In fact the *gahapati* cut across other social groups since the texts use the word *brāhmaṇa-gahapati* for *brāhmaṇas* who were based on land (that is for *brāhmaṇas* whose identity was based on ascribed status but who performed the functions of a *gahapati*). The failure to accommodate the *gahapati* in the Brahmanical system is the greatest failure of the Brahmanical model: it shows up clearly the model's rigidity and utter distance from empirical reality.

The Brahmanical model is weakest in explaining the politico-economic domain. On the other hand, the inclusion of the *gahapati* in the system of stratification is the strength of the Buddhist scheme. The evidence of the Buddhist texts is unambiguous in its representation of the *gahapati* as an economic category but this does not mean that the *gahapati* can be mechanically equated with the *vessa* and thereby fitted into the Brahmanical scheme. Such an equation militates against the entire weight of evidence available in the Buddhist sources. The *vessa* and the *suddas* are theoretical categories in the Brahmanical scheme based on ascribed status. The *gahapati* on the other hand is clearly a category in the system of production. He is one who commands and hires the labour of the *dāsa-kammakara*. The term *brāhmaṇa-gahapati* shows the need to move beyond the Brahmanical caste categories in order to explain existing reality. It should be noted that it was not the ordinary *brāhmaṇa* who drew services from the *suddas* in the Buddhist texts. It was only the *brāhmaṇa-gahapatis* who drew services from the *dāsa-kammakaras* in a relationship that originated from the *brāhmaṇa-gahapati's* control over land rather than from any notion of ritual superiority of the *brāhmaṇas*.

The inability of the caste framework to depict the social reality of the period and of the Brahmanical scheme to accommodate the *gahapati* has resulted in portraying not merely a partial view of society but also a distorted view of it. This conclusion is more than borne out by early inscriptional evidence. While there are no inscriptions available for the pre-Mauryan period with which we are mainly concerned, there is considerable inscriptional evidence for the period 200 B.C. to A.D. 200.[125] What is striking from an analysis of the empirical categories of the inscriptions is not just their close correspondence, but their near absolute similarity, with the social categories of Buddhist literature.[126] The inscriptions make the same distinct use of the words *gahapati*, *seṭṭhi-gahapati* and *seṭṭhi*; likewise, of *vāṇijja*, *cammakāra*, *karmāra and dantakāra*. There are no direct references to *khattiyas*, and this fact is very significant for us. It has earlier been pointed out that there are no references to *khattiyas* in the Buddhist texts except in the *gaṇa-saṅghas* which were restricted to specific areas in north-eastern India. Since the sites of the inscriptions are mostly concentrated in central and south-central India, the absence of *khattiyas* supports our conclusion that the *khattiyas* were numerically significant only in the *gaṇa-sanghas*. Similarly, there are numerous references to *brāhmaṇas*, but none to *suddas*. Instead, there are references to occupational categories which include both skilled and unskilled workers. If these categories were supposed to be *suddas* according to Brahmanical theory, it was irrelevant to the

[125] The inscriptions relate to gifts of various kinds made to the Buddhist *saṅgha* by donors from a wide range of social groups.

[126] See Appendix B.

donors. They, and others, saw themselves as members of an occupational category which gave them a sense of identity. The debate on the question of whether the *gahapati* was *vessa*, or the *kammakara* a *sudda*, was not the major problem for Buddhists and others at that time, and so it has not been the main focus of this study. It is time that students of the period shed the Brahmanical spectacles that have been used so long. A more meaningful understanding of social reality should then emerge.

CHAPTER V

The Social Background of the Early Buddhists

The problem

Buddhism was primarily a religious movement, not a social one. However, it had an important social dimension to it. In order to comprehend the social dimensions of the Buddhist movement it is necessary to identify the elements in society which became closely involved with it. No published work that is based on a comprehensive analysis of references available in the early Pāli canon exists to date on the social background of the early Buddhists.[1] Despite this, several opinions have been expressed on the relationship between Buddhism and certain sections of society, largely in the form of broad generalizations unsupported by firm data. These generalizations have possibly been made either on the basis of an impressionistic survey of Buddhist texts in which certain names have struck the eye of the reader, or because Buddhist literature has been treated as a homogeneous unit, without much regard for the chronological stratification of the texts. Some analysis exists of certain names available in the *Theragāthā* and *Therīgāthā*, the compilations of verses attributed to the *theras* and *therīs* (elders) of the *saṅgha*. These texts feature in the *Khuddaka Nikāya*, the fifth division of the *Sutta Piṭaka*, along with thirteen other texts, most of which are somewhat later than the *Vinaya Piṭaka*, and the first four *Nikāyas* of the *Sutta Piṭaka* (see Introduction). The commentary on the *Theragāthā* and *Therīgāthā*, written by Dhammapāla in the fifth century A.D., contains crucial evidence for the social and locational background of these elder members of the *saṅgha*. In her introduction to these texts, Mrs Rhys Davids has classified the *theras and therīs* according to their social and regional backgrounds.[2] Subsequently, a more detailed analysis of the information available in the *Ther-*

[1] J.W. Jong has pointed to this lacuna too ('The Background of Early Buddhism', *Journal of Indian Buddhist Studies*, Vol. XII, 1964, p. 45).

[2] C.A.F. Rhys Davids, *Psalms of the Early Buddhists*, p. xxviii.

agāthā and *Therīgāthā* has been attempted by Gokhale.[3] However, since the analyses in both works are based on evidence provided in a comparatively late commentary, they suffer from serious flaws. The commentary cannot be relied upon for its categorization of the *theras and* therīs for a variety of reasons. Many of the categories of the early Pāli canon had changed their connotation by the time the commentaries were written. We have already referred to the problem of a number of *gahapatis* mentioned in the early Pāli canon being converted into *seṭṭhis* by the *Jātakas* and the commentaries. Other discrepancies have been revealed in a comparison of names available in the *Vinaya* and the first four *nikāyas* of the *Sutta Piṭaka* with the commentary on the *Theragāthā* and the *Therīgāthā*.

The method

In this chapter we propose to analyse all the names mentioned in the early Pāli canon where social and economic backgrounds are indicated. We shall divide the Buddhists into two categories: those who joined the *saṅgha*, and those who supported it from outside the *sangha*. In the interests of accuracy we shall discuss only those names in this analysis for which our sources themselves indicate the social background, either directly (where status or occupational indications are given), or indirectly (where reasonable inferences can be drawn from the texts themselves). This has meant the non-inclusion of several names for which the commentaries have provided information, but for whom specific information is lacking in the texts themselves. Our analysis also leaves out certain group references, specially where these pertain to large round numbers of entrants into the *saṅgḥa* for whom other information is extremely vague in our sources. It has, however, taken note of some specific group references in the case of the laity, but since exact figures are not available they have been listed separately (see Appendix C).

In classifying names according to their social backgrounds we have followed the principles of social stratification reflected in the Buddhist texts as indicated in the previous chapter. Thus, there are four groups among the categories normally characterized as *ucca kulas* in the Buddhist texts. These are the specific social groups of *khattiyas*, *brāhmaṇas* and *gahapatis*, and a miscellaneous fourth group

[3] B.G. Gokhale, 'The Early Buddhist Elite', *Journal of Indian History*, Vol. XLIII, 1965, pp. 391–402.

consisting of *ucca kulas* other than these three.[4] This scheme is used in order to narrow down the groups as far as possible, so that we may determine more accurately the actual social base of the categories concerned. We have placed certain individuals, such as people who were employed by the king in some capacity among the *ucca kulas*, since such employment is listed as one of the occupations associated with *kula-puttas*. In addition to the four categories listed above, we have two other social groups, one consisting of *nīca kulas*, and the other comprising *paribbājakas*. All the *nīca kulas* are placed here together, in one group, partly for convenience but also because they frequently appear thus in the texts. Since there is a correspondence between *nīca kula, hīna kamma*, and *hīna sippa*, the low occupational categories are grouped as *nīca kulas*. Similarly, because the social base of *paribbājakas* has been submerged by the act of renunciation, thereby placing them outside the system of stratification, they are listed at the end of the Appendix in a category by themselves.

The saṅgha

There are 105 references to individuals who joined the *saṅgha* and whose social background is indicated in the texts. The largest group consists of *brāhmaṇas* (39), followed by *khattiyas* (28); 21 *bhikkhus* and *bhikkhunīs* originated from *ucca kulas* and one from a *gahapatikula*. The *nīca kulas* are represented by eight *bhikkhus*. Finally, there are eight *bhikkhus* who were *paribbājakas* before they joined the *saṅgha*. In addition to the 39 *brāhmaṇas* who are mentioned as joining the *saṅgha*, eight *brāhmaṇas* are cited as becoming *arahants* after hearing the Buddha preach, but it is not clear that they joined the *saṅgha*; seven were students of the famous sage Bavari and the eighth was Bavari himself. They have been classified separately, since they are clearly distinct from lay supporters of the *saṅgha*.

These figures require some elaboration. The *brāhmaṇa* component of the *saṅgha* included six *brāhmaṇas* who had already become *paribbājakas* before they met the Buddha and joined the *saṅgha*; the others are described as being students of other *brāhmaṇa* teachers. Of the 39 *brāhmaṇas* who joined the *saṅgha*, eight were therefore already associated with the pursuit of religious goals. Some of the

[4] We have placed the *seṭṭhi's* among the *ucca kulas*, rather than among the *gahapatis*, in order to distinguish the different roles that the two categories played.

most important disciples of the Buddha, like Sāriputta, Moggallāna and Mahā Kassapa belong to this group. The remaining 31 *brāhmaṇas* who joined the *saṅgha* were householders.

The *khattiya* component of the *saṅgha* consisted of 22 representatives from the *gaṇa-sanghas*; five members belonged to *rājakulas* or families of kings, and for one *bhikkhu* there are no details apart from the fact that he was a *khattiya*. Of the 22 *bhikkhus* from the *gaṇa-saṅghas*, 16 were Sākyans (of those nine were immediate kinsmen of the Buddha); one was a Lichcchavi; two were Vajjians; two were Mallās; and one was a Koliyan. Those belonging to royal families were all located in the kingdoms, two being from Magadha.

A striking feature of the composition of the *saṅgha* was the extremely small *gahapati* component consisting merely of one member. Even more important is the fact that no *gahapatis* or *gahapati-puttas* joined the *saṅgha*. The sole *gahapati* representative in the *saṅgha* was a *bhikkhunī* who had originally been the wife of a *gahapati*. In contrast, out of 21 *bhikkhus* belonging to *ucca kulas*, as many as 14 were from *seṭṭhi kulas*. Two representatives of the *ucca kulas* were the prosperous *gopaka* couple, Dhaniya and his wife. The others in the *ucca kula* group consisted of two *kula-puttas*, a son of a provincial governor, a courtesan,[5] a son of a minister and two others from genteel backgrounds.

The *nīca kula* component of the *saṅgha* was both small and disparate. It consisted of two *nahāpitas* (barbers); one *kumbhakāra* (potter); one *kevaṭṭa* (fisherman); one vulture trainer; one *dāsiputta* (the son of a slave woman); one actor; and one elephant trainer.

Social origins of important bhikkhus

Apart from forming the largest group within the *saṅgha*, *brāhmaṇas* also figure significantly among the inner circle of disciples surrounding the Buddha whom he relied upon for the propagation of the doctrine. The names of Sāriputta and Moggallāna in particular stand out in this context. Both were already *paribbājakas* when they met the Buddha in the early stages of his career as a teacher.[6] They had been followers of the *titthiya* leader Sanjaya and duly informed

[5] We have classified the courtesan among the *ucca kulas* since there is nothing in the Buddhist texts to show that the courtesan had low status. For similar reasons we have classified Tālapuṭa the *naṭa gāmaṇī* as low because of the grave disapproval shown by the Buddha against Tālapuṭa's profession.

[6] *Mahāvagga*, pp. 38–41.

him before they joined the Buddhist *saṅgha*. In an attempt to prevent them from going over to the Buddha, Sanjaya offered to share the leadership with them. Sāriputta and Moggallāna however declined the offer, and carried most of the followers of the sect over to the new faith.[7] When the Buddha first saw the two approaching him he announced to the other *bhikkhus* present: 'There, O *bhikkhus* two companions arrive; these will be a pair of true pupils, a most distinguished auspicious pair'.[8] Elsewhere, it is stated that they were the constant chief disciples of the Buddha in many previous births.[9] The closeness of Sāriputta and Moggallāna to the Buddha is too well known to require elaboration but some examples are being included for the non-specialist reader.

While Moggallāna came to be known for his *iddhi* (psychic) powers, Sāriputta had the singular honour of being referred to as the *dhamma senapati* of the Buddha. In the *Sela Sutta* of the *Sutta Nipāta*, the *Buddha* is compared to a *cakkavatti* and declares Sāriputta to be his general.[10] The *Saṁyutta Nikāya* contains a collection of *suttas* devoted to *Sāriputta's* achievements.[11]

The Buddha's dependence on Sāriputta is also attested by the fact that he entrusted his only son Rāhula to him for ordination.[12] Mention is made of a special *sutta* in the *Majjhima Nikāya* in which Sāriputta urged Rāhula to practice breathing exercises.[13] Sāriputta's wisdom was recognized and appreciated by others within the *Saṅgha*.[14] Sāriputta is described as the *aggasāvaka*[15] (chief disciple) of the Buddha and he often preached to the brethren as well as the laymen.[16]

Moggallāna may be treated as the second of the chief disciples of the Buddha since Sāriputta and Moggallāna are together declared to be the ideal disciples, whose example other *bhikkhus* should try and emulate.[17] Since Moggallāna's pre-eminence lay in his possession of *iddhi* power he was frequently called Mahā Moggallāna. Like Sāriputta, Moggallāna too could substitute for the Buddha and preach to the *bhikkhus*.[18] Buddha gave great importance to Sāriput-

[7] Ibid. [8] Ibid., B.O.D., IV, p. 55.
[9] *D.N.*, II, p. 6. [10] *Sutta Nipāta, Khuddaka Nikāya*, Vol. I, p. 358.
[11] *S.N.*, II, pp. 450–5. [12] *Mahāvagga*, p. 86; *B.O.D.*, IV, p. 103.
[13] *M.N.*, II, p. 100; *M.L.S.*, II, p. 91. [14] *S.N.*, I, p. 61; *K.S.*, I, p. 87.
[15] *Cullavagga*, p. 301. [16] *M.N.*, I, p. 20; *M.N.*, III, p. 347.
[17] *S.N.*, II, p. 198; *A.N.*, I, p. 71; *A.N.*, II, p. 174.
[18] *Cullavagga*, p. 285.

ta and Moggallāna to keep the *saṅgha* pure. The *Aṅguttara Nikāya* records an instance of Moggallāna seizing a wicked monk and thrusting him outside the door.[19] The trust the Buddha reposed in and the responsibility he gave his two lieutenants is demonstrated by the fact that it is they who are sent to win back the *bhikkhus* who have seceded with Devadatta.[20]

Another very important *brāhmaṇa* to be closely associated with the Buddha and the *saṅgha* was Mahā Kassapa. He is recorded as chief among the Buddha's disciples who kept the stricter observances, and as having very few wants.[21] He lived for many years as a forest dweller[22] and the Buddha was unable to persuade Mahā Kassapa to remain near him. This may be one reason why he is referred to less frequently than Sāriputta and Moggallāna while the Buddha was alive, although he too features in a collection of *suttas* based on him.[23] Mahā Kassapa appears to have been a *paribbājaka* earlier, according to the adverse remarks of a critical *bhikkhunī*.[24] He stood consistently for discipline and in the *Mahāgosinga Sutta* declared the need for stricter observances.[25] Mahā Kassapa rose to great prominence after the death of the Buddha, and his initiative resulted in the convening of the First Council, over which he presided. He foresaw the possibility of the break-up of the *sangha* and the individual anarchy of *bhikkhus* in the absence of the Buddha.[26] Kassapa's tremendous presence of mind, organizational skill, and qualities of leadership played a significant role in strengthening the *saṅgha* and preventing it from sliding into obscurity in the crucial days after the Buddha's death. According to the *Mahāparinibbāna Sutta*, the Buddha's body refused to burn till Mahā Kassapa could come and pay homage to it.[27] Later, Mahā Kassapa's regard for discipline carried the day at the Council of Rājagaha, when the question of dropping the lesser and minor rules of the *Pātimokkha* was debated.[28] The *Vinaya* and the *Sutta Piṭaka* were compiled at the

[19] *A.N.*, III, p. 312. [20] *Cullavagga*, p. 300.

[21] The eremetical stage of early Buddhism probably died out ultimately but, in the lifetime of the Buddha, a few monks at least continued to live according to it. *S.N.*, II, p. 132; *K.S.*, II, p. 109.

[22] In the *Majjhima Nikāya* he recommends forest dwelling for the monks (*M.N.*, I, p. 265; *M.L.S*, I, p. 266).

[23] *S.N.*, II, pp. 165–88; [24] Ibid., p. 183.

[25] *M.N.*, I, p. 265; *M.L.S.*, I, p. 266.

[26] *Cullavagga*, p. 406. [27] *D.N.*, II, p. 125. [28] *Cullavagga*, p. 410.

First Council at Rājagaha under the guidance of the venerable Mahā Kassapa.[29]

Important bhikkhus *of* khattiya *origin*

Perhaps the best known figure apart from the Buddha himself in Buddhist legend is Ānanda, who was a close kinsman of the Master. He had joined the *saṅgha* along with five other kinsmen of the Buddha: Bhaddiya, Bhagu, Kimbila, Anuruddha and Devadatta. Of all these kinsmen, the closest associate of the Buddha was Ānanda, for whom the Buddha had the greatest affection. Ānanda considered himself to be the Buddha's spiritual heir.[30] Throughout the later years of the Buddha's life Ānanda was his personal assistant, and was constantly in his company like a faithful shadow. This accounts for Ānanda's major role in compiling the teachings of the Buddha in the form of the *Sutta Piṭaka*.[31] Every *sutta* in the first four *nikāyas* begins with the statement '*evam me sutam*' ('thus I have heard').

The most striking feature of Ānanda's personality was his very human quality, a characteristic that makes him such an endearing figure. It was probably his deep attachment to the Buddha that accounted for the fact that he did not become an *arahant* in the lifetime of the Buddha.[32] When he realized that the Buddha was about to die he stood at the door, weeping inconsolably.[33] Earlier, he is spoken of as becoming sympathetically sick along with the Buddha.[34] In his concern for the Buddha's health he could not be bothered with rules. Ānanda was also a great champion of good causes.[35] It was entirely due to his intervention that women were allowed entry into the *saṅgha*. Even in this action Ānanda was moved to compassion by the sight of Mahāpajāpatī Gotamī, the Buddha's foster mother, who stood outside at the entrance hall, 'with swollen feet and covered with dust, sad and sorrowful'.[36] She had arrived after travelling a long distance, disregarding the heat and cold in order to seek permission to enter the *saṅgha*. When Ānanda failed to persuade the Buddha initially, he did not give up but tried again, using different tactics this time. Finally the doors of

[29] *Cullavagga*, pp. 408–9. [30] *M.N.*, II, p. 378. [31] *Cullavagga*, p. 409.
[32] *D.N.*, II, p. 110; *D.B.*, II, p. 158. [33] *D.N.*, II, p. 110; *D.B.*, II, p. 158.
[34] *D.N.*, II, p. 79; *D.B.*, II, p. 107. [35] *Cullavagga*, p. 374.
[36] *Vinaya Texts*, tr. by T. W. Rhys Davids and Hermann Oldenberg, Vol. III, p. 321.

the *saṅgha* were thrown open to women.[37] Subsequently his championing of the cause of women was one of the charges against him at the First Council held at Rājagaha. In all humility Ānanda replied that *he* saw no wrong in doing so, but nevertheless if the Council held him guilty he would accept its censure.[38]

Ānanda's generally helpful nature seems to have encouraged his colleagues to consult him about their various problems. He was like Buddha's antennae, conveying to him the news of Devadatta's attempts to split the *saṅgha*.[39] He preached not only to monks but also to other *paribbājakas* like Sandaka, whom he won over to the Buddha.[40] Sometimes he suggested similes to the Buddha.[41] When prominent members of the laity were sick (like the *gahapatis* Anāthapiṇḍika, Sirivaḍḍha, and Mānadiṇṇa) he went to console them.[42] Ānanda was extolled by the Buddha for his erudition, good behaviour, endurance in walking,[43] resoluteness and personal attention. He was called a *dhamma bhandāgarika* or the treasurer of *dhamma*.[44] So pervasive is Ānanda's presence in the Buddhist texts that it is impossible to imagine them without him.

Another kinsman of the Buddha who appears to have a prominent position among the founder's close associates is Anuruddha. He is described in the texts as being delicately nurtured and having three storeyed residences, 'one for the cold season, one for the hot season, and one for the rains'.[45] Anuruddha was reluctant initially to go forth into the houseless state because of his delicate upbringing, but when he discovered that it was even more hazardous to lead a household life, he renounced the world in the company of his kinsmen.[46]

Anuruddha features in the *Aṅguttara Nikāya's* list of eminent disciples as being the most clairvoyant of the Buddha's disciples.[47] Anuruddha was present along with Ānanda when the *mahāparinibbāna* of the Buddha took place. Immediately thereafter and up to

[37] *Cullavagga*, p. 374. [38] *Cullavagga*, p. 411.

[39] *Vinaya Texts*, tr. by T.W. Rhys Davids and Hermann Oldenberg. Vol. III, p. 255.

[40] *M.N.*, II, pp. 212–13. [41] *D.P.P.N.*, Vol. I, p. 254.

[42] *M.N.*, III, p. 350; *S.N.*, IV, pp. 151, 152.

[43] *A.N.*, I, p. 25. [44] *D.P.P.N.*, Vol. I, p. 262.

[45] *Vinaya Texts*, tr. by T.W. Rhys Davids and Hermann Oldenberg, Vol. III, p. 224.

[46] *Cullavagga*, p. 281. [47] *A.N.*, I, p. 23.

the arrival of Mahā Kassapa, Anuruddha seems to have taken charge of the situation. He showed philosophic calm, in contrast to Ānanda's grief, and exhorted the weeping brethren: 'Enough my brethren! Weep not, neither lament. Has not the Exalted One formerly declared this to us, that it is in the very nature of all things near and dear to us, that we must divide ourselves from them, leave them, sever ourselves from them?'[48] Later, he asked Ānanda to inform the Mallās of Kusinārā about the Buddha's death so that arrangements could be made for the funeral.[49] The Mallās consulted Anuruddha when they were unable to lift the body of the *tathāgata* and he advised them to take a different direction since it was the wish of the spirits that they do so.[50] Similarly, when the funeral pyre refused to catch fire the Mallās consulted Anuruddha[51] who said that spirits were waiting for the venerable Mahā Kassapa to reverently salute the feet of the Exalted One.[52] It was only after Mahā Kassapa came that Anuruddha retreated into the background.

The only representative of the *nīca kulas* among the prominent disciples of the Buddha was Upāli, who was a barber of Sākyan noblemen. According to the narration in the *Cullavagga*, Upāli appears to have been merely accompanying the Sākyans up to the edge of their territory on their journey to seek ordination from the Buddha. At the border, the Sākyans took off their finery, wrapped them in their robes and gave them to Upāli, asking him to turn back saying, 'These things will be sufficient for you to live upon'. Upāli turned back initially, but, after a while, he felt uneasy about taking the bundle. He thought to himself, 'These Sākyans are fierce. They will think that these young men have been brought by me to destruction and they will slay me.'[53] Instead of returning to Kapilavatthu, he decided to join the *saṅgha* along with the Sākyans. The Sākyans requested the Buddha to ordain Upāli first and place him before them in the *saṅgha* so that their excessive pride would be humbled.

Once he joined the *saṅgha*, Upāli seems to have quickly carved a niche for himself because of his mastery of the *vinaya*. He was

[48] *D.N.*, II, p. 121; *D.B.*, II, p. 177. [49] *D.N.*, II, pp. 121–2; *D.B.*, II, p. 179.

[50] *D.N.*, II, p. 123; *D.B.*, II, p. 181.

[51] *D.N.*, II, p. 125; *D.B.*, II, p. 185. [52] *D.N.*, II, p. 126.

[53] *Cullavagga*, p. 281; *Vinaya Texts*, tr. by T.W. Rhys Davids and Hermann Oldenberg, Vol. III, p. 229.

taught the *vinaya* by the Buddha himself and was known as *vinayadhārānam*.[54] In the *Aṅguttara Nikāya's* enumeration of eminent disciples he is listed as the one who knew the disciplinary rules by heart.[55] Even in the lifetime of the Buddha, Upāli was sometimes called upon to give his judgement on disputes, as in the case of the *bhikkhus* Ajjuka and Bharu Kacchaka.[56] Upāli played a significant role in the First Council of Rājagaha where he helped Mahā Kassapa to codify the rules on discipline in the form of the *Vinaya Piṭaka*.[57]

Other figures who are enumerated as close associates of the Buddha include Mahā Koṭṭhita, Mahā Kappina, Rāhula, Devadatta, Mahā Cunda, Puṇṇa Mantāniputta, and Mahā Kaccana; of these Mahā Koṭṭhita, Mahā Cunda, Mahā Kaccana[58] and Puṇṇa Mantāniputta were *brāhmaṇas*. Mahā Cunda was also the younger brother of Sāriputta. Mahā Kappina, Rāhula, and Devadatta were *khattiyas*; Rāhula was Buddha's son and Devadatta his cousin. Thus we find that within the small circle of Buddha's closest associates there were four who were related to the Buddha himself (Ānanda, Anuruddha, Devadatta, and Rāhula), and two others were related to each other (Sāriputta and Mahā Cunda).

The laity

We use the word laity in its widest sense to include all those who were sympathetic to the Buddha's ideas but who did not actually join the *saṅgha*. The laity comprised many individuals who are described as *upāsakas*, having accepted the *tiraratana* (triplegems) of the Buddha, *dhamma*, and *saṅgha*. It also includes many people who are simply stated to have supported the *saṅgha*. Support might take the form of donating land, constructing *vihāras*, gifting robes, medicines or supplies, but most often it meant simply feeding the monks. This was by no means an insignificant function. On the other hand, it may be treated as the primary function of the laity who looked after the basic needs of the monks. Without this

[54] *A.N.*, I, p. 25. [55] Ibid. [56] *D.P.P.N.*, I, p. 408 [57] *Cullavagga*, p. 408.

[58] *S.N.*, II, pp. 132–3; *K.S.*, II, p. 108. See also *Pācittiya*, p. 96. The two lists differ in their compilation of the names. The *Vinaya* list is more comprehensive. It includes the following names: (1) Sāriputta, (2) Mahā Moggallāna, (3) Mahā Kaccana, (4) Mahā Koṭṭhita, (5) Mahā Kappina, (6) Mahā Cunda, (7) Anuruddha, (8) Revata, (9) Upāli, (10) Ānanda, (11) Rāhula, and (12) Devadatta. The *Saṃyutta Nikāya* list consists of only eight names and includes the name of Puṇṇa Mantāniputta.

minimum support the *bhikkhus* would have been unable to pursue their goal of *nibbāna*. The feeding of the monks was the most important tie between them and the laity, in return for which the *bhikkhus* taught *dhamma* to the laity.

There are 175 names mentioned in the texts as followers or supporters and these constitute our list of the laity in the Buddha's time (see Appendix C). Here again, the largest component consists of *brāhmaṇas* (76). They are followed by *gahapatis* who comprise 33 members; 26 people belong to other *ucca kulas*; and 22 were *khattiyas*. The *nīca kulas* are a small group here too and are represented by 11 people. Finally, we have seven *paribbājakas* and this appears to be something of an anomaly in the list. Since *paribbājakas* were wanderers who had renounced the household state, it is not clear how they could have supported the *sangha* in any way. The significance of the term *upāsaka* is not clear from the sources in the context of the *paribbājakas*. It is possible that they accepted the teachings of the Buddha without formally joining the *saṅgha* and complying with its discipline. However, at least in one instance a *paribbājaka* appears as a supporter of the *saṅgha* since he invites the Buddha and other *bhikkhus* to a meal. This was probably possible because he had the steady support of the Lichchhavis, who had undertaken to provide his material needs. He is described as a reputed teacher who was respected by the people.[59]

The brāhmaṇa *component of the laity*

Of the 76 *brāhmaṇas* listed among the laity, eight are described as wealthy and were obviously prestigious figures. Pokkarasādi,[60] Soṇadaṇḍa,[61] Caṇkī,[62] Kūṭadanta[63] and Lohicca[64] appear to have enjoyed *brahmadeya* lands in the *brāhmaṇa-gāmas* of Kosala and Magadha. Their acceptance of the Buddha's teaching is given considerable importance in early Pāli texts. Many *suttas* in the *Dīgha Nikāya*[65] and the *Majjhima Nikāya*[66] are wholly devoted to the meeting between the Buddha and various prominent *brāhmaṇas* and their ultimate decision to become lay disciples of his. Since they were leading members of the *brāhmaṇa* community, their support to the Buddha would have had considerable influence upon the rest

[59] *M.N.*, I, p. 308. [60] *D.N.*, I, p. 76. [61] Ibid.
[62] *M.N.*, II, p. 427. [63] *D.N.*, I, p. 109. [64] *D.N.*, I, p. 191.
[65] *D.N.*, I, pp. 76, 97, 109. [66] *M.N.*, II, p. 427.

of the people. Pokkarasādi, a teacher with a large following, is described as accepting the Buddha as his guide. His wives and children are also said to have done the same.[67] This obviously created an impact, for Pokkarasādi's example is quoted by Soṇadaṇḍa, another famous *brāhmaṇa*, as good reason for visiting the Buddha.[68] Most of these *brāhmaṇas* had large numbers of followers, and their decision to accept the Buddha could have adversely affected their standing among their own followers. They had to therefore judiciously balance their old status as teachers with their new one as followers.

The case of Soṇadaṇḍa illustrates many of these points. Soṇadaṇḍa is described as dwelling at Campa in Magadha on a flourishing piece of land.[69] When the Buddha was staying in the vicinity of Campa many *brāhmaṇa-gahapatis* decided to visit him. Soṇadaṇḍa also expressed his desire to accompany them, but other *brāhmaṇas* who were visiting Campa on business tried to dissuade him from doing so.[70] They said: 'Let not the venerable Soṇadaṇḍa do that. . . . If the venerable Soṇadaṇḍa went to call upon (Gotama) then the venerable Soṇadaṇḍa's reputation would decrease and the *samaṇa* Gotama's would increase.'[71] They further declared that since Soṇadaṇḍa was well born, of pure descent, both prosperous and virtuous, a teacher of 300 *brāhmaṇas*, and honoured and esteemed by King Bimbisāra and by Pokkarasādi, it was the Buddha who should visit him and not the other way round.[72] In response Soṇadaṇḍa enumerated the reasons for his decision to visit the Buddha, which included the Buddha's pure descent, his having gone forth at a young age leaving much wealth behind, and the fact that King Bimbisāra and the eminent *brāhmaṇa* Pokkarasādi had put their trust in him.[73] However, as Soṇadaṇḍa proceeded, he was struck with doubts about his reputation in case he failed to frame his question to the Buddha properly. He thought: 'The company might thereupon speak of me with disrespect, and my reputation would decrease, and with my reputation my income would grow less, for what we have to enjoy, that depends on our reputation.'[74] Fortunately for him, the Buddha did not embarrass him. They had a discussion on the question of who was a real *brāhmaṇa*. At the end

[67] *D.N.*, I, p. 95. [68] *D.N.*, I, p. 101. [69] *D.N.*, I, pp. 97 ff.
[70] *D.N.*, I, p. 98. [71] *D.B.*, I, p. 146. [72] *D.N.*, I, p. 99.
[73] *D.N.*, I, pp. 100–1. [74] *D.N.*, I, p. 102; *D.B.*, I, p. 151.

of the discussion Soṇadaṇḍa became a lay disciple and invited the Buddha to a meal.[75] Soṇadaṇḍa however requested the Buddha to excuse him from bowing before the Buddha in the presence of the assembly: 'If O Gotama after I have entered the assembly I should rise from my seat to bow down before the venerable Gotama then the assembly would find fault with me . . . now he who should lose his reputation, his income would grow less. . . . If then, when I am seated in the assembly, I stretch forth my joined palms in salutation let the venerable Gotama accept that from me as rising from my seat.'[76]

A large number (30) of the *brāhmaṇas* that we have listed became *upāsakas* in groups, having obviously influenced each other in the process. These include the *brāhmaṇa-gahapatis* of Verañja,[77] Sāla,[78] Veḷudvāra,[79] Venāgapura[80] and Khomadussa.[81] They are described in the texts as having approached the Buddha with some question which bothered them. At the end of the session after having had their doubts resolved they declared themselves *upāsakas* of the Buddha.

Important gahapati *supporters of the Buddha*

While many prominent *brāhmaṇas* are described as becoming *upāsakas* of the Buddha, they are rarely depicted as being continuously important in the early Pāli texts. Soṇadaṇḍa, Pokkarasādi or Kūṭadanta do not appear to have contributed any further support to the *saṅgha* other than having fed the Buddha and his band of *bhikkhus* when they declared themselves his *upāsakas*. Although they were themselves frequently land-based, they never gifted any land to the *saṅgha*. Nor is there any reference to them in the context of the construction of *vihāras* for the *saṅgha*. Even the gift of robes was hardly ever made.

The *gahapatis*, on the other hand, feature as continuing supporters of the *saṅgha*. They figure prominently in the early canon as the most important component of the laity and their acceptance of the Buddha's teachings is given considerable importance. The narration of the *gahapati* Anāthapiṇḍika's first meeting with the Buddha is probably as significant as the Buddha's first meeting with the Kings Bimbisāra or Ajātasattu. A long passage in the *Cullavagga* of the *Vinaya-Piṭaka* recounts the episode in considerable detail.[82]

[75] *D.N.*, I, p. 103. [76] *D.N.*, I, p. 108; *D.B.*, I, p. 158. [77] *M.N.*, I, p. 359.
[78] *M.N.*, I, p. 355. [79] *S.N.*, IV, p. 303. [80] *A.N.*, I, p. 171.
[81] *S.N.*, I, p. 184. [82] *Cullavagga*, pp. 249–53.

Beginning with Anāthapiṇḍika first hearing of the Buddha through his brother-in-law, the *seṭṭhi* of Rājagaha, the narrative goes on to describe Anāthapiṇḍika's great excitement, which mounted by the hour and made sleep impossible the night before he came face to face with the Buddha, and the joy which he experienced when the Buddha addressed him by his personal name, Sudatta (which was not known to most people).[83] The subsequent account of his purchase of the Jetavana from prince Jeta Kumāra at a fabulous price and its presentation to the Buddha[84] indicates the importance with which he was treated by the *saṅgha*. Anāthapiṇḍika features right through the texts, frequently visiting the Buddha and demonstrating his deep faith in him. Many *suttas* in the texts are addressed to Anāthapiṇḍika. Towards the end of his life he seems to have been reduced to poverty,[85] and was unhappy that he could no longer provide for the monks in the same fashion as in the past. The Buddha then preached the *Velāma Sutta* to encourage him.[86] As he lay on his death-bed he sent a special message to Sāriputta to visit him.[87] Sāriputta went along with Ānanda and preached the *Anāthapiṇḍikovada Sutta*. He is described as being reborn as a *deva* in the *deva* world.[88] In the *Aṅguttara* list of eminent people *Anāthapiṇḍika* is described as the chief alms-giver amongst Buddha's disciples.[89]

Another prominent *upāsaka* of the Buddha was Citta *gahapati* of Macchikāsaṇḍa. Citta also features in the list of prominent disciples in the *Aṅguttara Nikāya*, where he is declared to be chief among the *upāsakas* and a *dhamma* teacher.[90] A collection of *suttas* is named after him in the *Saṁyutta Nikāya*.[91] Citta *gahapati* is recorded as having played host to a number of *theras* (elders) who stayed at Macchikāsaṇḍa in the wild mango grove belonging to him.[92] Apart from his support of the *saṅgha* what marked him out from other *gahapati* supporters was his deep knowledge of Buddhism and his skill at expounding his knowledge.

He is described as being able to understand the full meaning of a pithy saying of the Buddha.[93]

[83] Ibid., p. 250. [84] Ibid., p. 253.
[85] *D.P.P.N.*, I, p. 71. [86] *A.N.*, IV, pp. 35–7. [87] *M.N.*, III, p. 345.
[88] Ibid., p. 348. [89] *A.N.*, I, p. 26. [90] Ibid. [91] *S.N.*, III, pp. 252–70.
[92] *S.N.*, III, p. 253. In addition he offered food, lodgings, robes and medicines to Isidatta, Acela Kassappa and Mahā Kassappa (*S.N.*, III, p. 257).
[93] *S.N.*, III, 259–60.

Citta even features as answering a question raised by the *bhikkhu* Godatta.[94] Further, he cornered Nigaṇṭha Ñataputta in an argument and it is obvious that he found Nigaṇṭha unsatisfactory as a teacher.[95]

The only example of a *bhikkhu* having to seek the forgiveness of an *upāsaka* concerns Citta, who had been offended by the behaviour of the *bhikkhu* Sudhamma. The Buddha admonished the latter, saying: 'How can you, foolish man, jeer at the *gahapati* Citta who has faith and is a benefactor, a supporter of the order'?[96] The Buddha then arranged a formal act of reconciliation in which Citta was requested to forgive the *bhikkhu*.[97] We have earlier referred to the exhortation of Citta's relatives who asked him on his deathbed to fix his aspiration on being reborn as a *rāja*, a *cakkavatti*.[98] It is significant that the texts considered him worthy of being reborn a *cakkavatti*, the counterpart of the Buddha in the lay world.

Other *gahapatis* who appear to be significant in the texts include Meṇḍaka, who possessed psychic powers,[99] Sandhana,[100] Nakulamātā and Nakulapitār.[101] Nakulamātā and Nakulapitār are said to have welcomed the Buddha like a long-lost son when they first met him because they had been his parents in many previous births.[102] They are depicted as an ideal couple and appear in the *Aṅguttara Nikāya's* list of eminent disciples, as the most intimate disciples of the Buddha.[103] Among the Buddha's best known *upāsikās* is Visākhā Migārmātā, who also belonged to the *gahapati* category. She is listed as an ideal lay woman, as well as chief among those who ministered to the order.[104] She features right through the texts, donating robes and alms to the *saṅgha* and was a special patron of the *bhikkhunīs*. Visākhā Migāramātā requested Buddha to grant her eight permanent boons, which he did. These were that as long as she lived, she should be allowed to give robes to members of the order for the rainy season; food for monks coming into Sāvatthi; food for those going out; food for the sick; food for those waiting on the sick; medicine for the sick; a constant supply of rice gruel for anyone needing it; and bathing robes for the nuns.[105] As a dynamic member of the laity Visākhā was called upon to judge

[94] *S.N.*, III, pp. 263–5. [95] Ibid., pp. 265–6.
[96] *Cullavagga*, pp. 32–5; *B.O.D.*, V, p. 25. [97] Ibid. [98] *S.N.*, III, pp. 268–70.
[99] *Mahāvagga*, pp. 254–9. [100] *A.N.*, III, p. 149. [101] *D.P.P.N.*, II, p. 3.
[102] Ibid. [103] *A.N.*, III, pp. 17–19. [104] *A.N.*, I, pp. 26–7.
[105] *A.N.*, I, p. 27.

questions related to disciplinary matters in the *saṅgha*. She was also treated as a very trustworthy witness and her word was accepted in a charge of impropriety levelled against the *bhikkhu* Udayin at a formal meeting of the *saṅgha* called to lay down punishment against the offender.[106] Visākhā was the object of many *suttas* preached by the Buddha during her frequent visits to him. These include the famous discourse on the keeping of the *uposatha*;[107] the discourse on the eight qualities which win power for women in the world and power and happiness in the next; and the eight qualities which enable women to be born among the *devas*.[108]

Apart from the examples already given, it is *gahapatis* who generally feature most frequently in the list of eminent *upāsakas*. Of the twenty personalities in this list, twelve are described as *gahapatis*.[109] They formed the largest single group amongst the lay followers of the Buddha. We shall pursue this point in the conclusion of this chapter.

Other prominent supporters of the Buddha

Prominent lay followers of the Buddha included the ruling kings of Magadha and Kosala, where the Buddha spent a great deal of time. Both the kings of Magadha who were contemporaries of the Buddha, Bimbisāra and Ajātasattu, are described as becoming his *upāsakas*.[110] The sketch of the Buddha's early career in the *Mahāvagga* describes the first meeting between the Buddha and Bimbisāra, his subsequent acceptance of the Buddha's teachings, and the gifting of the Veḷuvana, which was the first property given to the *saṅgha*.[111] The significance that the Buddha attached to the patronage of Bimbisāra is evident from numerous references in the early Pāli canon. The *pātimokkha*, or custom of the fortnightly assembly of monks, was introduced at the suggestion of Bimbisāra.[112] Similarly, the extremely severe rule that monks bathe only once a fortnight followed an occasion when Bimbisāra had to wait for his bath while *bhikkhus* indulged in some merriment when bathing in the river.[113]

[106] *Mahāvagga*, pp. 306–10; *B.O.D.*, IV, p. 416.

[107] *Pārājika*, pp. 278–9. [108] *A.N.*, III, pp. 352, 364, 366.

[109] *A.N.*, III, p. 149. The *gahapatis* include Bhallika, Anāthapiṇḍika, Citta, Ugga, Nakulapitā, Tavakaṇṇika, Vicchayo, Vijayamāhita, Meṇḍaka, Ugga of Vesali, Isidatta, and Pūraṇo.

[110] *Mahāvagga*, p. 37; *D.N.*, I, p. 74 [111] *Mahāvagga*, pp. 35–8.

[112] *Mahāvagga*, p. 105. [113] *Pācittiya*, pp. 159–60.

Ajātasattu's question regarding the utility of the life of a recluse was the occasion for the preaching of the *Samaññaphala Sutta.*[114] Ajātasattu is also depicted as seeking the advice of the Buddha before attacking the Vajjian confederacy.[115] He is described as becoming an *upāsaka,*[116] a status that was not denied to him despite the grievous wrong he committed in killing his father.

Pasenadi, the king of Kosala, was also a steady supporter of the Buddha and the *Saṁyutta Nikāya* contains a collection of *suttas* addressed to him.[117] Initially, Pasenadi seems to have been somewhat sceptical of the Buddha's claim to be a perfectly and supremely enlightened person, since the Buddha was young in comparison with the six contemporary *titthiya* leaders.[118] However, the Buddha was able to convince Pasenadi that youth was no bar to wisdom and subsequently Pasenadi became an *upāsaka.*[119] His favourite wife, Mallika, was also an important follower of the Buddha and is depicted as being a more steadfast devotee than her husband. Through her efforts, some of Pasenadi's doubts were resolved.[120]

Some other *upāsakas* belonging to *rājakulas* were also among the prominent lay disciples of the Buddha. They included the princes Jeta,[121] Abhaya,[122] Jīvaka Komārabhacca[123] and Bodhirājakumāra.[124] Jivaka was the best known of these and is listed as the most loved of the Buddhas *upāsakas,*[125] probably because of his great skill as a physician. The *Vinaya* relates how a large number of sick people joined the *saṅgha* since that was the only way they could have access to his treatment. Jivaka was otherwise busy ministering to the king's family apart from the *saṅgha.*[126] Jivaka also built a *vihāra* for the Buddha and gifted robes to the *bhikkhus.*[127] Jeta Kumāra had become an *upāsaka* following the purchase by Anāthapiṇḍika of the Jetavana for the *saṅgha.* He was so moved

[114] *D.N.*, I, pp. 39–75. [115] *D.N.*, II, pp. 78–9.
[116] *D.N.*, I, p. 75. [117] *S.N.*, I, pp. 67–102. [118] *S.N.*, I, pp. 67–8.
[119] Ibid., p. 69. [120] *M.N.*, II, pp. 353–8.
[121] *Cullavagga*, p. 253. [122] *M.N.*, II, p. 71.
[123] *Mahāvagga*, pp. 297–8; *B.O.D.*, IV, pp. 394–6. [124] *M.N.*, II, p. 342.
[125] *A.N.*, I, p. 26. The *Mahāvagga* contains an entire section on Jivaka's birth and subsequent career as a physician. Jivaka is described as the son of the courtesan Salavati of Rājagaha. Since he was brought up by Abhayarājakumāra, who regarded himself as Jivaka's father, we have listed him as *khattiya*. Jivaka also regards himself as a member of a king's family when he says, 'It is hard to make a living in these king's families', and goes off to train as a physician (*Mahāvagga*, p. 287).
[126] *Mahāvagga*, p. 76. [127] *Mahāvagga*, p. 297.

by Anāthapiṇḍika's faith in the Buddha that he built and donated a gateway in the corner of the Jetavana at his own expense.[128]

A few *khattiyas* belonging to the *gaṇa-saṅghas* were also important figures among the Buddhist laity. Chief of these was Mahānama the Sākyan, who gave choice alms-food.[129] Sīha the Lichcchavi, who was originally a follower of the Nigaṇṭhas, was an important convert to the Buddhist faith and his transference of allegiance was resented by the Jainas.[130] Similarly, Roja the Mallā did not originally have faith in the Buddha, unlike other Mallās. He went to see the Buddha only to comply with a decision of the Mallās which decreed that whoever failed to pay him homage would be fined 500 coins.[131] Ānanda was disappointed that Roja had not come out of faith and requested the master to discover some means by which Roja Mallā would become a disciple since that would create a definite impact on others. Buddha drew Roja into the faith by the power of his compassion.[132] Roja then requested the Buddha to henceforth accept hospitality only from him and, although this request was turned down, Roja discovered that the *saṅgha* needed green vegetables and supplied it with them.[133]

Among the *upāsakas* belonging to *ucca kulas* other than *brāhmaṇa*, *khattiya* and *gahapati*, were the *vāṇijjas*, Tapussa and Bhallika, the *seṭṭhi* of Rājagaha, and the courtesan Ambapali. Tapussa and Bhallika appear in the list of eminent disciples in the *Aṅguttara Nikāya* amongst the Buddha's first disciples.[134] The wealthy *seṭṭhi* of Rajagaha is depicted as noticing the discomfort of *bhikkhus* living in the open and expressing a desire to build *vihāras* for the *saṅgha*. This was brought to the notice of the Buddha, who gave the *seṭṭhi* permission to do so.[135] The *seṭṭhi* then built 60 *vihāras* in a day. He invited the Buddha and other *bhikkhus* for a meal and dedicated the 60 dwellings for the *cātudisa saṅgha* (*saṅgha* of the four quarters), both of the present and the future.[136] This formula, which appears so often in the texts and inscriptions, first appears in the context of the gift of *vihāras* by the *seṭṭhi* of Rājagaha. The incident of Ambapali's visit to the Buddha, his acceptance of her invitation to a meal which she refused to withdraw at the request of the Lichchhavis of Vesāli, and her subsequent gifting of the Ambavana to the *saṅgha* is

[128] *Cullavagga*, p. 253.
[129] *A.N.*, I, p. 26. [130] *Mahāvagga*, pp. 248–53. [131] *Mahāvagga*, pp. 260–1.
[132] Ibid., p. 262. [133] Ibid. [134] *A.N.*, I, p. 26.
[135] *Cullavagga*, p. 239. [136] Ibid., p. 240.

described both in the *Vinaya Piṭaka* and the *Dīgha Nikāya.*[137]

The only prominent *upāsaka* who belonged to the *nīca kulas* was Cunda the *kammara-putta* of Pāva. It was at Cunda's house that the Buddha had his last meal which brought on an illness leading to death. The Buddha apparently knew that a part of the menu would have harmful consequences and thus asked Cunda not to serve it to the other *bhikkhus.*[138] He also probably anticipated a certain amount of censure against Cunda for he specifically stated before his death that no blame should be attached to Cunda. On the other hand, he said that in providing the *tathāgata* his last meal, Cunda had achieved an honourable position, equal to that of the server of the first meal immediately after his enlightment. Both acts were credited with unique merit.[139]

Khattiya, brāhmaṇa, *and* gahapati: *key figures in the Buddhist texts*

In presenting details concerning the social composition of the Buddhist *saṅgha* and the laity, an enumeration of figures alone cannot convey the flavour of the texts, which throw considerable light on the prominence attributed to various social groups. We shall take up some of these features before concluding this chapter and analyse the facts that have already been enumerated.

If one looks at the structure of the texts as a whole, the narration of the meetings between the Buddha and the *jaṭila* Uruvela Kassapa, King Bimbisāra, and the *gahapati* Anāthapiṇḍika are given special importance. All three appear in *Khandhaka* portion of the *Vinaya Piṭaka* from which it is possible to piece together a sketch of the Buddha's career as a teacher. It is likely that the acceptance of Buddhist teachings by these key figures (along with certain other similar situations interspersed in the texts) were specially significant for their 'demonstration effect' on the people, and explains the prominence given to them in the narrative.[140]

Bimbisāra and Anāthapiṇḍika appear frequently in the early Pāli canon and we have already discussed them in the preceding sections of this chapter. Uruvela Kassapa, on the other hand, appears only in the context of his first meeting with the Buddha, and his gradual

[137] *D.N.*, II, pp. 76–8; *Mahāvaga*, p. 246. We have placed Ambapāli among the category of *uccakulas* because there is nothing in the early Pāli texts that suggests low status for a courtesan. We have also classified her as a supporter because our sources do not indicate that she joined the *saṅgha*.

[138] *D.N.*, II, pp. 98–9. [139] *D.N.*, II, pp. 105–6. [140] Ibid.

but total acceptance of the Buddha as his teacher.[141] He was a reputed *jaṭila*, the eldest of three brothers, each of whom had his own following. All had settled at different points along the Nerañjara river.

According to the narration, the Buddha visited Uruvela Kassapa and spent the night in a room where the sacred Brahmanical fire was kept despite Kassapa's warning that the spot was inhabited by a fierce *nāga* (serpent). In a rare display of magical powers,[142] the Buddha overcame first this *nāga* and then another. Although Uruvela Kassapa was very favourably impressed, he still considered the Buddha to be a great ascetic with magical powers, but not an *arahant* like himself.[143] The Buddha spent some time living in the neighbourhood till Uruvela Kassapa was ready for conversion. Uruvela Kassapa was finally convinced that he was not an *arahant*, and that the path he was following would not lead him to *arahantship*. He thereupon acknowledged defeat and asked for ordination.[144] All his pupils also joined, having shaved off their hair and thrown away their fire implements into the river. Uruvela Kassapa's brothers, Nadi Kassapa and Gaya Kassapa, also joined the *saṅgha* along with their respective followers.[145]

From Gayāsīsa, the Buddha went to Rājagaha accompanied by the three Kassapa brothers and their pupils. When King Bimbisāra and the assembly of *brāhmaṇas* and *gahapatis* saw them approaching they wondered whether the Buddha had accepted Uruvela Kassapa as his teacher or vice versa. In the presence of the entire assembly Uruvela Kassapa declared his allegiance to the Buddha[146] and immediately after this Bimbisāra also declared himself a lay follower and made the first gift to the *saṅgha* in the form of Veḷuvana (bamboo grove) just outside Rājagaha.[147] The tremendous impact created by Uruvela Kassapa's acceptance of the Buddha as his teacher is attested by later evidence. The incident is depicted in later sculptures and Hieun Tsang refers to a stupa being erected at the spot

[141] It may be noted here that the three key figures represent the three social categories of *brāhmaṇa* (Uruvela Kassapa), *khattiya* (King Bimbisāra), and *gahapati* (Anāthapiṇḍika). The three categories feature prominently in the structure of the text (see Chapter III).

[142] The Buddha often speaks critically of magic and the display of magical powers. The use of these powers by him is therefore doubly significant.

[143] *Mahāvagga*, p. 32. [144] Ibid., p. 33. [145] Ibid., p. 34.

[146] Ibid., p. 35. [147] Ibid., p. 38.

where the conversion took place.[148] Uruvela Kassapa does not feature anywhere else in the texts, except in the list of eminent disciples. He is described as chief of those who had a large following,[149] but we do not know what influence he had on the *saṅgha*. It is possible, however, to deduce the importance of the *jaṭilas* as a group within the *saṅgha* from the Buddha's ruling that the probationary period of four months mandatory for all other *paribbājakas* who wished to join the *saṅgha* could be waived only in the case of *jaṭilas*.[150]

Wealthy supporters of Buddhism

Among those significant in the narrative are also included people who once enjoyed great wealth and pleasures and renounced them, such as the *seṭṭhi-puttas* Yasa,[151] Soṇa Koḷivisa[152] and Soṇa Kuṭikaṇṇa.[153] The case of Yasa in particular appears to symbolize the value attached to giving up great wealth and luxury. He is depicted as having been a very sheltered *seṭṭhi-putta* who lived in great opulence.[154] Nevertheless Yasa was dissatisfied with his existence and slipped out one night exclaiming, 'Alas! What danger'.[155] The Buddha saw him from a distance and called out to him, 'Come Yasa, here is neither distress nor danger.'[156] While the Buddha preached to him, Yasa was filled with great joy. Soon, however, his father discovered his absence and came in search of him. He asked Yasa to return to his grieving mother, but the Buddha interceded and declared that household life had no attraction for Yasa and ordained him.[157] Yasa's father was himself impressed by the Buddha and became the first *upāsaka*, while Yasa's mother and wife became the first *upāsikās*.[158] Immediately afterwards, four friends of Yasa also joined the *saṅgha*.[159] The section on Yasa in the *Mahāvagga* ends with the information that fifty young acquaintances who were *seṭṭhi's* and *seṭṭhi-anuseṭṭhis*, also joined the *saṅgha*.[160] Yasa does not feature elsewhere in the early Pāli canon, but whenever he is referred to in the later commentaries the great luxury of his lay

[148] C.S. Basak, 'The Role of Uruvela Kassapa in the Spread of Buddhism' in A.K. Narain (ed.), *Studies in Pāli and Buddhism*, p. 374, n. 31.
[149] *A.N.*, I, p. 25. [150] *Mahāvagga*, p. 76. [151] *Mahāvagga*, p. 18.
[152] Ibid., p. 199. [153] Ibid., p. 213. [154] Ibid., p. 18.
[155] Ibid., *B.O.D.*, IV, p. 22. [156] Ibid., p. 19; *B.O.D.*, IV, p. 23.
[157] Ibid. [158] Ibid., p. 21. [159] Ibid., p. 21. [160] *Mahāvagga*, p. 22.

life is mentioned. Similarly, Soṇa Koḷivisa[161] and Soṇa Kuṭikaṇṇa[162] are described as possessing great wealth and being delicately nurtured but nevertheless renouncing it to join the *saṅgha*. The renunciation of luxury was obviously invested with special significance. In contrast, Upāli, the only member of the *nīca kulas* to rise to importance in the *saṅgha*, is described as having joined the *saṅgha* almost by accident and not through any conscious decision on his part to lead the 'higher life'.[163] The narration of Upāli's ordination is only an appendage to the story of the ordination of Buddha's Sākyan kinsmen.[164] The text mentions the progress made by his erstwhile Sākyan lords immediately after joining the *saṅgha*, but ignores Upāli in the narration,[165] even though Upāli ultimately became the expert in the *vinaya*.

The importance of kinship ties in the extension of support to Buddhism

We have already briefly touched upon kinship ties in the social composition of the *saṅgha*. This appears to have been a very important factor in the development of both the Buddhist *saṅgha* and laity. The texts themselves give frequent examples of the relevance of kinship ties and we shall briefly mention some here. The inner circle of twelve prominent disciples of the Buddha consisted of three people who were kinsmen of the Buddha, one being Rāhula, the Buddha's son. Rāhula's depiction as a member of the group is extremely difficult to explain, unless we accept the importance given to kinship ties. He is not referred to as possessing any special powers, unlike other members of the core group.[166] In fact, whenever reference is made to him it is in the context of being exhorted to strive harder.[167] Not many *suttas* are devoted to Rāhula, and he is never shown preaching to anyone and was clearly still under training.[168] Yet he is listed as one of the twelve prominent figures around the Buddha.[169]

Other kinsmen of the Buddha within this small circle included Ānanda and Anuruddha.[170] The narrative relates the events which lead to their joining the *saṅgha*. Mahānama, an elder and a respected Sākyan, laments that there were no representatives from his family

[161] Ibid., p. 199. [162] Ibid., p. 213. [163] *Cullavagga*, pp. 281–2.
[164] Ibid., p. 282. [165] Ibid. [166] *M.N.*, II, p. 92. [167] Ibid., p. 100.
[168] *S.N.*, II, pp. 203–5; the *Aṅguttara Nikāya* speaks of him as foremost among those anxious for training (*A.N.*, I, p. 24).
[169] *Pācittiya*, p. 96. [170] Ibid.

who had gone forth to join the *saṅgha*[171] and told his younger brother Anuruddha that either he or Anuruddha should join it. The account earlier suggests that each family had sent a representative to join the *saṅgha* and this itself demonstrates the strength of kinship ties amongst the early Buddhists. When Anuruddha decided to join the *saṅgha*, he was accompanied by five other Sākyan kinsmen including Bhaddiya the Sākya *rāja*. According to the record in the *Mahāvagga*, Bhaddiya the Sākya rāja, Anuruddha, Ānanda, Bhagu, Kimbila and Devadatta, 'just as they had so often previously gone out to the pleasure ground with fourfold array, even so did they now go out with fourfold array.'[172]

We have already pointed to the prominent role that Ānanda and Anuruddha went on to play in the *saṅgha*. Apart from Buddha's kinsmen among the twelve inner disciples, three other members were related to each other. These were Sāriputta, Revata and Mahā Cunda,[173] all of whom were brothers. Sāriputta's family is a notable example of the kinship factor operating in the building of an organization. According to later Buddhist tradition represented in the *Theragāthā, Therīgāthā* and the *Apādana*, three of Sāriputta's brothers joined the *saṅgha*, and so did three of his sisters. In fact, the entire family seems to have been a part of the rising Buddhist movement.[174] Sāriputta was the most important *bhikkhu* in the *saṅgha* apart from the Buddha, and his kinsmen seem to have been as much a part of the new movement as the kinsmen of the founder.

Other examples can be cited where kinship ties were relevant both in attracting members into the *saṅgha* as well as spreading Buddhism amongst the laity. As already listed, Uruvela Kassapa joined the *saṅgha* along with two brothers.[175] Similarly, four Bharadvāja *brāhmaṇa* brothers joined the *saṅgha*, although three brothers had initially resented the action of the first brother.[176] Anāthapiṇḍika, the most prominent *upāsaka* of the Buddha, came to hear of the *tathāgata* through his brother-in-law, the *seṭṭhi* of Rājagaha,[177] and consequently became a follower himself.[178] Not only was Meṇḍaka *gahapati* an *upāsaka* of the Buddha,[179] but also his grand-daughter, Visākhā Migāramātā.[180] Visākha was responsible for the conversion of her father-in-law who had earlier been a follower of Nigaṇ-

171 *Cullavagga*, pp. 279–81. 172 Ibid., p. 281. 173 *Pārājika*, p. 96.
174 *D.P.P.N.*, II, p. 1109. 175 *Mahāvagga*, p. 34.
176 *S.N.*, I, pp. 160–4. 177 *Cullavagga*, pp. 249–50.
178 Ibid. 179 *Mahāvagga*, p. 257. 180 *D.P.P.N.*, II, p. 900.

ṭha Ñātaputta.[181] Her younger sister Sújāta was a daughter-in-law of Anāthapiṇḍika[182] and received special attention from the Buddha in a sermon on the duties of women.[183]

It is reasonable to infer from the available evidence that kinship was an important basis for recruitment into the *saṅgha* and in the spread of Buddhism. It was particularly relevant within the narrower circle surrounding the Buddha. The importance of kinship ties in Buddhist society was recognized by the Buddha himself when he allowed exceptions to a series of rules on grounds of kinship.[184] Apart from waiving the probationary period of four months applicable to the *paribbājakas* in the case of the *jaṭilas* the Buddha waived the probationary period for the Sākyas too. While allowing the exception Buddha explicitly stated that he did so on grounds of kinship. He says, 'If a Sākya by birth, O *bhikkhus*, who has belonged to a *titthiya* school comes to you, he is to receive the *upasampada* ordination directly and no *parivāsa* is to be imposed on him. The exceptional privilege, O *bhikkhus*, I grant to my kinsmen'.[185] The relaxation of rules on grounds of kinship was likely to have been the accepted norm since it appears not to have been criticized. Kinship bonds were likely to have had some influence generally in the inclusion of followers for the various sects.

Another area where the kinship factor operated in a very decisive manner was over the question of the entry of women into the *sangha*.[186] The initial request came from Mahāpajāpatī Gotamī, the Buddha's aunt and foster mother, but it was turned down by the Buddha. When Ānanda took up the cause of Mahāpajāpatī he used the kinship bond between the Buddha and Mahāpajāpatī to press his point.[187] The Buddha then acceded to the request and Mahāpajāpatī became the first *bhikkhunī* to be ordained. As its seniormost member, she also headed the *bhikkhunī saṅgha* and acted as the mediator between the Buddha and the *bhikkhunī saṅgha*.[188]

Analysis of the social composition of the early Buddhists

The large *brāhmaṇa* component among the early Buddhists both within the *saṅgha* and outside it needs some explanation. It has commonly been assumed that Buddhism was antagonistic to the

[181] Ibid., p. 902. [182] Ibid., p. 904. [183] *A.N.*, III, pp. 223–5.
[184] *Pārājika*, pp. 301–4; *Pācittiya*, pp. 87–90. [185] *Mahāvagga*, p.76.
[186] *Cullavagga*, pp. 373–7. [187] Ibid., p. 374. [188] *Cullavagga*, pp. 377–9.

brāhmaṇas, and as already noticed, there is some basis for such an assumption.[189] But how then can we explain the participation of the *brāhmaṇas* in such large numbers? One reason which seems plausible is that Buddhism was essentially a 'salvation' religion in which it was necessary to renounce the world and lead the 'higher life' in order to achieve the goal of *nibbāna*. This was by no means easy for most people. That *brāhmaṇas* responded in considerable numbers was because they were primarily a religious group whose precise function, ideally at least, was the pursuit of salvation. The Buddha frequently dwelt on this theme and his antagonism was directed against the *brāhmaṇas* for defaulting from their original pursuit of religious goals, and for leading a mundane existence instead.[190] It has been suggested by Lillie that the Buddhist movement was a revolt of higher Brahmanism against the lower and he argues that the Buddha drew a sharp contrast between the lower Brahmanism of the householder with the higher Brahmanism of the houseless one.[191] We have earlier shown that *brāhmaṇas* were opposed to the ascetic tradition, but it is also clear that many *brāhmaṇas* had responded to that tradition and often became *paribbājakas*. These *brāhmaṇas* would have seen in Buddhism an alternative to the decadent values exhibited by the existing Brahmanism. Some of the Buddha's most prominent disciples, such as Sāriputta, Moggallāna, and Mahā Kassapa were *brāhmaṇas* who had become *paribbājakas* even before they met him.

Many other *brāhmaṇas* who were not capable of renouncing the world nevertheless became lay followers of the Buddha by accepting his teachings. The Buddhist texts often refer to *brāhmaṇas* raising questions regarding the importance of sacrifice and its true meaning. The acceptance of the Buddha's views on these subjects by prominent *brāhmaṇas* would probably have generated a debate even among those *brāhmaṇas* who remained outside the direct orbit of Buddhism, and this may have helped in a transformation of the Brahmanical system itself over a period of time. On the other hand, the participation of significant numbers of *brāhmaṇas* in the Buddh-

[189] See Chapters II and IV.

[190] We have already demonstrated that the Buddha used the word *brāhmaṇa* in two different senses (see Chapter II) as a term of value as well as a social category, and that when he used the term *brāhmaṇa* in the sense of a 'value' he was identifying with it.

[191] Arthur Lillie, *The Life of the Buddha*, p. 127.

ist movement worked in the opposite direction too. However honest their acceptance of the Buddha's teachings, the *brāhmaṇas* carried along with them many ideas and beliefs from their earlier environment. We have an example of this in the case of the *brāhmaṇa* brothers Yamelu and Tekula, who requested the Buddha to allow the use of Sanskrit in teaching the *dhamma*.[192] While the Buddha was alive his charisma and unquestioned leadership of the *saṅgha* resisted such moves, but later on the *brāhmaṇa* component probably influenced the development of Buddhism in a variety of ways.

The *khattiyas* formed the second largest unit within the *saṅgha* and this feature also requires some explanation. Scholars like Oldenberg[193] and Weber[194] have seen Buddhism as a *khattiya* reaction to the increased social dominance of *brāhmaṇas* and their claim to pre-eminence. We have already pointed to the special tension between these two groups. However, the status of the *khattiyas* as wielders of political power should have placed them in a position of opposition to the ascetic tradition and the world-renouncing ideal. Nevertheless, *khattiyas* adopted Buddhism in significant numbers. It is possible to argue that, since the Buddha was a *khattiya* he would naturally have drawn into the new movement other members of his own social group. While this is very likely, a more important reason is the nature of the society in which Buddhism arose.

It is significant that the bulk of *khattiya* representation came from the *gaṇa-saṅghas*. They accounted for 22 out of a total of 28 *khattiyas* in the *saṅgha*. In discussing the religious propensities of various status groups, Weber has argued that concepts like salvation are remote from all ruling strata and that their religious propensities would normally be low, except at times when they were faced with a crisis of declining political power.[195] According to Weber, 'The development of a strong salvation religion by socially privileged groups normally has the best chance when demilitarization has set in for these groups and when they have lost . . . the possibility of political activity. . . . Consequently, salvation religions usually emerge when the ruling strata . . .have lost their political power.'[196] This was exactly the situation in the *gaṇa-saṅghas* in the sixth century

[192] *Cullavagga*, pp. 228–9.
[193] H. Oldenberg, *The Buddha: His Life, His Doctrine, His Order,* p. 156.
[194] Max Weber, *Religion of India*, pp. 226–7.
[195] Max Weber, *Economy and Society*, Vol. I, p. 472.

B.C. During the lifetime of the Buddha the *gaṇa-saṅghas* were steadily being crushed by the growing monarchical kingdoms of Kosala and Magadha. The Sākyas had lost their state to Kosala, and even the powerful Vajjian Confederacy was facing the onslaught of Ajātasattu. The proud and independent Sākyas and Lichchhavis, so conscious of their *khattiya* status, were being rendered irrelevant in their roles as wielders of political power. They witnessed with heightened consciousness the fact that all things are transitory and subject to change, which was exactly what the Buddha taught. No wonder, then, that they responded to the call of the Buddha. Kosambi has also remarked upon the collapse of the *gaṇa-saṅghas*, which could no longer contain its ablest members, and the effects this had upon the individuals within it.[197] A few sought outlets in political careers in the neighbouring monarchical kingdoms, while others turned to monkhood.[198]

Before this chapter is concluded it is necessary to account for the absence of *gahapatis* in the ranks of *bhikkhus*. This is unusual, given the fact that the *gahapati* was a vital component of the laity and an intrinsic part of Buddhism. One could reasonably expect the composition of the *saṅgha* to reflect society outside the *saṅgha*, as was largely the case as far as the representation of other social groups was concerned. The only exception was that of the *gahapatis*. This feature is even more noticeable if we consider that many *seṭṭhi-puttas* joined the *saṅgha*.

It is possible to argue that certain categories did not experience the special 'tension' required to renounce the world, and that this tension was not easily generated among certain groups, such as the land-based. It is also possible that the economic and social system in which the *gahapati* was located did not create the conditions for renunciation. We must remember that the period was one in which a primarily agrarian economy had emerged and that this economy supported a rising urban population. We have already established that the *gahapati* was the pivot of this economy and the primary tax payer. The withdrawal of such a category from the social world would have had a crucial, negative impact on the economic and social system. The two areas which the *bhikkhu* rigorously ab-

[197] D.D. Kosambi, 'Ancient Kosala and Magadha', *Journal of Bombay Branch of the Royal Asiatic Society*, Vol. XXVII, 1952, p. 183.

[198] The Mallā Bandhula and his nephew Kārāyana joined King Pasenadi's service (*D.P.P.N.*, I, p. 1079, II, p. 266).

stained from were production and reproduction. The *gahapati* on the other hand was specially concerned with both aspects,[199] and thus, while he was not debarred from the *saṅgha*, he tended to remain outside it. Instead, the *gahapati* became the most important category of the laity, particularly in terms of support to the *saṅgha*, which was also a vital part of the new movement.

[199] See Chapter III.

CHAPTER VI

The King in Early Buddhism

General ideas on kingship

The theme of power and its exercise occur frequently in early Buddhist literature. Ideas on power are invariably expressed through the medium of the king and the Buddhists do not seem to envisage a political and social system without the institution of kingship. Nevertheless, the importance of the king in relation to the central conception of Buddhism, in the form of a Buddhist society, has been a matter of controversy. While some scholars have held that the king had an extremely significant status in Buddhism,[1] others hold that Buddhism was apolitical in its orientation.[2] The fact that the Pāli canon does not directly outline a theory of the power and authority of the temporal ruler, but only provides numerous scattered references reflecting diverse opinions, has, to some extent, been responsible for this controversy. In our analysis of the role of power in Buddhism we shall begin with the general political ideas reflected in Buddhism before taking up the controversy about the significance of the king in the total world-view of Buddhism. The political ideas of the Buddhists themselves reflect various themes, such as general ideas on kingship; contemporary kingship, which included both the legitimate and despotic exercise of power; and ideal kingship, as articulated through the concept of the *cakkavatti dhammiko dhammarāja*, or the righteous universal ruler. We shall take up the various strands separately in this chapter.[3]

[1] S.J. Tambiah, *World Conqueror World Renouncer*, p. 8; Trevor Ling, *The Buddha*, p. 180.

[2] M. Weber, *The Religion of India*, p. 206.

[3] B.G. Gokhale ('The Early Buddhist View of the State', *Journal of American Oriental Society*, Vol. 89 (4), 1969, pp. 731–8) has suggested an evolutionary model for Buddhist thinking on the nature and functions of the state which, according to him, passed through three distinct phases. The first phase concerns the theory of the origin of the state as given in the *Aggañña Sutta*, where the state begins as a quasi-contractual arrangement in which the king agrees to perform specific functions on

The origin of kingship in the Buddhist genesis myth

The *Aggañña Sutta* of the *Dīgha Nikāya*[4] has a considerable range of ideas on the origin of the state with its concomitant in the form of the social contract theory,[5] within which the rise of kingship is located. These political ideas are expressed in a myth which deals with the origin of the world, the evolution of man and the rise of various institutions. The myth has been described in the chapter dealing with the genesis of the world by the famous Pāli commentator Buddhaghosha,[6] and is extremely significant for an understanding of the political ideas of Buddhism. The major stages of the myth describe the gradual deterioration of men from a state that has been compared with the ideal condition described by Rousseau, to the state of nature described by Hobbes.[7] In the original state of nature beings lived in godlike perfection, but as they succumbed to greed and passion they gradually lost their superior moral and physical attributes and were transformed into ordinary human beings. A direct consequence of this progressive fall of man was the growth of the institutions of family, private property, the political state and social differentiation, in successive stages. The crucial part of the myth dealing with the origin of kingship links the rise of the family and the rise of private property to the need for the exercise of power in maintaining a social order based on the two. Sharma has pointed out that the political compact between the ruler and the people in the *Aggañña Sutta* is preceded by a social compact which, though not explicitly stated, is implicit in the people's minds. There is an implicit obligation to respect the family and the private

---

behalf of the people. The second concerns the problems of relations between Buddhism and a well-entrenched and all-powerful monarchical despotism, and a solution is proposed in the theory of the two spheres of life, one of the *dhamma* and the other of *āṇā* (authority). In the third and final phase the Buddhists explicate their own ideal state in which the state simply becomes an instrument of *dhamma*, which now assumes the form of a cosmic force capable not only of containing the challenge of the power of the state but also of regulating its behaviour. In this sense the state becomes an ethical institution drawing its authority from the *dhamma* and guided by its repository the *saṅgha*. The major themes we have taken up for consideration are similar to Gokhale's model, but we have seen the ideas as existing at the same time acting and reacting upon each other in a dialectical manner.

[4] *D.N.*, III, pp. 63–76.

[5] R.S. Sharma, *Aspects of Political Ideas and Institutions in Ancient India*, pp. 49–50.

[6] *D.B.*, I, p. 106.

[7] R.S. Sharma, *Aspects of Political Ideas and Institutions in Ancient India*, p. 49.

rice fields of one another when the people agree to the establishment of a king over them.[8]

The Buddhist account of the genesis of the world is significant for its opposition to the Brahmanical world view, particularly on two major points which are related to each other and flow from the fact that the social order based on *vaṇṇa* divisions is intrinsic to Brahmanical political theory but is peripheral to the Buddhist. Ghoshal has pointed out that the ideas contained in the *Aggañña Sutta* present in a dramatic and vigorous form an open challenge to the Vedic dogma of the divine creation of the social order.[9] In the *Aggañña Sutta* social divisions are related to the functional distinctions among men and arise as a matter of convenience. Some people teach, others perform economic functions, and still others live by hunting and fishing.[10] This feature of the *Aggañña Sutta* has important implications for the Buddhist notion of kingship. In the Brahmanical conception the maintenance of the social order based on *vaṇṇa* divisions was one of the most important duties of the king. In contrast, it was the maintenance of the social order based on property with which the king was most often associated in Buddhism.

Seven symbols of sovereignty

Kingship is invariably associated with the possession of seven precious gems (*sattharatana*) which appear to be symbols of sovereignty and are unique to Buddhist philosophy in this form.[11] We shall analyse these symbols since we believe that the *sattharatana* represent the constituent elements of kingship as envisaged in Buddhism. It has been pointed out by Horner[12] that the number seven had

[8] Ibid., p. 50. Similarly Drekmeier (Charles Drekmeier, *Kingship and Community in Early India*, p. 109 and footnote) has suggested that the government, which grew out of the need for order, was rooted in a secular compact, and that one can infer from the myth that the social contract is between the *Kṣatriyas* as a group and the rest of society.

[9] U.N. Ghoshal, *A History of Indian Political Ideas*, p. 62; S.J. Tambiah, *World Conqueror, World Renouncer*, p. 22.

[10] *D.N.*, III, pp. 72–4.

[11] A series of sculptural representations of the *cakkavatti* surrounded by the seven precious gems have been found in Jaggayapeta in the Amaravati region. They are a graphic representation of kingship as conceived of in Buddhist political philosophy. All the sculptures are part of a Buddhist complex in Andhra.

[12] I.B. Horner, 'The Buddha's Co-natals' in A.K. Narain (ed.), *Studies in Pāli and Buddhism*, p. 115.

a special significance in the Indian tradition and was considered to be a symbol of perfection. According to Dumont[13] it represented a totality. The seven precious gems are: the *cakkaratana* or the wheel treasure; the *hatthiratana* or the elephant treasure; the *assaratana* or the horse treasure; the *maṇiratana* or the precious gem treasure; the *itthiratana* or the woman treasure; the *gahapatiratana*; and the *pariṇāyakaratana* or the councillor treasure.[14]

The *cakkaratana* is probably the most valued symbol of sovereignty possessed by the king. Rhys Davids interprets the wheel as a representation of the solar disc of the sun.[15] In the *Mahāsuddasana Sutta*[16] it is described appearing in the sky as a heavenly treasure and is quite clearly a mystical object rather than a material one, unlike the six other treasures which are enumerated as being among the material possessions of the great king, Mahā Sudāssana.[17] According to Zimmer,[18] the luminous apparition of the wheel in the firmament is a duplication of the neolithic symbol of the sun wheel, and Gonda[19] describes the wheel as a symbol of the sun which in its daily course illumines and *rules* the earth.

The *Mahāsudassana Sutta* describes the wheel as being sprinkled with water by the king who exhorts it to 'go forth and overcome'. The wheel then moves forward successively in all the four directions followed by the *cāturangini senā* or the four-fold army.[20] The entire operation seems to represent physical control over dominion, which is an integral aspect of kingship. According to the Petrograd dictionary *cakra* is sometimes equivalent to *rāshṭra* or dominion and signifies the realm or sovereignty with the wheel of monarch's chariot rolling over his dominions.[21] Gonda describes the *cakkarata-*

[13] L. Dumont, 'Kingship in Ancient India', *Contributions to Indian Sociology*, Vol. VI, 1962, p. 73.

[14] *D.N.*, II, pp. 133–5; *M.N.*, II, p. 398; *D.N.*, III, p. 48, *A.N.*, I, p. 335.

[15] *D.B.*, II, p. 202, n. 3.

[16] A.K. Coomaraswamy ('A Royal Gesture; and Some other Motifs', *Feestbundel v.d.k. Bataviaasch Genootschap Van Kunstenen Wetenschapen, Weltevreden*, Pt. I, 1929, p. 58) has suggested that the sculptural representations of the *cakkavatti* from Jaggayapeta are probably a representation of the legendary king *Mahāsudassana* through whom the *cakkavatti* concept was articulated in Buddhist literature.

[17] *D.N.*, II, pp. 133–5. [18] H. Zimmer, *The Philosophies of India*, p. 129.

[19] J. Gonda, *Ancient Indian Kingship from the Religious Point of View*, p. 124.

[20] *D.N.*, II, p. 132; *D.N.*, III, p. 49. The *cāturangini sena* itself appears to be an attribute of kingship and the king is invariably accompanied by the *cāturangini sena* even when he visits the pleasure garden (*uyyāna bhūmi*). *D.N.*, II, p. 136.

[21] Otto Bohtlingk and Rudolf Roth, *Sanskrit Worterbuch*, p. 906.

na as the main treasure of the emperor, a sort of 'palladium of dominions,' and winning the various quarters of the world for the king.[22] The wheel is also described as beginning to slip down from its position at the approach of the king's death.[23] We suggest that this symbolizes the weakening control of the dying king over his dominion and the fact that each succeeding king had to establish control over his dominion for himself. The possession of the wheel by the new king cannot be taken for granted since it was clearly not a paternal heritage (*petakam dāyajjang*),[24] but had to be won by each succeeding king. The fact that control over dominion was intrinsic to kingship appears more directly in the Pāli canon. The state is sometimes referred to as *vijita*,[25] or subjugated territory, and one of the terms expressing sovereignty is *issariya*,[26] which signifies variously rulership, mastership, supremacy, and dominion, according to the Pāli dictionary.[27]

The *hatthiratana* and *assaratana*, as described in the *Mahāsudassana Sutta*, are related to the *cakkaratana* in that they represent the *means* of physical control over dominion. Both are described as *sabbeseto* (all white), *idhima* (wonderful in power) and *vehaṅgasāmo* (able to fly through the air).[28] The king's ability to make both of them submit to his control is considered an auspicious sign. Since they are well-trained, both submit to the king's control and carry him over his entire dominion and bring him back to his capital.[29] The elephant and cavalry corps were very important organs of the traditional *cāturangini senā* in Pāli literature, and the possession of large numbers of elephants and horses, led by the *hatthiratana* and the *assaratana*, along with a large number of chariots, led by a chariot called *vejayanta* (flag of victory), are listed among the treasured possessions of king Mahā Sudassana.[30] They presented themselves every morning before the king in order to be of service to him.[31] Apart from indicating that the army was one of the elements of

[22] J. Gonda, *Ancient Indian Kingship from the Religious Point of View*, p. 126n. See also A Wijesekhara ('Wheel Symbolism in Chakravartin Concept' in A.S. Altekar et al. (eds), *S.K. Belvalkar Felicitation Volume*, p. 267), who argues that the evidence of the Pāli texts should symbolize in its original state the militaristic *power* of a conquering hero which Buddhism borrowed from the pre-Buddhist Vedic culture. He suggests that it is based on the legend of the all-conquering hero Indra, who was the wielder and turner of the wheel of power.

[23] *D.N.*, III, pp. 50–1. [24] *Ibid.*, p. 47. [25] *M.N.*, II, p. 398. [26] *M.N.*, I, p. 355.

[27] T.W. Rhys Davids and W. Stede, *Pāli Dictionary*, p. 123.

[28] *D.N.*, II, p. 138. [29] Ibid., pp. 133–4. [30] Ibid., p. 143. [31] Ibid.

kingship, the description also indicates the king's *actual* control of the instruments of dominion.

The fourth treasure which appears before king Mahā Sudassana is the *maṇiratana*, or the gem treasure called *veḷuriya*, which was perfect in every way. Its brightness and splendour is said to transform night into day.[32] Remarking on the significance of possession of precious gems, Gonda writes:

> In India as elsewhere a great magic value is attached to gems and jewels. Whoever wears a wonderful stone is proof against all fear and danger, hunger and want, sickness and weapons; spirits and demons have no hold upon him. Even the Gods are said to be in possession of such priceless objects. The *syamantaka* jewel for instance, which is worn by Krisna on his wrist, yields daily eight loads of gold and preserves the wearer from all dangers.[33]

While this elucidation throws some light on the significance of the possession of priceless gems in general, it does not explain its importance in the specific context of kingship. The *Mahāsudassana Sutta's* elaboration of the effects of its possession by the king might help explain its symbolism. The jewel is said to have spread its splendour around for a *yojana* (about a league) on every side. Mahā Sudassana, in order to test its glory, set his four-fold army in array and raised aloft the gem on top of a *dhajjang* (standard) which enabled him to march into the darkness with the help of its light. Similarly, all the inhabitants of the villages around set about their work thinking that the day had begun.[34] The association of the priceless gem with the armed forces of the king marching out, as well as with the inhabitants of the countryside going to work, represents two sides of the same coin. The priceless gem was symbolic of the financial basis of kingship in the form of a full treasury. The full treasury supported the army, while the hard work of the inhabitants of the dominion contributed in turn to the maintenance of a full treasury. Gokhale has also pointed out that a full treasury and the army are two important constituents of kingship. He writes: 'The power of the king . . . rested on certain tangibles and intangibles. Among the material possessions two are commonly mentioned—one is a full treasury (*pari-puṇṇakosa koṭṭhakaro*)[35] and

[32] Ibid., p. 134.
[33] J. Gonda, *Ancient Indian Kingship from the Religious Point of View*, p. 38.
[34] *D.N.* II, p. 134. [35] *D.N.*, I, p. 115.

another is a large, strong and well-equipped four-fold[36] army'.[37]

The fifth priceless possession of Mahā Sudassana was the *itthiratana* or the woman treasure. This refers to the perfect queen and consort, beautiful in appearance, fragrant and possessed of a wondrous touch which was cool in summer and warm in winter. She was ever alert to hear what she might do to please the king and is described as being completely faithful to him both in body and mind.[38] The possession of the *itthiratana* by the king may merely symbolize the family and householder aspect of the king, through which succession could be ensured and kingship continued and perpetuated in subsequent generations. However, the context in which the *itthiratana* appears in the *Mahāsudassana Sutta* might also suggest that it represents the earth. In Brahmanical literature[39] the king is sometimes referred to as the husband of the earth, and it is not unlikely that the *itthiratana* is symbolic of the productive and fertile aspects of the earth. It is also possible to relate the *itthiratana* of Buddhist kingship to the *mahīsī* or chief queen, one of the twelve *ratniṇs* of the Vedic king whose presence was vital in the *ratnahaviṁṣi* ceremony of the *rājasūya* sacrifice where the king offers oblations to the Gods at the homes of the *ratnins* such as the *senani* and *purobhita*.[40] The *mahīsī* or chief queen was herself related to the fertility principle in Vedic consecration ceremonies. Vedic texts describe the *mahīsī* as one in whose house oblations are to be offered to Aditī, the Earth Goddess. Aditī is likened to a milch cow or mother who sustains men and fulfils their desires.[41] The *itthiratana* of Buddhist kingship probably reflects a survival of certain elements of Vedic kingship.

The sixth treasure of the king is the *gahapatiratana*. In Chapter III we have already touched upon the *gahapati's* inclusion among the seven treasures of the king. We reiterate the point here since the *gahapati* is not only the base of the system of production, and conse-

[36] The *Saṁyutta Nikāya* (S.N., I, p. 83) describes the fourfold army as infantry, cavalry, chariot and elephant corps.

[37] B.G. Gokhale, 'Early Buddhist Kingship', *Journal of Asian Studies*, Vol. XXVI, 1966, pp. 17–28.

[38] *D.N.*, II, p. 134.

[39] J.W. Spellman, *Political Theory of Ancient India*, p. 209.

[40] J.C.Heesterman, *Ancient Indian Royal Consecration*, p. 49.

[41] *Śatapatha Brāhmaṇa*, V, 3.1.4.; R.S. Sharma, *Aspects of Political Ideas and Institutions*, p. 135.

quently the base of the system of taxation (without whose effort the king could not locate the treasure in the narration), but the *gahapati* also represents here the people who inhabit the territory or dominion of the king

The last of the seven treasures is the *pariṇāyaka ratana.*[42] The word *pariṇāyaka* has been explained in the *Pāli Dictionary* as a leader, a guide, an adviser. In the *Mahāsudassana Sutta* Rhys Davids translates *pariṇāyaka* as adviser. The later work *Lalita Vistara* (approximately first century A.D.) describes him as a general,[43] and this might be closer to his more specific function as a leader of the king's forces. The *Mahāsudassana Sutta* narration itself suggests such an interpretation since the *pariṇāyaka* is associated with being the chief of 84,000 *khattiyas* of the king.[44] The king communicated his orders on the daily elephant and cavalry parade through the *pariṇāyaka.*[45] The queen summoned the *pariṇāyaka* when she wished the four-fold army to accompany her to visit the king.[46] The *pariṇāyaka* was the agent through whom the king ruled. He was meant to be wise and learned, knowing what should be done and what should be left undone, and he actually executed both civil and military power on behalf of the king.[47] There is also some evidence of the eldest son and heir apparent performing the functions of the commander of the forces, and of being trained as a general during the lifetime of his father. Thus, Viḍūḍabha is described as the *senāpati* of Kosala in the *Majjhima Nikāya.*[48] The *pariṇāyaka* could therefore have been the heir apparent of the king and symbolized at the same time the king's military strength. This is supported by a sculptural representation of the *cakkavatti* at Jaggayapeta, where the *pariṇāyaka* is represented as a boy.

These seven precious gems, the possession of which enhanced the king's prestige, represent the constituent elements of kingship and can be reduced to three basic ideas: (1) dominion or territory represented by the wheel or the *cakkaratana*; (2) the means of control over dominion represented by the *hatthiratana*, the *assaratana*, and the *pariṇāyaka*; and (3) the basis of control over dominion, represented by the *itthiratana*, *gahapati ratana*, and *maṇiratana*. Reduced to this form, the Buddhist notion of the constituent elements of

[42] *D.N.*, II, p. 135. [43] *D.B.*, II, p. 208n.
[44] *D.N.*, p. 143. [45] Ibid. [46] Ibid., p. 144.
[47] Ibid., p. 135. [48] *M.N.*, II, p. 357.

kingship are comparable to the *saptāṅga prakritis* of Kauṭilya,[49] although individual elements may differ. In the *Arthaśāstra* the *swāmi* and *janapada* represent dominion and its mastery; and *durga, daṇḍa,* and *amātya*, signify the means of control over dominion. We may also include here the *mitra*, or ally, enumerated by Kauṭilya, since he was described as always ready to help when occasion demanded it; and the *kośa*, which stands for the basis of control over dominion.

A notable feature of both theories is their secular orientation in conceptualizing the polity. Both eliminate the *purohita* or representative of spiritual authority in the temporal area of the state. The Buddhist conception of kingship also reflects a certain continuity with Vedic ideas of kingship. The use of the term *ratana* clearly demonstrates this. The Vedic *ratniṇs* who participated in the *rājasūya* ceremony are referred to as limbs (*aṅga*) of dominion, which together make up kingship.[50] Kingship in Buddhism as symbolized by the seven precious gems thus seems to share certain basic elements with Vedic political ideas on the one hand, and with those of Kauṭilya on the other.

A survey of the scattered references to kingship in early Buddhist literature suggests a clear dichotomy of ideas into two opposed types of kingship: one reflecting the *actual* or *existing* exercise of power by contemporary kings; and the other reflecting the *ideal* or *normative* exercise of power by the king. We shall classify them as the actual king and the normative king and examine the two ideas separately.

Despotic kingship at the time of the Buddha

Kingship as reflected in early Buddhist literature appears to be marked by an absolute exercise of power unrestrained by any institutional controls. No checks upon the king were exercised by any agency and there is no indication of the idea of limitations being recognized by the existing wielders of power. This is a notable feature of the institution of kingship as represented by kings of the Buddha's day. The king had complete control over the people and the material resources of the kingdom. On the other hand, we can discern two separate features of contemporary kingship in the Pāli

[49]. *Kauṭilya's Arthaśāstra*, R.P. Kangle, Vol. I, p. 164.
[50] J.C. Heesterman, *Ancient Indian Royal Consceration*, p. 51.

canon. One reflects the acceptance by society of the need to exercise power in order to maintain law and order within society. We may term this the legitimate basis of kingship. The term legitimate is used here to apply to the exercise of power by the king within the sanctioned framework of the original contract between the king and the people in the *Aggañña Sutta*, which was to preserve the social order based on property and family. The other aspect of contemporary kingship was the fact that kingship had clearly stepped outside the original sanctioned framework, leading to the frequent exercise of power outside it. The exercise of power therefore could be legitimate or arbitrary according to the individual predilections of the king, but it is important to remember that there is no evidence of any *effective control* upon the king's ability to impose his will upon the dominion.

Legitimate exercise of power

The exercise of power by the legitimate king was concerned directly with two major threats to the social order: offences against property, and offences against the family. These were areas in which the people expected the king to act and also use force in order to effectively exercise control. The exercise of power in these two areas was the minimum requirement of kingship and enjoyed considerable support from the people. The *Aṅgulimāla Sutta* of the *Majjhima Nikāya* gives an account of the robber Aṅgulimāla's misdeeds in the kingdom of Kosala, ruled over by King Pasenadi. Aṅgulimāla had struck such terror that whole villages became depopulated. The people are described as having collected at the gate of the palace and vociferously demanded that the king suppress Aṅgulimāla.[51] The king was also expected to suitably punish offences brought to his notice by the people. Three such offences communicated to the kings included stealing, adultery, and destroying the *gahapati's* home by making false allegations.[52] These offences were punished by the king with imprisonment, banishment or death. The power to punish is one of the definitions of a king in the *Vinaya*, which states that those who 'administer torture and maim are called kings'.[53]

The ruler and the robber stand in opposition to each other in

[51] *M.N.*, II, p. 346. [52] *A.N.*, II, pp. 455–6.
[53] *B.O.D.*, I, p. 74; *Pārājika*, p. 57.

Buddhist texts, one as the protector of property, the other as its violator. Thus, the weakness of the ruler is immediately associated with the strength of robbers who paralysed a kingdom. In such an insecure situation the *rājas* were unable to control their borders, and *brāhmaṇas* and *gahapatis* were adversely affected because they could not conduct their normal business.[54] Since *brāhmaṇas* and *gahapatis* were the major property-holding categories, the weakness of the king resulted in the productive system being seriously dislocated. Certain misdeeds are depicted as resulting in punishment in the lifetime of the offender, and the example cited is that of a robber who was punished by the ruler.[55] Buddhist literature lists a series of violent punishments against robbers, and the king's imposition of severe punishments is described as having a deterrent effect upon prospective offenders.[56] The extreme harshness of punishments suggests that, apart from their expected deterrent effects, a very severe view was taken of such offences by society. In the *Vinaya Piṭaka* Bimbisāra, a supporter of the *saṅgha*, is nevertheless depicted as being annoyed with the *bhikkhu* Dhaniya for having helped himself to state property.[57] Dhaniya's action was also vigorously condemned by the people.[58] Both Gokhale[59] and Tambiah[60] have pointed to the association of the king with the protection of the social order based on the institutions of family and private property.

Other characteristic features of kingship as it is portrayed in early Buddhist literature include judicial functions;[61] the protection of the kingdom from external dangers, for which fortifications surrounded by moats were set up and maintained in the border regions and manned by wise and watchful wardens;[62] expansion of the kingdom and the maintenance of tight internal control;[63] recruiting a strong army based on skilled fighters regardless of their social origins;[64] marching through the kingdom and setting up camps from time to time;[65] and providing patronage to diverse religious groups.[66] However, it must be pointed out that, although kings are

54 *A.N.*, I, p. 65. 55 *A.N.*, I, p. 46. 56 *A.N.*, II, pp. 255–6.

57 *Pārājika*, p. 54. 58 Ibid.

59 B.G. Gokhale, 'Dhamma as a Political Concept', *Journal of Indian History*, Vol. XLVI, Pt. II, 1968, p. 254.

60 S.J. Tambiah, *World Conqueror World Renouncer*, pp. 13, 15.

61 *S.N.*, I, p. 73.

62 *A.N.*, III, pp. 234–5; *S.N.*, IV, p. 137.

63 *S.N.*, I, pp. 82–4; *A.N.*, I, p. 65.

64 *S.N.*, I, pp. 97–8. 65 *A.N.*, III, p. 105. 66 *S.N.*, I, pp. 76–7.

frequently portrayed as discussing philosophical questions with the leaders of various sects,[67] or even as patrons and lay-followers of particular sects,[68] the king never lost sight of his political role as head of state. The recurrent statement of Ajātasattu and Pasenadi as they take leave of the Buddha is, 'Well now sir, we must be going. We are busy folk and have much to do'.[69] Ajātasattu's question on the relevance of the life of a recluse in the *Sāmaññaphala Sutta* is particularly significant in this context. He could not ignore the non-economic status of *bhikkhus* and other *paribbājakas*. His contrasting the *bhikkhu* with other working categories like the *naḷakāra* (basket maker), *pesakāra* (weaver), *kumbhakāra* (potter), *gaṇakā* (accountant) and *muddikā* (computer), is pointed when he asked the Buddha to explain the visible fruits of the life of a recluse, which the king cannot perceive, unlike the fruits of the work of others.[70] Pragmatic control over the kingdom was never relaxed and the maintenance of power required perpetual vigilance and effort. In fact, the king is described in the *Aṅguttara Nikāya* as one who sleeps very little while conducting state business.[71]

Arbitrary exercise of power

The borderline between pragmatic control over the kingdom, within the sanctioned framework of the original contract in the *Aggañña Sutta*, and the arbitrary exercise of power, was obviously very fine and resulted in the frequent despotic wielding of power by kings. There are innumerable references to this in the early Buddhist literature, which may have resulted from erosion of the popular control and participation which once existed in the tribal kingship of earlier times.[72] This erosion of popular control of the king had yet to be replaced by any other form of control, institutional or otherwise. Thus *rājas* are more often then not, represented as exercising power in a wilful and capricious manner, rather than in a legitimate and controlled capacity. Apart from general statements about the arbitrariness of the kings, which we shall give below the king of Kosala, Pasenadi himself, is depicted in such an incident. The *Saṁyutta Nikāya* states that Pasenadi had many peo-

[67] *D.N.*, I, pp. 45–52. [68] *S.N.*, I, p. 69.

[69] *M.N.*, II, pp. 372, 380; *A.N.*, IV, p. 153; *D.N.*, I, p. 75.

[70] *D.N.*, I, p. 52. [71] *A.N.*, II, p. 409.

[72] For example, the decline of the role of the *sabhās* and *samitis* as the area governed by the king increased.

ple seized and bound by ropes and chains and in other ways taken prisoners.[73]

Buddhist texts strikingly demonstrate the arbitrary exercise of power and the exploitative capacity of kings. We have earlier argued that one of the two major functions of a king was the protection of property and the punishment of robbers who violated these rights, and that *rājas* and robbers were thus in a special relationship to each other. However, we also have a number of references where *rājas* and robbers are coupled together in a common relationship, with both violating the wealth of people. Accumulated wealth is stated to be equally vulnerable to expropriation by *rājas* and robbers alike.[74] The king here is not the protector of the people or a suppressor and punisher of offenders, but himself a violator of social norms and therefore equivalent to the robber. Collusion between kings and robbers is also suggested in the Buddhist texts. Robber chiefs could rely on powerful people like *rājas* and *rājas'* ministers to protect them by lying in defence of the robber and speaking up for him.[75] Similarly, kings and robbers are coupled together as subjects of objectionable conversation by *bhikkhus*.[76]

The law itself was not applied in a consistent or legitimate manner but in a highly personal and arbitrary one. Thus *rajas* are depicted as rewarding or punishing according to the way their personal interests were served.[77] Ānanda's attention was drawn to the king's absolute and unadulterated control over the people in his dominion in a conversation with Viḍūḍabha, the son of king Pasenadi of Kosala. He asks: 'In the kingdom of Kosala and within the range of his sovereignty and sway, has the king power to expel or banish any *samaṇa* or *brāhmaṇa*, anyone either virtuous or not, anyone either leading or not the higher life?' Viḍūḍabha acknowledged the king's power to do so within his dominion but not outside it.[78] There is no evidence that any curbs could be invoked to prevent the king from exercising authority in an arbitrary or irrational manner. An epithet of the king is *issariyamada*, or one who is 'drunk with the intoxication of power', and this was how Pasenadi described himself.[79] *Bhikkhus* are described as facing danger from the tyranny

[73] *S.N.*, I, p. 75. [74] *A.N.*, II, pp. 311, 424; *S.N.*, I, pp. 30, 89.
[75] *A.N.*, II, pp. 385, 497. [76] *D.N.*, I, p. 150; *D.N.*, III, p. 29.
[77] *S.N.*, III, pp. 301–3. [78] *M.N.*, II, p. 378; *M.L.S.*, II, p. 312.
[79] *S.N.*, I, pp. 99–100.

of kings[80] and there is a warning that even a young prince who is blessed with high birth should be treated with respect because he may seek revenge once he became a king.[81] Gokhale also points to the despotic potential of the state and the fact that private property rights and the sanctity of human beings were subject to royal pleasure, with the king often choosing to exercise his powers arbitrarily.[82]

Normative kingship: the cakkavatti dhammiko dhammarāja

The problem of containing the arbitrary exercise of power was particularly acute in a society in the process of change, where old institutions had collapsed but had yet to be replaced by others. The collective power of the people in early Indian society, which had been expressed through tribal institutions, was no longer feasible in the expanding territorial units of the Buddha's time. These changes altered the role of power itself. Instead of helping the community as a whole, power had increasingly become an end in itself.[83] In fact, the challenge of individualism which was confronting the *gaṇa-saṅghas*,[84] with other forces that resulted in their gradual decay, was being reflected in the institution of kingship too. As the exercise of power itself was nevertheless essential for the maintenance of the social order, the *Aggañña Sutta* demonstrates quite clearly the popular support for the institution of kingship. As Gokhale has argued:

> The authority [of the state] stems from the delegation by the people to the government powers of imprisonment, of imposing fines, banishment, confiscation of unlawfully gained property, and death. These powers were considered essential for the state to discharge the obligations entrusted to it by the citizens. The people have to come to terms with the state for without it they are helpless victims of anarchy.[85]

As we have shown this very necessity for vast powers by the state created the constant danger of their abuse and since effective popular control was no longer feasible, Buddhist political theory formulated the concept of a just and moral king, a *dhammiko dham-*

[80] *Mahāvagga*, p. 114. [81] *S.N.*, I, p. 67; *K.S.*, I, pp. 93–4.

[82] B.G. Gokhale, '*Dhamma* as a Political Concept', *Journal of Indian History*, Vol. XLVI, Pt. II, 1968, p. 252.

[83] C. Drekmeier, *Kingship and Community in Ancient India*, p. 93.

[84] J.P. Sharma, *Republics in Ancient India*, p. 241.

[85] B.G. Gokhale, 'The Early Buddhist View of the State', *Journal of American Oriental Society*, Vol. 89, 1969, p. 735.

marāja who would wield power according to certain norms unlike the existing kings. This *dhammiko dhammarāja* was also a *cakkavatti*,[86] a world ruler who would put an end to the petty tyranny of the many and establish instead a universe where not only social order but also a moral order would prevail. He is the normative king in Buddhist literature who is contrasted strikingly in every sense from the actual kings of the Buddha's day.

The normative king, the *dhammiko dhammarāja*, is described as protector of his people (*janapadatthaviriya patto*) and lord of the four quarters (*cāturanto vijitavi*).[87] He possesses the seven precious gems (*sattharatana samanagato*)[88] and conquers only by righteousness without having to resort to force (*adanḍena, assatthena, dhammena*).[89] The Buddha himself was an ideal *cakkavatti* in an earlier life and had ruled without force.[90] The fact that the *cakkavatti* establishes control over his dominion without the use of force, even though he is accompanied by the four-fold army, is a notable feature of the *dhammiko dhammarāja*.[91] Instead the rival kings welcome and submit to him, and ask him to teach them (*anusāsa mahārājāti*).[92] No situation of resistance by the rival kings is envisaged and it seems that the Buddhists believed that, if the righteous king (*dhammena dhammiko dhammarāja*) conquered by *dhamma* even his enemies would

[86] The idea of a *cakkavatti* or a universal emperor who would extend his sway to the limits of the land had been growing in India for sometime before the Buddha, and was expressed in terms such as *samrāṭ* and *sārvabhauma*. The Buddhists seem to have expressed the same idea through the term *cakkavatti* which subsequently gained currency, and became the most popular term for the supreme king. The *Vinaya Piṭaka* conceives of a hierarchy of power, which is implicit in the theory of the *cakkavatti*, in a definition of kingship as, 'kings of the earth, local kings, king's deputies, subordinate chieftains. . .' (*Pārājika*, p. 57; *B.O.D.*, I, p. 74). Similarly the *Dīgha Nikāya* represents the same idea of the hierarchy of power in a reference to a chieftain (*rajañño*) called Pāyāsi (*D.N.*, II, p. 236). Pasenadi the king of Kosala is described in the *Samyutta Nikāya* as the head of a group of five *rājas* (S.N., I, p. 75). Petty princes are followers or retainers of the *cakkavatti*, who is considered the chief among them (*G.S.* V, p. 17; *G.S.*, III, p. 260; *K.S.*, III, p. 133).

[87] *D.N.*, II, p. 130. [88] Ibid, pp. 132–5.

[89] *D.N.*, II, pp. 14–15, 46, *D.N.*, III, p. 110.

[90] *A.N.*, III, p. 221.

[91] *D.N.*, II, p. 132. The description of the *cakkavatti* who followed the wheel over the four quarters, accompanied by the four-fold army but not using it, is a structural inversion of the Brahmanical *aśvamedha* rite which is part of the coronation ceremonies of the king.

[92] *D.N.*, III, p. 47.

welcome him.[93] Of course the *cakkavatti* was not interested in mere territorial expansion or in controlling the material and physical resources of the dominion but in the establishment of a uniform and just moral and social order. In the Buddhist narration of the *cakkavatti's* expedition to the four quarters, rival kings have no fear that their territories will be confiscated by the *dhammarāja*. The *cakkavatti's* main concern is teaching the five moral precepts of Buddhism to the layman and to the newly subordinated kings, after which he exhorts them to enjoy their possessions as before (*yatthā bhutang cha bhuñjatha*).[94]

The creation of just social order

After the *cakkavatti* had brought the entire universe under his umbrella he must proceed to ensure that his people live in comparative comfort, in a world where destitution has been wiped out. The *dhammiko dhammarāja* thus provides for the basic needs of the people, before a stable social order can be established, and this stable social order appears to be a precondition for the establishment of a moral order in the world.[95] The *dhammiko dhammarāja* must not merely be concerned with upholding the property and family rights of people in society but go beyond these minimum obligations and also ensure that everyone's basic needs are met. The ideal king Mahā Sudassana, for instance, establishes a perpetual grant (*evarupang dānang paṭṭhapeyyang*),[95] to provide food for the hungry, drink for the thirsty, gold for the poor, money for those in want, as well as wives for those who required them.[96]

The breakdown of the moral order, and the problem of offences against the family and property which the king was expected to punish, were inter-related. Instead of only punishing offenders, which would merely ensure the stability of the social order but not make for moral order, the normative king first had to provide the poor and deprived with the essentials of existence. Theft and violation of property would disappear only when all have been given the means of subsistence. In the *Cakkavattisīhanāda Sutta* a variety of offences, such as stealing, violence, murder, lying, evil-speaking and adultery are described as the outcome of the poverty of the des-

[93] In this context the statement of the *Saṁyutta Nikāya* which speaks of the futility of war as a means of settling anything is relevant (*S.N.*, I, p. 83).

[94] *D.N.*, III, p. 50. [95] *D.N.*, II, p. 137. [96] *D.B.*, II, p. 211.

titute which the king had not succeeded in eliminating.[97] On the other hand, the king in the *Kuṭadanta Sutta* is told by his wise adviser that his country, which was being harassed by dacoits required a comprehensive approach to deal with the problem of disorder. Mere punishment of offences with fines or more serious penalties like death would not work because this would be just a piecemeal approach to the problem of disorder. The only method of ending disorder is to provide food and seed-corn to those who keep cattle and farms, capital to those in trade, and wages and food to those in the king's service.[98] In the words of Rhys Davids, 'Then those men following each his own business will no longer harass the realm'.[99] When the king followed these instructions disorder disappeared, the people were quiet and at peace and could dwell with open doors.

The elimination of destitution was the highest function of the normative king. For instance, in the *Cakkavattisīhanāda Sutta* a successor of the *cakkavatti* Dalhanemi who was a *rāja* and *khattiyo muddhavassitto* (an anointed king), does not however possess the *cakkaratana*, the first precious possession of a universal ruler, for as we have seen the *cakkaratana* was not a paternal heritage[100] but had to be gained by each *cakkavatti* through righteous government. Such government required the eradication of destitution, and the mere protection of his subjects by the king is not enough. The *Cakkavattisīhanāda Sutta* makes this point very clearly.

> Then brethren, the king, the anointed *khattiya*, having made all the ministers and all the rest sit down together, asked them about the āriyan duty of the sovereign war-lord. And they declared it unto him. And when he had heard them, he did provide the due watch and ward and protection (*rakkhavarana guting samviddhi*), *but on the destitute he bestowed* no wealth [italics mine] (*no cha kho addhanang dhanamanuppadasi*).[101]

This led to the breakdown of the social and moral order that we have outlined above. Protection of the people is, nevertheless, the second highest function of the king. The *dhammiko dhammarāja* must provide protection for his subjects, for his army, for *khattiyas* and other subordinates, for *brāhmaṇas* and *gahapatis*, for people in the towns and the countryside, for *samaṇas* and *brāhmaṇas*, and even for the birds and beasts.[102]

[97] *D.N.*, III, pp. 56–7. [98] *D.N.*, I, pp. 115–16.
[99] *D.B.*, I, p. 176. [100] *D.N.*, III, p. 47.
[101] *D.N.*, III, pp. 51–2; *D.B.*, III, p. 66. [102] *D.N.*, III, p. 48; *A.N.*, II, p. 403.

It is significant that the *dhammarāja* is portrayed as a complete antithesis of the actual kings depicted in the early Pāli canon, where he is frequently lumped with robbers and expropriators of the wealth of people. The normative king, on the other hand, takes from his people only the proceeds of just taxation (*dhammikena balikena*). He declines to accept more even when it is voluntarily offered by the *brāhmaṇas* and *gahapatis* of his kingdom. Instead, the *dhammarāja* asks them to keep what they have and take with them some of the king's wealth.[103]

The *cakkavatti dhammiko dhammarāja* is a charismatic leader with a popular base, dear to his people like a father to his sons. They look at him as he drives past them and request him to drive slowly, so that they can gaze longer at him.[104] The people are loyal to the *dhammarāja* and conform to his wishes. He cannot be overthrown by anyone.[105] On important occasions the *cakkavatti dhammiko dhammarāja* consults his people. King Mahāvijita, who wished to perform a large sacrifice, is advised by his chaplain to consult various categories of people in his kingdom. The king then consults *khattiyas*, *brāhmaṇas* and *gahapatis* of the towns and the countryside, and seeks their sanction. When they indicate their approval, they are all described as colleagues by consent.[106] Here again, the *dhammarāja* is clearly contrasted to the tyrannical and despotic kings portrayed in the literature.

Lastly, the *dhammiko dhammarāja* patronizes *samaṇas* and *brāhmaṇas* who are worthy, providing them with all the things necessary to pursue their goals.[107] The position attained by the righteous universal ruler is itself a reward for giving, self conquest, and self control, so that the status is associated with an already moral being, like King Mahā Sudassana. The leadership provided by the *dhammiko dhammarāja* is crucial to the establishment of social and moral order. If he errs, the *khattiyas*, *brāhmaṇas*, and *gahapatis* follow suit, and even Nature, is affected. Conversely, when kings are righteous all the reverse consequences follow,[108] in what has been termed the 'multiplier effect' by Tambiah.[109] The normative king is therefore intrinsic to the social and moral order of the world.

[103] *D.N.*, II, pp. 137–8. [104] *D.N.*, II, p. 136; *D.N.*, III, p. 129.
[105] *D.N.*, III, p. 135. [106] *D.N.*, I, p. 121; *D.B.*, I, p. 176.
[107] *D.N.*, II, p. 141; *D.B.*, II, p. 217.
[108] *A.N.*, II, pp. 79–80; *G.S.*, II, pp. 84–5.
[109] S.J. Tambiah, *World Conqueror, World Renouncer*, p. 50.

The righteous king as an alternative to the despotic king

Let us now attempt to assess the essential features of the Buddhist conception of normative kingship. The *dhammiko dhammarāja* was the Buddhist answer to the concentration of power in the person of the king and its consequent abuse by individual kings which was a characteristic feature of society at the time of the Buddha. It was an attempt to tame the institution of kingship and to contain the absolute exercise of power by the application of the principle of *dhamma*, which was to guide the king in his role as the head of the state. As Ghoshal observes,

> The most important contribution of the early Buddhist canonists to the store of our ancient political thought consists in their 'total' application of the principle of righteousness to the branches of the king's internal and foreign administration.[110]

The application of the principle of *dhamma* may also be viewed as an attempt to transform power into authority by infusing it with certain norms. The principle of *dhamma* helped fill the lacuna created by the breakdown of the king–people bond in the changing political scene witnessed by the Buddha, a process which began at the end of the Vedic period. Kingship in the early Vedic period had been qualitatively different from its manifestations in later times. On the basis of the Vedic texts, Sharma argues that the *vis* or the people of the tribe chose the king in the Ṛg Vedic period.[111] He also suggests that in the period of the *Brāhmaṇas* the monarchies of Vedic times appear to have undergone a change: whereas Vedic monarchies were limited, with the king being only *primus inter pares*, the monarchies of the *Brāhmaṇa* period had become autocratic.[112] Similarly, Drekmeier holds that, because of the existence of tribal councils and popular assemblies in the Vedic period, power was dispersed among the members of a community to an extent that was rare in Indian history.[113] Following the breakdown of the king–people bond, the need for a replacement resulted in the development of the *king-brāhmaṇa* relationship in the Brahmanical tradition and kingship came to be conceived as a marriage between

[110] U.N. Ghoshal, *History of Indian Political Ideas*, p. 69.

[111] J.P. Sharma, *Republics in Ancient India*, p. 27.

[112] Ibid., p. 62.

[113] C. Drekmeier, *Kingship and Community in Ancient India*, p. 284.

brahma and *kṣatra*, a relationship in which *kṣatra* could not survive without *brahma*.[114]

On the basis of a study of the royal consceration ceremony, Heesterman has argued that the *ratnahaviṁṣi* ceremony represented the important bond between the king and the people and showed the character of a *sacrum publicum* in which the people had fully participated.[115] However, the elaboration and refining of ritual technique turned the ceremony into the exclusive domain of ritual specialists, and the people were gradually excluded from the ritual. The king-people relationship then gave way to a king-*brāhmaṇa* relationship. We would however argue that the exclusion of the people from the ritual was itself a result of the gradual erosion of the king-people bond, following from the social, economic and political changes of the later Vedic period.

In a parallel but somewhat later development, Buddhism formulated the idea of a *cakkavatti dhammiko dhammarāja* who would be guided by the principle of *dhamma*. *Dhamma* was an immutable moral principle which was above the king, the *rāja* of the *rāja*. In response to the question of a *bhikkhu*; 'But who, lord, is the *rāja* of the *rāja*, the roller of the wheel, the *dhamma* man the *dhammarāja*?' The Buddha replied: 'It is *dhamma*. . . : Herein *bhikkhu*, the *rāja*, the *cakkavatti* the *dhammiko dhammarāja*, relies just on *dhamma*, honours *dhamma*, reveres *dhamma*, esteems *dhamma*: with *dhamma* as his standard, with *dhamma* as his mandate, he sets a *dhamma* watch for folk within his realm.'[116] The Buddhist formulation of the *cakkavatti dhammiko dhammarāja* also implied that power could be used not only negatively to punish, tame, and control society, but also more positively to create a new society and new social order. The new social order would in turn provide the basis for a new moral order.

The king and the saṅgha

Two related aspects of Buddhist normative kingship which are of some significance to us deal with the relationship between the king and the Buddha (or the *sangha*), that is, between the social and the asocial world; and the roles envisaged for the *cakkavatti* and the Buddha as charismatic leaders of these two different spheres of the

[114] A.K. Coomaraswamy, *Temporal Power and Spiritual Authority in the Indian Theory of Government*, p. 2.

[115] J.C. Heesterman, *Ancient Indian Royal Consecration*, p. 266.

[116] *G.S.*, III, pp. 114–15; *A.N.*, II, p. 463.

universe. The controversial aspect of Buddhist political theory centres on the relationship between the king and the *saṅgha*. This is a point over which we find considerable differences between the early texts and later commentaries and chronicles written in Sri Lanka. The differences suggest that Buddhist political theory grew dynamically, particularly after Buddhism became the state religion in Sri Lanka.

The early Buddhist texts reveal a definite separation between the social and asocial world, even in the realm of Buddhist political ideas. This does not mean that the Buddha was apolitical or that he consciously turned his attention away from temporal matters, for we have seen that he was concerned with the institution of kingship and the exercise of power. However, early Buddhism conceived of a separation between the sphere of the king, and that of the *saṅgha*, unlike Brahmanism, where *regnum* (*kṣatra*) and Sacerdotum (*brahma*) were united. Since the *bhikkhu* was not part of the social world he could not replace the *purohita* of the *brahma-kṣatra* relationship and in keeping with this separation the Buddha conceived of the *dhammiko dhammarāja* where *dhamma* would play the role of the guardian of the king. Even in the realm of the *dhammiko dhammarāja*, the *bhikkhu* stood outside the world of the king. The entire word and spirit of the early Pāli canon overwhelmingly points to this conclusion. *Bhikkhus* are explicitly barred from taking an interest in the temporal affairs of the world, or in talking about the king,[117] a ban which heads the list of objectionable items of conversation for *bhikkhus*.[118] *Khattavijja* (politics) is rated as a low skill and the *Jātakas*[119] reflect the sentiment that politics and ethics are irreconciliable with politics being opposed to salvation.[120] The Buddha condemned those *samaṇas* and *brāhmaṇas* who acted as emissaries of kings,[121] and stated that he was not interested in the problems of war, conquest, victory and the defeat of monarchs, unlike other degenerate *samaṇas* and *brāhmaṇas*.[122] He also listed ten disadvantages in entering royal courts[123] which were crowded with sense objects, and obstructed progress towards *nibbāna*.

[117] *D.N.*, I, p. 150; *D.N.*, III, p. 29.

[118] *D.N.*, I, p. 9.

[119] See *Jātaka*, ed. by V. Fausboll, Vol. V, p. 288, where according to the *Khattavijja* one's own interest was to be promoted even at the cost of killing one's parents.

[120] U.N. Ghoshal, *A History of Indian Political Ideas*, p. 66.

[121] *D.N.*, I, p. 9. [122] *D.N.*, I, p. 8. [123] *A.N.*, IV, pp. 163–4.

The separation between the temporal and the spiritual spheres is most forcefully brought out in the theory of the *mahāpurisa* (great man).[124] Every *mahāpurisa* bears on his person thirty-two bodily signs, and only two courses are open to the possessor of these characteristics: He can either become a *tathāgata* or Buddha and be a world renouncer, or he can become a *cakkavatti* and be a world conqueror.[125] The significant point is that every *mahāpurisa* had to make a conscious decision to be either one or the other. He could not be both at the same time, or combine within himself both *brahma* and *kṣatra*, because the two worlds are separate and opposed to each other.[126] Even under the aegis of the *dhammiko dhammarāja*, where the social world itself is ruled by the righteous king, the separation between the two worlds continues and cannot be blurred. The Buddha himself established the norms for the righteous king in one of his previous births and consciously took the decision to be a *cakkavatti* in many others.[127] In his current historic existence he just as consciously adopted the alternative model of the world renouncer for himself.

The really controversial point about the separation between the social and the asocial worlds centres on the nature of the relationship between the king and the *saṅgha*. Did Buddhism envisage a close relationship between the two, even if it is granted that the spheres of the king and the *saṅgha* were separate? Tambiah and Ling have argued that there was an intimate relationship between the king and the *saṅgha*,[128] and that Buddhist civilization is a triangular relationship between the king, the *saṅgha* and the people.[129] However, we suggest that, while this close relationship may have developed over time, it is not reflected in early Buddhist literature. The Buddha respected the power of the king, and therefore maintained good relations with all the prominent kings that came into his orbit, but there is no indication that the king had any crucial role

[124] *D.N.*, III, pp. 110–38. [125] Ibid., p. 110.

[126] Bimbisāra's statement to the overseers in his kingdom is significant in this context. He says, 'ye have now received from me instructions in the things of this world. Go now and wait upon the Blessed One. The Blessed One himself shall instruct you in the things of eternity.' (T.W. Rhys Davids and H. Oldenberg, *The Vinaya Texts*, *S.B.E.*, Vol. XVII, p. 2; *Mahāvagga*, p. 199.)

[127] *A.N.*, III, p. 221.

[128] S.J. Tambiah, *World Renouncer, World Conquerer*, p. 41.

[129] T. Ling, *The Buddha*, p. 180.

to play in the propagation of the *nibbānic* goals of Buddhism. The king was nothing more than the highest member of the laity, whose patronage as the head of the social world was significant. But this did not mean that the king would play a role in the world of the *saṅgha*. Also, while it is true that suggestions made to the Buddha by kings were accepted, too much should not be made of such incidents as the Buddha frequently accepted suggestions from other members of the laity too. Similarly, if a king's patronage was valuable, so was that of other important groups in society. The economic requirements of the *saṅgha* necessitated some contact with kings as well as with other members of the laity, but these contacts were firmly kept within certain boundaries. In fact, there is evidence to show that the use of political power, or *kṣatra*, to further goals within the *saṅgha* would end disastrously, as revealed by Devadatta's unsuccessful attempts to split the *saṅgha*. The higher morality of the Buddha, standing outside the world of *kṣatra*, triumphed.[130]

The divorce between *brahma* and *kṣatra* is also apparent in Buddha's dealings with contemporary kings. It is striking that, while the Buddha developed the concept of the *cakkavatti* who was a *dhammiko dhammarāja*, he never expounded this theory to any of the contemporary kings, even to those described as his *upāsakas*. Despite Pasenadi's extreme devotion to the Buddha,[131] he continued to rule in a despotic and arbitrary fashion, without any attempt being made by the Buddha to even introduce him to notions of more ethical kingship. Ajātasattu, who was a parricide, was as much an *upāsaka* of the Buddha as the learned and generous *gahapati* Citta was. The Buddha also stood apart from the power struggles of his day. He did not take sides in the conflict between Ajātasattu and the Vajjians, or even between Ajātasattu and Pasenadi, although he himself described Pasenadi as the more moral of the two.[132]

The separation between the social and the asocial world is logi-

[130] *Cullavagga*, pp. 283–304.

[131] In two unique passages Pasenadi is described as falling at the feet of the Buddha and kissing them. One one occasion Pasenadi had just returned from a sham fight, having attained his object and being victorious. Even here the Buddha did not attempt to convey his notions of ideal kingship to the Kosalan king (*M.N.*, II, p. 367; *A.N.*, IV, p. 150).

[132] *S.N.*, I, pp. 82–3.

cally consistent with the Buddhist *bhikkhus'* opposition to the *brāhmaṇas*, who, as we have seen, did not separate the two worlds but fused them instead. The *bhikkhu* was in constant opposition to the *brāhmaṇa*; in religion, economic activity and in the polity. The concept of the *dhammarāja* was conceived in order to bring morality into the social world, not to play any special role in the asocial world of the *saṅgha*. This is clear from a rare reference in the *Cakkavattisīhanāda Sutta* which predicts a time in the future when there will be a *cakkavatti* and an *arahant* Buddha at the same time.[133] (Normally the *cakkavatti* and the *tathāgata* do not exist simultaneously.)The relationship posited between the two in the narration is still one of separation, with the *cakkavatti* Sankha and the Metteya Buddha, occupying supreme positions in their respective spheres. The king would have control over universal dominion, and the Metteya Buddha over the spiritual world of *samaṇas* and *brāhmanas*, kings and people, to whom he will teach the *dhamma*. There is nothing explicit or even implicit in the *sutta* to suggest that the king would create ideal conditions for the Buddhist *sāsana* (teachings). The two worlds remain as separate as ever. At the end of his career the *cakkavatti* Sankha is depicted as renouncing the world under the Metteya Buddha and seeking his own salvation.[134] It may be noted that Sankha has to give up one world to enter the other. Apart from the act of renunciation, there is no relationship between Sankha and Metteya in the *Cakkavattisīhanāda Sutta*.[135]

As Buddhism developed, the relationship between the king and the *saṅgha* grew closer, transforming the original relationship based on the patronage of the *saṅgha* by the king, to one of active involvement in the affairs of the *saṅgha*. This was probably a natural outcome of kings using their state power to propagate the faith, and particularly followed from the fact that kings became the first converts in countries like Sri Lanka, and then helped establish Buddhism which percolated down to the people through the king and the court. This development can actually be seen in the comparative accounts of the first and second Buddhist Councils, initially in the

[133] *D.N.*, III, pp. 60–1.

[134] It is obvious that even the *cakkavatii* acquires no special merit and requires to renounce the world in order to progress towards *nibbāna*. The *gahapati* Citta who has the option to be reborn a *cakkavatti*, expresses dissatisfaction at the idea because it would not lead him to the real goal of *nibbāna* (*S.N.*, III, pp. 269–70).

[135] *D.N.*, II, pp. 60–2.

Cullavagga of the *Vinaya Piṭaka*, and then later in the *Mahāvaṃsa* and the commentary to the *Vinaya Piṭaka*, written approximately in the fifth-sixth century A.D. in Sri Lanka. In the *Cullavagga* account, the First Council is called to codify the rules and teachings of the *saṅgha*. The *bhikkhus* decide to hold the Council at Rājagaha because of the abundance of dwelling places available there. They spent the first month of the rainy season repairing the dwellings and subsequently proceeded with the task of the first council. In the *Mahāvaṃsa* account, however, the reigning king is introduced as playing a definite role. After the dwellings had been repaired the *bhikkhus* announce their intention of holding a council to the king, Ajātasattu. To his question, 'what should be done?' they answered that a place should be provided for the meetings. After the king had a hall built he retired saying: 'My work is finished.'[136] In the *Samanta Pāsādika* a fifth-century commentary on the *Vinaya* written by Buddhaghosha, also from Sri Lanka, Ajātasattu retires saying, 'Yours is the authority of the spirit (*dhammacakka*) as mine is of power' (*āṇācakka*).[137] Even though the king in both the later narrations concedes the separation between the asocial and the social world, and then retires from the scene, the very fact that he is informed and his patronage specifically sought, suggests that the later chroniclers from Sri Lanka could not conceive of any important event in the *saṅgha* taking place without the involvement of the king.

The account of the second Council is even more striking. The *Cullavagga* makes no mention of Kāḷāsoka during whose reign the Council was supposed to have been held. In contrast, the *Mahāvaṃsa* makes King Kāḷāsoka play a very significant role with the rival factions appealing to him for help.[138] Finally, the king went to the Mahāvana, assembled the *bhikkhus*, and when he had heard what was said by both sides, decided for himself which was *the true faith* [italics mine]. Then he retired saying to the rightly believing *bhikkhus*. 'Do what ye think well to further the doctrine'. He also promised to be their protector before returning to the capital.[139]

[136] The *Mahāvaṃsa*, tr. by W. Geiger, p. 16.

[137] Buddhaghosha, *Samanta Pāsādika*, ed. by Birbal Sharma, Vol. I, p. 11.

[138] *The Mahāvaṃsa*, pp. 22–3. In the *Cullavagga* the factions deal with the differences that has arisen between the two major groups entirely by themselves (pp. 416–30).

[139] *Mahāvaṃsa*, p. 23.

Two factors helped the establishment of close links between the *saṅgha* and the king. One was the powerful personality of the emperor Aśoka and his actions in supporting the *saṅgha* and the consequent dispatch of missions to various countries. The other was the rise of numerous sects within Buddhism which resulted in the king's increasing role as the ultimate judge of which sect represented the true faith among the various contending factions. This fact more than any other gave the king a lever to use in the internal affairs of the *saṅgha*, as from time to time he took upon himself the task of 'purifying' the *saṅgha* and expelling 'heretics'. Whereas in early Pāli literature the *saṅgha* quietly and without much fuss split if there were irreconciliable differences, in later Buddhism the king takes it upon himself to uphold the true faith and punish heretics. This probably occurred for the first time under Aśoka who states in the Allahabad pillar inscription that he had expelled the schismatics from the *saṅgha*.[140] The practice was subsequently followed from time to time by Buddhist kings of south and south-east Asia. A striking example of the penetration of temporal power into the *saṅgha's* spiritual arena, resulting in an erosion of the basic principles of the *saṅgha*, is cited by Gombrich.[141] A *bhikkhu's* explanation for the penetration of caste principles into the *saṅgha* held the king responsible for the practice.[142] He claimed that the impropriety of a low caste *bhikkhu* in the presence of the king had so shocked the king that he forthwith passed an edict banning the entry of low-caste *bhikkhus* in the Siyam Nikāya *saṅghas* of Sri Lanka.[143] We have here a clear example of the subversion of one of the fundamental principles of recruitment into the *saṅgha* based on an essential aspect of the Buddha's teaching: that one's origins were irrelevant in the asocial world of the *saṅgha*.[144]

[140] E. Hultzsch, *Corpus Inscriptionum Indicarum*, Vol. I, p. 160.

[141] R. Gombrich, *Precept and Practice*, p. 312.

[142] The first roots of the penetration of caste into the *saṅgha* can be traced back to an Ordinance (*katikāvata*) issued by the king in 1266 requiring that the ordinand be asked his caste in the *upasamapada* (higher ordination ceremony), D.B. Jayatilika (ed.), *Katikāvat Saṅgarā*, p. 9, cited in Gombrich, p. 307.

[143] One of the three major organizations of *bhikkhus* in Ceylon (R. Gombrich, *Precept and Practice*, p. 309).

[144] It must be pointed out that the option of disagreeing with the king was always open if the *bhikkhus* so desired. Rahula cites cases where the king's authority over ecclesiastical matters was subject to that of the *saṅgha*. The king had no power to force the hands of the *saṅgha* against their wishes. On one occasion the monks

These developments in the history of Buddhism resulted in the *brahma-kṣatra* division gradually giving way to a system closer to the Brahmanical model, where *brahma* and *kṣatra* were part of the same system. Buddhism had separated the two at one level but integrated them at another level by making *dhamma* an integral part of kingship. This principle of separation and simultaneous integration gave way gradually in later Buddhism to the king's *dhamma* including active involvement in the asocial world of the *saṅgha*.[145]

We have argued that early Buddhism separated the social and asocial worlds and conceived of a system in which the basic link between the two worlds was based on the patronage offered by the king, but that this did not give him any special role in relation to the *saṅgha*. However, Buddhism did envisage a special role for the king as the supreme head of the social world. The king as the *dhammiko dhammarāja* has as great a role in transforming the temporal world and creating a just and stable society as the Buddha had in transforming the spiritual world. In Ghoshal's words, 'they have a jointly unique role as universal benefactors.'[146] The Buddha was fully conscious of the collapse of the old order based on a more egalitarian and less arbitrary society in which there had been greater community participation. However he also realized that the old order had disappeared irrevocably. The collapse of the tribal republics and the rise of centralized monarchy made it obvious that the *political will* necessary to transform the social world would have to be exercised by the king. The Buddhists therefore developed the idea of the *cakkavatti dhammiko dhammarāja* who, by a just exercise of power, would play a pivotal role in transforming society. He would initiate a revolution from above, which would eradicate destitution through charity and welfare and thereby contain the extreme inequities otherwise inevitable in the social world. The *cakkavatti* and the Buddha were both instruments of change in their respective arenas, upon whom rested the responsibility of reordering human life.

---

actually applied the act of *pattanikkunjjana* (turning down the alms-bowl), which was the greatest possible insult to the layman, on a king who had acted against the wishes of the *mahāvihāra*. (Walpole Rahula, *History of Buddhism in Ceylon*, p. 68.)

[145] An extreme case of the collapse of the separation between the social and the asocial world of the *saṅgha* in relation to kingship was the system of lamaism in Tibet which sought to unite Imperium and Sacerdotium. (V.P. Varma, *Early Buddhism and its Origins*, p. 353.)

[146] U.N. Ghoshal, *A History of Indian Political Ideas*, p. 79.

CHAPTER VII

Conclusion: Early Buddhism in a Historical Perspective

In this work we have attempted to place early Buddhism against the background of the socio-economic and political changes occurring in India in the sixth century B.C. We have argued that Buddhism originated and was nurtured in a period characterized by an expanding economy, political consolidation and the emergence of new socio-economic categories. All these features were not only reflected in early Buddhism but were crucial to the shaping of its ethos.

The transition from the pastoralism of an earlier era to a surplus producing agrarian economy generated the second phase of urbanization in India and represented a process of considerable change. In this process, the *gaṇa-saṅghas*, which had a productive system centering on the communal holding of land, began to collapse one by one. The *gaṇa-saṅghas* gave way not merely to a process of political consolidation but to the expanding economy and an agrarian system based on the private control of land. The productive system of the *gaṇa-saṅghas* was organized around the clans and the labour performed by the *dāsa-kammakaras*. The social and economic system of the *gaṇa-saṅghas* was comparatively simple, in contrast to an economy based on the individual holding of land and organized around the *gahapati* who played a crucial role in the expansion of the economy elsewhere. The emergence of the *gahapati* as a significant social category was a special feature of this period and was as important as the collapse of the *gaṇa-saṅghas*. The two developments must be seen together as they are inter-related and constitute two aspects of the same phenomenon.

We have established that the *gahapati* represented the economy, but, more specifically, he was the head of the household as a producing unit; he was primarily land-based and frequently produced for the market. The *gahapatis* were a high-status group, recognized as such in the wider social milieu, including by the king.[1] This is apparent not only from the Pāli texts but from Jaina texts also. The *gahapatis* were prosperous, mobile, and dynamic, and it was through them that the expanding society was being articulated. In Buddhist texts, *gahapatis* do not represent a caste or a group whose status was based on birth. Instead, they represented an embryonic class, which controlled the means of production and occupied a dominant place in the economic system. We may view *gahapatis* as the dominant peasantry of society in the early Buddhist period, since they dominated the agrarian system in the area outside the *gaṇa-saṅghas*, and controlled the bulk of the land. It is important to emphasize that *gahapatis* included within their group not only the category of rich peasants but also the whole group of peasants who held enough land to supply the needs of their families without having to work for others. It was this group that employed the *dāsa-kammakaras* and served as a link between the rural and emerging urban centres of the sixth century B.C.

The social milieu of the sixth century B.C. was also reflected in the social origins of the early Buddhists. We have shown through a statistical analysis of the background of early Buddhists that early Buddhism drew most of its support from the *ucca kulas* of the *khattiyas*, *brāhmaṇas* and *gahapatis*, although it also drew some support from occupational categories like the *kumbhakāras, nahāpitas*, and *kammakaras*, who had a low status in the Buddhist system of stratification. The significant conclusion that emerges from the analysis of the background of the early Buddhists was the absence of *gahapatis* from the *saṅgha* and their prominent representation among the lay-supporters of Buddhism. We have argued that Buddhist recognition of the *gahapati's* high status is also a recognition of the significance of the economic function as being basic to any society, despite Buddhism's advocacy of renunciation as a means to salvation.

[1] It should be emphasized that the early Buddhist texts convey a picture of society in which the producing groups were protected by the king. They present a sharp contrast to the view in the Brahmanical texts that peasants were helpless and dominated by a ruling elite. In these texts the peasant producers are treated as an eminently exploitable group: thus in formulating the status hierarchy they are regarded as marginal and subservient to those who dominated the ritual and political domains. In the Buddhist texts however such producing groups are highly esteemed for their substantial contribution to the expanding peasant economy.

The *gahapati's* role in the system of production not only merited high social status but also the acceptance of his continuing participation in the economy without which the *saṅgha* itself could not afford to pursue its *nibbānic* goal through renunciation. The *gahapati's* support from outside the *saṅgha* was therefore vital and it is in this context that the Buddha's discourse to the young *gahapati* Sigāla in the *Sigālovāda Sutta* should be seen.

The *SigālovādaSutta*,[2] which has been called the layman's social *vinaya*, is of considerable significance in depicting the responsiveness of Buddhism to its social milieu. It not only stresses the importance of support to the renouncers (*samaṇa-brāhmaṇas*) as one of the central duties of the *ariyasāvaka*, but also indicates the ideal layman as one who works hard, does not dissipate his wealth but makes the maximum use of it; preserves and expands his property, and saves a portion of his wealth for times of need. The idler is condemned as one who finds reasons to avoid work and complains of the cold, heat, and so on, resulting in a dissipation of such wealth as he already possesses and an inability to acquire new wealth.[3]

In this context the account of a conversation between the Buddha and Mahanāma the Lichchhavi is of particular significance.[4] The incident describes a group of young Lichchhavis 'stalking and ranging' in the great forest outside Vesāli. These young men, armed with bows and surrounded by a pack of dogs, appear to have been dissipating their energy, plundering, eating, and teasing the women of the clan. Mahānāma complains of their behaviour to the Buddha who responds by setting out five conditions for growth and prosperity. The conditions are headed by endorsing hard work and wealth gained by the sweat of the brow and the strength of the arm. Since *khattiya* clan-holders of land in the *gaṇa-saṅghas* did not have to work because the *dāsa-kammakaras* laboured for them, the Buddha's homily about hard work to them is specially significant. The Buddha ends by reiterating that a *kula-putta* who acquired wealth by hard work, zeal, and the strength of the arm, and who also honoured and revered the *samaṇa-brāhmaṇas*, would prosper and not decline.[5]

The *ariyasāvaka* of the Buddha therefore grows both in this

[2] *D.N.*, III, pp. 139–49.
[3] *D.N.*, III, 142; *D.B.*, III, p. 176.
[4] *A.N.*, II, pp. 338–40; *G.S.*, III, pp. 62–4. [5] *A.N.*, II, p. 339.

world and the next. By continuing to participate in the productive system, he can support the *saṅgha* from outside. Along with growth in wisdom, faith, virtue, love and generosity, the *ariyasāvaka* prospers as far as landed property, wealth and grain, his family, his *dasa-kammakara-porisas* and cattle are concerned.[6]

Apart from recognizing the central place that economic functions occupied in society and urging a proper work ethic for *ariyasāvakas* (almost invariably addressed to *gahapatis*),[7] the Buddha also outlined certain social responsibilities for his lay-followers. These focus on a series of paternalistic relationships between parents and children, husband and wife, teacher and pupil, and master and worker, and these are the basis of an ordered society. The relations between master and worker are particularly significant. The employer must treat his workers humanely by giving them work according to their capacity, feeding them well, and giving them occasional respite from work.[8] In return, the *dāsa-kammakaras* will respect and obey their masters and serve them dutifully.[9] The Buddha disapproves of a *dāsa* or '*upavāsa*'[10] of a *gahapati* being envious of the *gahapati's* affluence. This is described as wrongful envy (*pāpika issā*). For those who were really low in the social and economic system there was no real redemption as long as they lived in the social world. The only escape was to renounce the world and join the *saṅgha*, where their low origin would not count, since it would be submerged in their new status as *bhikkhus*. Their potential for salvation was equal to that of those who had high status in the social world. Apart from this, their status in relation to the social world itself would rise, and they would be equally entitled to respect and honour from everyone, including the king.[11] For those who remained in the social world, however, there was no escape from their low status: only the possibility of birth in a higher status in the next life through a generous and virtuous life in this one. The social order envisaged by Buddhists was clearly one in which the *gahapati* was the nodal point.

While Buddhism did not envisage the complete eradication of inequalities in society, it certainly sought to contain them. The vision

[6] *A.N.*, IV, p. 208; *A.N.*, II, p. 423.

[7] *A.N.*, II, pp. 67–9. [8] *D.N.*, III, p. 147. [9] Ibid.

[10] An 'underling' according to F.L. Woodword (*The Book Gradual Sayings*, V, p. 27).

[11] *D.N.*, I, p. 53.

of the new society conceived by the Buddha was ordered on more rational principles than the Brahmanical system, and the creation of this ideal society was the responsibility of the king in his new role as a *cakkavatti* and *dhammiko dhammarāja*. The existing political system based on absolute kingship as reflected in Buddhist literature had to be transformed into one in which kingship would be an instrument of social and political change. The new political system would be based on charismatic kingship in which the *cakkavatti* was morally responsible for the elimination of destitution and the creation of a new socio-political order. The king had to play a major role in stabilizing a society which was displaying the stresses of an era of change. Thus, the *cakkavatti* was the counterpart in the social world of the *tathāgata* in the asocial spiritual world. The two *mahaporisas* together would reorder human existence.

The Buddha had a positive attitude to the expanding economy and the contemporary social world despite his ideal of renunciation. His new society, although not perfect and therefore no Utopia, was, however, more attuned to a period of rapid change than the Brahmanical system, which explains its appeal and its success at that time.

APPENDIX A

Select List of Terms Depicting Various Strata in Early Buddhist Literature

I. *Vaṇṇa*

Reference	*Context*
(1) *D.N.*, I, p. 80.	The young *brāhmaṇa* Ambaṭṭha states that there are four *vaṇṇas-khattiyas, brāhmaṇas, vessas* and *suddas*. Of the four, *khattiyas, vessas,* and *suddas* are attendants of the *brāhmaṇas*.
(2) *D.N.*, III, pp. 63, 64, 72, 74.	The Buddha interprets the myth of the origin of the four *vaṇṇas* to two *brāhmaṇas* who have become *bhikkhus*. First to be demarcated as a *vaṇṇa* were *khattiyas*, who were created to maintain the social order. They were followed by the *brāhmaṇas*, *vessas* and *suddas*.
(3) *M.N.*, II, pp. 375 ff	King Pasenadi asks the Buddha if there was any difference between the four *vaṇṇas*. The Buddha replies that from the manner in which they are addressed and saluted the *khattiya* and *brāhmaṇa* are pointed to as chief.
(4) *M.N.*, II, p. 377.	King Pasenadi asks the Buddha if there could be any difference between the four *vaṇṇas* if they were possessed of the five qualities for striving (for salvation). The Buddha replies that there would be no difference between them.
(5) M.N., II, pp. 403–4.	The *brāhmaṇa* Assalāyana comes to inquire from the Buddha about his views on the purity of the four *vaṇṇas*. He tells the Buddha that *brāhmaṇas* are the best, and all the others are low; only *brāhmaṇas* are the sons of Brahmā and heirs to Brahmā being born from Brahmā's mouth.
(6) *M.N.*, II, pp. 405–6.	In his reply, the Buddha cites the example of Yona and Kamboja, where there were only two *vaṇṇas*, *ayya* (master) and *dāsa*; further, the

	ayya could become a *dāsa* and the *dāsa* an *ayya*. He argues that all four, *khattiyas, brāhmaṇas, vessas,* and *suddas*, were all equally capable of salvation.
(7) *M.N.*, II, pp. 311–15.	Avantiputta, the king of Madhurā approaches the venerable Kaccāna and says that *brāhmaṇas* consider themselves to be the best *vaṇṇa* and regard all others as low. He asks for Kaccāna's opinion on this claim. In reply Kaccāna states that anyone, whether *khattiya, brāhmaṇa, vessa* or *sudda* could employ others if they were rich enough to do so. All would be equally punishable regardless of their *vaṇṇa*. Thus, the four *vaṇṇas* were all exactly the same. Similarly, in their potential for salvation they were exactly the same.
(8) *A.N.*, II, pp. 480–2.	The Buddha describes his dream about four birds of different colours (*vaṇṇa*) which come and sit at his feet. Likewise, people from the four *vaṇṇas* come within his fold by joining the *saṅgha*.
(9) *A.N.*, IV, p. 270.	When a man joins the *saṅgha* he becomes *vevaṇṇiyanti*, one without a *vaṇṇa*.
(10) *Cullavagga*, p. 356.	Once the *bhikkhu* joins the *saṅgha* the four *vaṇṇas* are likened to the river losing its identity after joining the sea.
(11) *A.N.*, II, p. 117.	A horse trainer destroys his untrainable horse lest his teacher's family (*ācariyakula*) loses its status (*avaṇṇo ahositi*).

II. *Jāti*

(1) *Pācittiya*, pp. 11, 22.	There are high *jātis* (*ukkaṭṭa jāti*) and low *jātis* (*hīna jāti*). The high are the *khattiya* and *brāhmaṇa*. The low are the *caṇḍāla, nesāda, veṇa ratthakāra* and *pukkusā jāti*.
(2) *A.N.*, I. p. 149.	Whatever be a person's birth (*eva-meva manussesu yasmim kasmiṅcha jātiyo*), whether a *khattiya, brāhmaṇa, vessa, sudda* or a *caṇḍāla pukkusā*, he can reach the final goal if detached from wordly ties.
(3) *S.N.*, I, p. 165.	The Buddha tells the *brāhmaṇa* Suddhi, who claims a special status for the *brāhmaṇas* based

	on birth, that *brāhmaṇas* are not *brāhmaṇas* on the basis of their inherent status. Any person can attain the supreme goal if he exerts himself.
(4) *Sutta Nipāta, Khuddaka Nikāya*, I, p. 314.	When *brāhmaṇas* lost their *dhamma*, the *suddas*, *vessas* and *khattiyas* disagreed amongst themselves; the wife despised the husband; and the *khattiyas* and *brāhmaṇas* who are protected by their *jāti*, forgot their breed and fell to the power of lust.
(5) *Sutta Nipāta, Khuddaka Nikāya*, I, pp. 334–6; See also *S.N.*, I, p. 167.	The *brāhmaṇa* Sundarika Bhāradvāja asks the Buddha which *jāti* he belongs to. The Buddha answers saying that he is neither a *brāhmaṇa*, *rāja putta* or *vessa*, and that even the fact of having originated in a *nīca kula* is irrelevant for a *muni*.
(6) *D.N.*, I, p. 79.	The young *brāhmaṇa* Ambaṭṭha abuses the Sākyas for being rough and disrespectful to the *brāhmaṇas*. He refers to the Buddha as of Sākya *jāti*.
(7) *D.N.*, I, pp. 86–7.	The Buddha discounts the relevance of *jāti* and says that only in the context of marriage are references made to *jāti* and *gotta*.
(8) *Pācittiya*, p. 421.	Upāli, the great master of the *vinaya*, is abused as a *nihīno jacco* (of low birth) and *mala majjano* (one who shampoos others) by angry nuns.
(9) *M.N.*, II, p. 273.	Ghatīkāra, the *kumbhakāra*, is referred to as *itara jacco* (of low birth) by his *brāhmaṇa* friend, Jotipāla.
(10) *Sutta Nipāta, Khuddaka Nikāya*, I, pp. 329–30.	King Bimbisāra, on seeing the Buddha approaching from a distance, is convinced from the Buddha's noble bearing that he could not be of low birth, and could only be of the *khattiya jāti*. In his reply to the king's question, the Buddha says that he is of the Sākya *jāti*, his *gotta* affiliation Ādicca, and that he has 'gone forth' from that *kula*.
(11) *D.N.*, III, p. 63.	The Buddha asks the *bhikkhus* Vaseṭṭha and Bhāradvāja, both *brāhmaṇas*, whether they were reviled by other *brāhmaṇas* for having joined the *saṅgha*. They reply in the affirmative and say that *brāhmaṇas* consider themselves to be the best *vaṇṇa*.

(12) *Sutta Nipāta, Khuddaka Nikāya*, I, p. 363.	The *brāhmaṇa*, Bhāradvāja tells the Buddha that *brāhmaṇas* consider one who is a *jātiyo brāhmaṇa* to be a real *brāhmaṇa*.
(13) *Pārājika*, pp. 253–4.	The Buddha gives a ruling that insulting *bhikkhus* by *jāti* was forbidden. The various *jātis* mentioned are *khattiya, brāhmaṇa, vessa* and *sudda*.
(14) *A.N.*, III, pp. 93–4	A grouping attributed to Pūraṇa Kassapa, one of the six *titthiya* leaders, which consists of six *jātis*. These are (i) the black *jāti* which includes mutton butchers, pork butchers, fowlers, etc. Also included are robbers, violent men, jailors, and all who follow a bloody trade. (ii) The blue *jāti* applies to *bhikkhus* who live as though they have a thorn in their side and all others who profess the theory of action [*kammavadin* and *kiriyavadin*]. (iii) The red *jāti* applies to the Jainas and the ascetics with one cloth. (iv) The yellow *jāti* consists of the white-robed and the followers of naked ascetics. (v) The white *jāti* consists of Ājīvikas and their followers. (vi) The purest white *jāti* consists of Ājīvika leaders such as Nanda Vaccha, Kisa Sankicca, and Makkhali Gosāla. In his interpretation of the colours, the Buddha reduces the categories to two, but uses the term *kula* rather than *jāti* (see below).
(15) *A.N.*, II, pp. 467 ff.	The *brāhmaṇa* Dona accuses the Buddha of not respecting aged *brāhmaṇas*. The Buddha replies by stating that there are five types of *brāhmaṇas*. The first is a Brahmā-like *brāhmaṇa* and the fifth the *brāhmaṇa caṇḍāla*. *The* Brahmā like *brāhmaṇa* is well born on both his mother's and father's side, has pure descent as far back as seven generations. He is a *brahmacariya* for 48 years and does not live by agriculture, cattle-keeping, trade, bowmanship and the king's service. Instead, he lives by mendicancy.
(16) *M.N.*, II, p. 404	According to Assalāyana, the *brāhmaṇas* are Brahmā's sons born from the Brahmā's mouth and heirs to the God Brahmā. Therefore they are the best *vaṇṇa*.

III. *Kula*

(1) *A.N.*, II, pp. 89–90.	The two-fold division of *kulas* is mentioned: those born in low *kulas* in the past are the *caṇḍāla, nesāda, veṇa, ratthakāra* and *pukkusā kulas*; those born in high *kulas* in the past are the *khattiya, brāhmaṇas* and *gahapati kulas*.
(2) *M.N.*, III, p.248.	High *kulas* are associated with wealth, beauty, eminence and wisdom.
(3) *M.N.*, III, p. 240.	Conversely the low *kulas* are associated with stupidity, poverty, ugliness and deformity.
(4) *A.N.*, III, pp. 94–5.	The Buddha re-interprets the six colour classification of Pūraṇa Kassapa. Instead he uses a two-colour scheme of black and white. White is associated with the high *kulas* and black with the low *kulas*.
(5) *Sutta Nipāta, Khuddaka Nikāya*, I, p. 336; see also *S.N.*, I, p. 167.	The Buddha tells the *brāhmaṇa* Sundarika Bhāradvāja that for a *muni* his origin in a low *kula* is irrelevant.
(6) *Sutta Nipāta, Khuddaka Nikāya*, I, p.330.	The Buddha tells Bimbisāra that he has 'gone forth' from the *kula* of the Ādicca *gotta* and is of Sākya *jāti*.
(7) *D.N.*, III, p. 63.	The *brāhmaṇas* Vaseṭṭha and Bhāradvāja are reviled for having joined the *saṅgha* by other *brāhmaṇas*.
(8) *M.N.*, II, p. 447.	*Khattiya, brāhmaṇa* and *rajañña kulas* are contrasted with the *caṇḍāla nesāda, veṇa, ratthakāra* and *pukkusā kulas* in an implicit division of high and low.
(9) *M.N.*, II, p. 281.	Raṭṭhapala, the son of a *gahapati*, is described as a *kula-putta*. He has much wealth which he gives up to join the *saṅgha*.
(10) *M.N.*, I, p. 119.	*Kula-puttas* are associated with certain *sippas* such as agriculture, cattle-keeping, trade, bowmanship, king's service and with reckoning on the finger, accounting and computing.
(11) *A.N.*, III, p. 375.	The Buddha tells Dīghajānu Koliyaputta that *kula-puttas* should associate with *gahapatis* and *gahapati-puttas*, and engage in agriculture, cattle-keeping and trade, or counting, reckoning and computing.

(12) *M.N.*, III, p. 430.	The *brāhmaṇa* Caṅkī, who wishes to visit the Buddha, is dissuaded from doing so by other *brāhmaṇas*. He replies that, since the Buddha has 'gone forth' from a high and eminent *kula*, he is worth visiting.
(13) *Cullavagga*, p. 255.	The Buddha asks *bhikkhus* the principle according to which allotment of the best facilities should be made in the *saṅgha*. Some reply that these should go to *bhikkhus* who are from *khattiya*, *brāhmaṇa* and *gahapati kulas*. The Buddha rejects this argument and says that the best facilities should be allotted to *bhikkhus* on the basis of seniority.
(14) *Pārājika*, p. 274.	The four *kulas* are defined as *khattiyas*, *brāhmaṇas*, *vessas* and *suddas*.
(15) *M.N.*, II, p. 445.	Whether one is from a *brāhmaṇa*, *khattiya*, *vessa* or *sudda kula*, all have equal potential in the quest for salvation.
(16) *M.N.*, I, pp. 35, 40.	Reference is made to *Kammārakula* (family of a metalsmith).

IV. *Unmarked Categories*

(1) *A.N.*, III, p. 339.	A gift of alms will ensure rebirth as a wealthy *khattiya*, a wealthy *brāhmaṇa*, or a wealthy *gahapati*.
(2) *S.N.*, II, p. 247.	While travelling *bhikkhus* are likely to come across learned *khattiyas*, learned *brāhmaṇas* and learned *gahapatis*, and be questioned by them.
(3) *S.N.*, I, p. 73.	Pasenadi complains to the Buddha that he has seen wealthy *khattiyas*, wealthy *brāhmaṇas* and wealthy *gahapatis* deliberately lying in order to fulfil worldly desires.
(4) *A.N.*, II, p. 219	Queen Mallika tells the Buddha that in the *rāja's* family there are *khattiya*, *brāhmaṇa* and *gahapati* maidens over whom she holds supremacy.
(5) *A.N.*, III, pp. 75–6.	The Buddha tells the *brāhmaṇa* Jāṇussoni, who questions him on the aspirations of various categories, that the *khattiya* aspires for power and territory and has dominion as his ideal; the *brāhmaṇa* wants *mantras* and sacrifices and has *brahmaloka* as his ideal; and the *gahapati* wants

	work and craft and has the completion or the fruit of work as his ideal.
(6) *M.N.*, I, p. 103; A.N., II pp. 305, 491; *S.N.*, II, p. 246; *M.N.*, II, p. 199.	All references use the categories of *khattiya*, *brāhmaṇa*, *gahapati* and *samaṇa*, indicating an implicit division of the world into the social and the asocial. Within the social world the *khattiya*, *brāhmaṇa* and *gahapati* represent social categories and the *samaṇa* the asocial world.
(7) *D.N.*, II, pp. 69, 86.	There are eight assemblies. Four of these are in the world of men and four in world of the gods. The former in the world of men are assemblies of *khattiyas*, *brāhmaṇas*, *gahapatis* and *samaṇas*.
(8) *S.N.*, I, pp. 97–8.	The king recruits *kumāras* from the *brāhmaṇas*, *khattiyas*, *vessas* and *suddas*, regardless of their origins.
(9) *D.N.*, I, p. 204.	The Buddha gives the example of a man who says, 'How I long for, how I love the most beautiful woman in this land', without knowing any other details about the woman. The details include information about whether the beautiful woman is a *khattiya*, a *brāhmaṇa*, a *vessa* or a *sudda*.
(10) *Pārājika*, p. 192.	Women are of four kinds: *khattiyani*, *brāhmaṇi*, *vessi* or *suddi*.

V. *Kamma* (work)

(1) *Pācittiya*, p. 11.	There are two kinds of work: high and low work. High work is described as agriculture, cattle-keeping, or trade. Low work is that of a storeroom keeper, and of a flower sweeper. Further, high work is associated with what is not disdained and not despised in the area, and low work is the opposite.
(2) *A.N.*, III, pp. 375, 378.	Worthwhile occupations or livelihoods fit for *kula-puttas* to pursue are: agriculture, cattle-keeping, trade, bowmanship, king's service, counting, accounting and computing.
(3) *Theragāthā*, *Khuddaka Nikāya*, II, p. 330.	The *thera* (elder *bhikkhu*), Sunīta says that he was of low origin and had performed the low work of the flower sweeper before becoming a *bhikkhu*.

VI. *Sippa*

(1) *Pācittiya*, p. 11.	There are two kinds of *sippas* (occupation of crafts): High and low. The high consists of counting, accounting, and writing. Low crafts are described as basket-making, leather worker, barber, and that of the weaver.
(2) *D.N.*, I, p. 52; *D.B.*, I, p. 68.	Ajātasattu mentions a variety of craftsmen. Their pursuit of these crafts leads to visible results. The various craftsmen are: mahouts, horsemen, charioteers, archers, standard bearers, camp marshalls, camp followers, high military officers of royal birth, military scouts, men brave as elephants, champions, warriors in buckskins, homeborn slaves, cooks, barbers, bath attendants, confectioners, garland makers, washermen, weavers, basket makers, potters, arithmeticians, accountants.
(3) *Pācittiya*, pp. 14, 18, 24.	*Pesakāra* (weaver).
(4) *Pārājika*, p. 365.	*Tantavāya* (weaver).
(5) *S.N.*, IV, p. 145.	An *Antevāsi* (acrobat) calls his activity a craft.
(6) *M.N.*, II, pp. 478–9.	Basket makers are described as being in their own settlement.
(7) *Pārājika*, p. 51.	Mentions Dhaniya the *bhikkhu* who had been a potter in the past and who made himself a beautiful house of clay.
(8) *Mahāvagga*, p. 262.	A *bhikkhu* who had been a barber in the past.
(9) *D.N.*, I, p. 191.	Bhesika, a barber, who is a sympathizer of the Buddha's teachings.
(10) *M.N.*, pp. 272–3.	Ghaṭīkāra is a potter and of low birth.

VII. *Artisans or Other Service Groups*

(1) *M.N.*, I, p. 41.	Samiti, son of a chariotmaker
(2) *D.N.*, II, p. 98.	Cunda, son of a metalsmith.
(3) *Pācittiya*, p. 221.	*Daṅtakara* (ivory worker).
(4) *Pārājika*, pp. 321–2.	*Kosiya kāra* (silk weaver).
(5) *M.N.*, I, p. 159.	*Paḷaganda* (carpenter). He has an assistant.

VIII. *Economic Categories* (with no other term of descriptions)

(1) *Mahāvagga*, p. 255.	Meṇḍaka *gahapati* employs a large number of *dāsa-kammakaras*, and *porisas* whom the family feeds and pays wages to.
(2) *Mahāvagga*, p. 255.	Meṇḍaka *gahapati* has a slave who possesses the psychic powers of Meṇḍaka's family. When the *dāsa* ploughs, seven furrows are made with one ploughshare.
(3) *D.N.*, III, p. 147.	The young *gahapati* Sigāla is asked to treat his *dāsa-kammakaras* humanely by giving them work according to their capacity and a certain amount of leisure. In return the *dāsa-kammakaras* will be obedient to their masters.
(4) *A.N.*, IV, p. 130.	*dāsas* and *upavāsas* (underlings) should not be envious of their master's wealth.
(5) *A.N.*, I, p. 134.	Normal food for the *dāsa-kammakaras* is sour gruel and broken rice.
(6) *M.N.*, I, pp. 167–8.	Kaḷī the *dāsi* of her mistress (a *gahapatnī*) tries an experiment and reveals the true temper of her mistress.
(7) *Pācittiya*, p. 241.	Slaves and workmen (*dāsa-kammakaras*) of the Sākyans attack their master's womenfolk as an act of revenge.
(8) *S.N.*, I, p. 91.	A *seṭṭhi-gahapati* regrets his gift of alms to *samaṇa-brāhmaṇas*. He thinks that he should have given the alms to his *dāsa-kammakaras* instead.
(9) *D.N.*, I, pp. 52–3.	The *dāsa* will get respect, even from the king, if he has renounced the world and becomes a *bhikkhu*.
(10) *Cullavagga*, p. 249.	The *seṭṭhi* of Rājagaha exhorts his *dāsa-kammakaras* to prepare a meal for the Buddha.

APPENDIX B

List of Categories appearing in Early Brahmi Inscriptions*

S. No	Ins-crip-tion number	Page No.	Location	Category	Other details	Additional references for original inscriptions
1.	181	28	Sanchi	*kamika* (labourer)	Gift of the labourer, Aṭṭha.	*Aṭṭhas kamikas dānang* (Jas Burgess, *Epigraphica Indica*, II, p. 98).
2.	201	29	Sanchi	*gahapati*	Gift of Vesasamandatā, daughter-in-law of Patiṭhiya *gahapati*	
3.	202	29	Sanchi	*gahapati*	Gift of the *gahapati* Patiṭhiya from Tumbavana.	
4.	206	30	Sanchi	*seṭṭhin*	Gift of Nāgā, the wife of the Kaṁdaḍigāmiya *seṭṭhin*.	
5	209	30	Sanchi	*lēkhaka* (clerk)	Gift of the *lēkhaka* Mūlagiri.	
6.	246	33	Sanchi	*seṭṭhin*	Gift of Kaniyāsi, mother of *seṭṭhin*.	
7.	248	33	Sanchi	*seṭṭhin*	Gift of a *seṭṭhin*, an executor of repairs.	*seṭṭhino paṭikam kārikāna dānang* (*Epigraphica Indica*, II, p. 100).
8.	255	34	Sanchi	*Seṭṭhin*	Gift of Kujara, brother of a *seṭṭhin*.	
9.	269	35	Sanchi	*vāṇija*	Gift of *vāṇija* Sirigupta	
10.	271	35	Sanchi	*rājalipikāra* (royal scribe)	Gift of the *rājalipikāra* Subāhita.	
11.	283	36	Sanchi	*seṭṭhin*	Gift of the *sāmanera* the Abeyaka *seṭṭhin*.	
12.	320	39	Sanchi	*vāṇija*	Gift of the *vāṇija* Saghadēva.	

*Source: H. Ludders Berlin, *A List of Brahmi Inscriptions*. All references are to the inscription number and page number listed therein. It should be noted that the inscriptions use the term *seṭṭhi* less rigorously than the Buddhist texts.

13.	331	40	Sanchi	*sotika* (weaver)	Gift of the *sotika* Damaka.	
14.	345	42	Sanchi	*daṁtakaras*	The inscription records that the carving (*rupakaṁma*) was done by the *daṁtakaras* of Vedisa.	
15.	346	42	Sanchi	*āvēsanin*	Gift of Ānanda the foreman (*āvēsanin*) of rājan Siri Sātakaṇi.	
16.	348	42	Sanchi	*seṭṭhin*	Gift of the Kurariya *seṭṭhin* at Acchāvaḍa.	
17.	355	43	Sanchi	*vāṇija*	Gift of the *vāṇija* Isiguta from Asvavati.	
18.	363	43	Sanchi	*seṭṭhin*	Gift of the *seṭṭhin* Sīha, the inhabitant of Kuraghara.	
19.	379	44	Sanchi	*seṭṭhin*	Gift of the *seṭṭhin* Nagadina, the inhabitant of Rōhaṇīpada.	
20.	416	47	Sanchi	*rajuka*	Gift of the surveyor (*rajuka*) Uttara.	
21.	422	47	Sanchi	*seṭṭhin*	Inscription mentions a *seṭṭhin* from Kaṁdaḍigāma.	
22.	423	47	Sanchi	*seṭṭhin*	Gift of Dēvabhāga, wife of the Kaṁdaḍigāmiya *seṭṭhin*.	
23.	449	48	Sanchi	*seṭṭhin*	Gift of the *gahapati* Patiṭhiya from Tuṁbavana.	
24.	450	49	Sanchi	*gahapati*	Gift of Dhañā, wife of the brother of the *gahapati* from Tuṁbavana.	*Tuṁbavana gahapatino patiṭhiyasa bhātu [jā] yaya dh [ā] ya dānang* (*Epigraphica Indica*, II, p. 384).
25.	470	50	Sanchi	*seṭṭhin*	Gift of the *seṭṭhin* Nāgila.	
26.	495	52	Sanchi	*vaḍakin*	Gift of the carpenter (*vaḍakin*) Manōrama.	
27.	576	36	Sanchi	*seṭṭhin*	Gift of the *seṭṭhin* Buddhapālita, the inhabitant of Pāṇḍukulikā.	
28.	581	57	Sanchi	*seṭṭhin*	Gift of Nāgapiya *seṭṭhin* of Achchāvaḍa.	

29.	725	70	Bharaut	*gahapati*	Gift of the *gahapati* Budhi from Bibikānadikaṭa.	
30.	728	70	Bharaut	*asavārika*	Gift of the *asavārika* (trooper) Suladha from Bibikānadikaṭa.	
31.	788	7	Bharaut	*brāhmaṇa* (*mānavaka*)	Inscription mentions the young *brāhmaṇa* (*mānavaka*) Brahmadēva.	
32.	857	86	Bharaut	*rupakāraka*	Gift of the sculptor (*rupakāraka*) Buddharakhita.	
33.	900	91	Bitha	*gahapatika*	Gift of some *gahapatika*, son of Eṇajā.	
34.	986	102	Kanheri	*suvaṇa-kōkāra*	Gift of the goldsmith (*suvaṇakō kāra*) Samidata of Kalyāṇa.	
35.	987	102	Kanheri	*vāṇijaka*	Gift of the *vāṇijaka* (trader) brothers, Gajasēna and Gajamita.	
36.	993	103	Kanheri	*hēraṇika* (treasurer)	Gift of Sivapālitanikā, (wife of the *hēraṇika* Dhamnaka).	
37.	1001	105	Kanheri	*nēgama gahapati*	Establishment of a cave (*leṇa*) by the *nēgama gahapati*.	*putasa negamassa gahapatisa* (Jas Burgess, *Archaeological Survey of Western India*, IV, p. 86).
38.	1005	105	Kanheri	*maṇikāra*	Gift of the jeweller (*maṇikāra*) Nāgapālita, the inhabitant of Soparaka.	
39.	1032	108	Kanheri	*kammāra*	Gift of the *kammāra* Nada from Kalyāṇa.	
40.	1035	109	Mahakal	*brāhmaṇa*	Gift of a *brāhmaṇa* of the Gotama *gōtra*.	
41.	1050	111	Kuda	*brāhmaṇa*	Gift of the *bammani* (*brāhmaṇa* woman) Bhaiyilā, wife of the *bammhana upāsaka* Ayitilu.	
42.	1051	111	Kuda	*mālākara*	Gift of the *mālākara* (gardener) Śivapīrīta, son of the *mālākara* Vadhuka.	
43.	1053	111	Kuda	*rājamaccha*	Gift of Gōyammā, the	

					daughter of the royal minister (*rājamaccha*) Hāla.	
44.	1052	112	Kuda	*lōhavāṇiyiya*	Gift of the ironmonger (*lōha-vāṇiyiya*) Mahika, the inhabitant of Karahāḍaka.	
45.	1056	112	Kuda	*seṭṭhi-gahapati*	Gift of the *gahapati*, the *seṭṭhi*, Vasula.	*gahapatino vasulasa seṭṭhino* (*Archaeological Survey of Western India*, IV, p. 87).
46.	1061	112	Kuda	*mālākara*	The gift of the gardener (*mālākara*) Mugudā [sa].	
47.	1062	113	Kuda	*satthavāha-gahapati*	Gift of the *satthavāha gahapati* Naga, the son of Svāmin.	*gaha [pu] tino sathavāhasa nagasa leṇa deyadhamma* (*Archaeological Survey of Western India*, IV, p. 88).
48.	1063 1064	113	Kuda	*seṭṭhin*	Gift of the *seṭṭhin* Vasulanaka.	
49.	1066	113	Kuda	*satthavāha*	Gift of the son of a *satthavāha*.	
50.	1073	114	Mahad	*seṭṭhi-gahapati*	Gift of a cave by Vadasiri [the wife of] . . . the son of the *gahapati-seṭṭhi* Saṃgharakhita, and the endowment of certain fields situated below the cave.	*gahapatisa seṭṭhisa Saṃgharakhita saputasa vi . . .* (*Archaeological Survey of Western India*, IV, p. 88).
51.	1075	114	Kol	*gahapati-putasa seṭṭhi*	Gift of Saṃgharakhita, the son of a *gahapati*, a *seṭṭhi*.	*gahapatiputasa seṭṭhi Saṃgharakitasa deya dhammaṃ* (*Archaeological Survey of Western India*, IV, p. 88).
52.	1084	115	Bhaja	*hālika*	Gift of Badha, wife of *hālika*.	
53.	1087	116	Karle	*seṭṭhin*	Establishment of a cave-dwelling, the most excellent one in Jambudipa by the *seṭṭhin* Bhutapāla.	
54.	1092	117	Karle	*vaḍhaki*	Making of the door of the cave by the *vaḍhaki* (carpenter) Sāmi.	

55.	1121	112	Sailarwadi	*hālikaya, kuḍubika, gahapati*	Gift of a cave by Siagutanika, wife of the *hālikaya* (ploughman) and *kuḍubika* (householder) Usabhanaka, together with her son the *gahapati* Namda.	
56.	1127	124 125	Nasik	*nyēgama gahapati*	Gift of a four-celled *leṇa* (cave) by the *nyēgama gahapati* Vira.	*gahapatisa nyēgamasa leṇa* (*Archaeological Survey of Western India*, IV, p. 116).
57.	1131	125 126	Nasik	*kṣatriya, brāhmaṇa*	Dedication of a cave by Ushavadata and his achievement in releasing Utamabhadra who had been beseiged by the Mālayas and his defeat of the Utamabhādraka *Kṣatriyas* (warriors), and his donation of a field bought at the hands of the *brāhmaṇa* Aśvibhūti.	*Utamabhadrakānām cha kṣatriyā nam . . . brāhmaṇasa hathe kinita mulena* (*Archaeological Survey of Western India*, IV, p. 99f).
58.	1138	127 128	Nasik	*lēkhaka*	Gift of a *lēṇa* (cave) by Ramanaka, son of the *lēkhaka* Sivamita.	
59.	1153	131	Junnar	*gahapati*	Gift of a *caitya* by the pious hamlet (*dhammanigama*) Vīrasēnaka, headed by the *gahapatis*.	*gahapati pamugasa* (*Archaeological Survey of Western India*, IV, p. 93).
60.	1157	131	Junnar	*gahapati*	Gift of a five-celled cave (*pachagabha*) by two brothers . . . the sons of a *gahapati*.	
61.	1170	133	Junnar	*gahapati*	Gift of the *gahapati* Sivadāsa, son of the *gahapati* Sayiti.	
62.	1171	134	Junnar	*gahapati*	Donation by various people and Nadaṇaka, the grandson of some *gahapati*.	
63.	1177	135	Junnar	*suvaṇakāra*	Gift of a cistern by the *suvaṇakāra* Saghaka.	
64.	1187	137	Pitalkhora	*gādhika* (perfumer)	Gift of a pillar by the family of the *gādhika* Mitadēva from Patiṭhana.	

65.	1198	138	Ajanta	*vāṇija*	Gift of a shrine by the *vāṇija* Ghanāmadaḍa.
66.	1206	141	Amaravati	*gahapati*	Gift of an *upāsikā*, the daughter of a *gahapati*.
67.	1209	141	Amaravati	*gahapati*	Gift of Sivaka, the son of the *gahapati* Pusila.
68.	1213	142	Amaravati	*vāṇija*	Gift of Mūlasiri, the son of the *vāṇija* Bodhisamma, along with his mother.
69.	1214	142	Amaravati	*vāṇiya*	Gift of Budhi, son of the *vāṇiya* Kanha.
70.	1216	142	Amaravati	*gahapati*	Gift of a *caitya* by the *gahapati* Hagha.
71.	1220	143	Amaravati	*gahapati*	Gift of the son of the *gahapati* Kanhati.
72.	1221	143	Amaravati	*gahapati*	Gift of a coping stone by Ajuṇa the grandson of the *gahapati* Mariti.
73.	1222	143	Amaravati	*gahapati*	Gift of the grandson of the *gahapati* Pāpin.
74.	1229	144	Amaravati	*vāṇiya*	Gift of a caitya pillar by the *vāṇiya* Kuṭa.
75.	1230	144	Amaravati	*gadhika vāṇiya*	Gift to the *saṅgha* by the *gadhika* (perfumer) *vāṇiya* Siridata, the son of the *vāṇiya* Dhammila.
76.	1239	146	Amaravati	*vāṇiya, hēraṇika*	Gift of the wife of an *upāsaka* the *vāṇiya* Nāgatisa, together with her sons the *hēraṇika* (treasurer) Buddhi.
77.	1244	147	Amaravati	*gahapati*	Erection of a pillar for lamps by the wife of a *gahapati* Sidhatha.
78.	1253	148	Amaravati	*gahapati*	Gift of the *upāsika* Kamā, daughter of the *gahapati* Iḍa.
79.	1254	148 149	Amaravati	*gahapati*	Gift of Makhabudhi, the son of the *gahapati* Budhi.
80.	1255	149	Amaravati	*gahapati*	Fragment which mentions a *gahapati* and the son of a *gahapati*.
81.	1260	149	Amaravati	*gahapati*	Gift by the grandsons of Kaṁmā, daughter of Bhagī, wife of the *gahapati* Rāhula.

82.	1273	151 152	Amaravati	*cammakāra*	Gift of a slab with a filled vase (*punaghaḍakapaṭa*) by the *cammakāra* Vidhika, son of the *upajhāya* (teacher) Naga.	
83.	1277	152	Amaravati	*gahapati*	Gift by Himala, son of a *gahapati*.	
84.	1285	153	Amaravati	*vāṇiya*	Records the erection of a coping stone by the *vāṇiyini* Sidhi.	
85.	1333	158 159	Bhattiprolu	*gāmaṇi*	Inscription mentions a treasurer (*hiraṇkāra*) Būba, the son of the *gāmaṇī*.	*hiraṇakāra gāmaṇī puto Būbo* (*Epigraphica Indica*, II, p. 328).

APPENDIX C

The Social Background of the Bhikkhus and Upāsakas

S. No.	Name	Social back-ground	*bhikkhu* or *upāsaka*	Other details	Reference
1.	Akkosaka Bhāradv-āja	*brāhmaṇa*	*bhikkhu*	He was incensed that his brothers had joined the *saṅgha*. He came to insult the Buddha but was converted.	*S.N.*, I, pp. 161–3.
2.	Aggika Bhāradv-āja	*brāhmaṇa*	*upāsaka*	The Buddha went to Aggika's house on his alms round and was insulted by Aggika who called him a *vasala* (an out-caste). Later he was won over and became an *upāsaka*.	*Sutta Nipāta, Khuddaka Nikāya*, I, pp. 287–90.
3.	Aṅguli-māla	*brāhmaṇa*	*bhikkhu*	Angulimāla was a terrible criminal who harassed the kingdom of Kosala. He was subdued and converted by the Buddha.	*M.N.*, II, pp. 344–51.
4.	Ajita	*brāhmaṇa*	Became an *arahant* but there is no specific mention of his joining the *saṅgha*.	A disciple of Bāvarī.	*Sutta Nipāta, Khuddaka Nikāya*, I, p. 424; *D.P.P.N.*, I, p. 36.
5.	Aññata Koṇḍañña	*brāhmaṇa*	*bhikkhu*	Very distinguished *brāhmaṇa* who left home with the Buddha.	*A.N.*, I, p. 33.
6.	Asurind-aka Bhāradv-āja	*brāhmaṇa*	*bhikkhu*	He was the third of the Bhāradvāja brothers.	*S.N.*, I, p. 163
7.	Assālaya-na	*brāhmaṇa*	*upāsaka*	He was a young *brāhmaṇa* who asked the	*M.N.*, II, pp. 403–13.

			Buddha about the superiority of the *brāhmaṇas*.	
8. Ahimsaka Bharadvaja	*brāhmaṇa*	*bhikkhu*	One of the Bhāradvāja brothers who was initially antagonistic to the Buddha.	*S.N.*, I, p. 164.
9. Āmagandha	*brāhmaṇa*	*bhikkhu*	He believed in the defilement of certain foods before he joined the *saṅgha*.	*Sutta Nipāta, Khuddaka Nikāya*, I, pp. 304–6.
10. Ārāmadaṇḍa	*brāhmaṇa*	*upāsaka*	Enquires from Mahā Kaccana why *khattiyas* quarrel with *khattiyas*, *brāhmaṇas* quarrel with *brāhmaṇas*, and *gahapatis* quarrel with *gahapatis*. He wishes to know if people can rise above their bondage to sensual lusts.	*A.N.* I, pp. 62–4.
11. Uggatasarīra	*brāhmaṇa*	*upāsaka*	Wishes to perform a great sacrifice. Becomes an *upāsaka*.	*A.N.*, III, pp. 184–8.
12. Ujjaya	*brāhmaṇa*	*upāsaka*	Asks the Buddha his opinion on the efficacy of sacrifice.	*A.N.*, II, p. 44.
13. Uṇṇābha	*brāhmaṇa*	*upāsaka*		*S.N.*, IV, p. 188; p. 233.
14. Uttara	*brāhmaṇa*	*upāsaka*	Pupil of the *brāhmaṇa* Brahmāyu at Mithila, but an admirer of the Buddha. He is sent to see the Buddha and gives a favourable report about the Buddha when he returns.	*M.N.*, II, pp. 383 ff.
15. Udaya	*brahmaṇa*	becomes an *arahant*. (there is no information of his having joined the *saṅgha*)	He was a pupil of Bāvarī and along with some other pupils he visited the Buddha. All the pupils questioned the Buddha and are described as realizing the truth.	*Sutta Nipāta, Khuddaka Nikāya*, I, pp. 435–8.
16. Udaya	*brāhmaṇa*	*upāsaka*	He and his family all became lay followers following the Buddha's repeated visits to seek alms. Udaya was hostile to the Buddha initially.	*S.N.*, I, p. 174.

17.	Devahita	*brāhmaṇa*	*upāsaka*		*S.N.*, I, p. 175.
18.	Upavāna	*brāhmaṇa*	*bhikkhu*	He was an *upaṭhaka* (attendant) of the Buddha.	*S.N.*, I, p. 175; *D.P.P.N.*, I, p. 399.
19.	Uruvela Kassapa	*brāhmaṇa*	*bhikkhu*	He was already a *paribbājaka* since he was a very famous *jaṭila*. His acceptance of the teachings is given considerable importance in the text.	*Mahāvagga*, pp. 29–33.
20.	Nadī Kassapa	*brāhmaṇa*	*bhikkhu*	Brother of Uruvela Kassapa.	*Mahāvagga*, p. 33.
21.	Gayā Kassapa	*brāhmaṇa*	*bhikkhu*	Another brother of Uruvela Kassapa.	*Mahāvagga*, p. 34.
22.	Esukāri	*brāhmaṇa*	*upāsaka*	He tells the Buddha that *brāhmaṇas* lay down four types of service for the various *vaṇṇas*. After listening to the Buddha's teachings he becomes an *upāsaka*.	*M.N.*, II, p. 447.
23.	Upasena	*brāhmaṇa*	*bhikkhu*	Brother of Sāriputta. He is listed as chief among those who was charming.	*A.N.*, I, p. 24.
24.	Kasī Bhāradvāja	*brāhmaṇa*	*upāsaka*	He was a very wealthy *brāhmaṇa* of Ekanaḷagāma. He operated 500 ploughs on his lands. When the Buddha asked for alms Kasī Bhāradvāja told him that the Buddha should plough, sow, and then eat. Later he accepted the Buddha's teachings.	*Sutta Nipāta*, *Khuddaka Nikāya*, I, pp. 280–3; *S.N.*, I, pp. 171–3. pp. up to 363
25.	Kandrayāna	*brāhmaṇa*	*upāsaka*		*A.N.*, I, pp. 64–5.
26.	Kuṇḍadhāna *thera*	*brāhmaṇa*	*bhikkhu*	Joined the *saṅgha* when he was very old.	*A.N.*, I, p. 24; *D.P.P.N.*, I, p. 625
27.	Kūṭadanta	*brāhmaṇa*	*upāsaka*	Very wealthy and well known *brāhmaṇa* who lived on *brahmadeya* land.	*D.N.*, I, pp. 109–26.

28.	Keṇiya	*brāhmaṇa*	supporter	Keṇiy'a was a *jaṭila* who invited the Buddha for a meal.	*Mahāvagga*, pp. 259–60; *B.O.D.*, IV, p. 336.
29.	Karaṇa-pāli	*brāhmaṇa*	expresses homage by kneeling	He was employed as a superintendent of works by the Lichchhavis.	*A.N.*, II, pp. 477–9.
30.	Mahā Cunda	*brāhmaṇa*	*bhikkhu*	He was a brother of Sāriputta and one of the chief elders of the *saṅgha*.	*A.N.*, III, p. 68; *D.P.P.N.*, I, p. 878.
31.	Jānusso-ṇi	*brāhmaṇa*	*upāsaka*	Very wealthy and prestigious *brāhmaṇa* who rode around in a luxurious chariot with white trimmings. He lived from time to time at Icchānaṅgala but was a permanent resident of Sāvatthi. In the *Aṅguttara Nikāya* he tells the Buddha that gifts of barley and milk should be given to *tevijja brāhmaṇas* (brāhmaṇas who knew the Vedas).	*S.N.*, II, p. 64. *A.N.*, I, p. 153.
32.	Gaṇaka Mogga-llāna	*brāhmaṇa*	*upāsaka*	He was a teacher of Sāvatthi.	*M.N.*, III, pp. 61–7.
33.	Ajita	*brāhmaṇa*	became *arahants* (33–35)	They were students of Bāvarī (33–35)	Sutta Nipāta, Khuddaka Nikāya, I, p. 438.
34	Tissa Metteya	*brāhmaṇa*			
35.	Todeyya	*brāhmaṇa*			
36.	Tikaṇṇa	*brāhmaṇa*	*upāsaka*	Speaks in praise of *tevijja brāhmaṇas* initially.	*A.N.*, I, pp. 150–3.
37.	Doṇa	*brāhmaṇa*	became an *anāgāmin* (according to the commentary he would be reborn only once more).	A very prestigious *brāhmaṇa* who distributed the Buddha's relics.	*D.N.*, II, p. 128.
38.	Dhāna-ñjāni Taṇḍul-apāla dvāra	*brāhmaṇa*	Reached (the highest) heaven	He was taught union with Brahma.	*M.N.*, II, pp. 449–61.

39.	Dhānañjānī (Female [F])	*brāhmaṇa*		*upāsikā*		*M.N.*, II, p. 493; *S.N.*, I, p. 160.
40	Dhānañjānī's husband	*brāhmaṇa*	*bhikkhu*		A *brāhmaṇa* of the Bhāradvāja *gotta* who was initially indifferent to the Buddha. He was influenced by his wife. He was called Bhāradvāja *thera*.	*S.N.*, I, p. 160.
41.	Dhotaka	*brāhmaṇa*	became an *arahant*		Disciple of Bāvarī	*Sutta Nipāta*, *Khuddaka Nikāya*, I, p. 438.
42.	Nāgita *thera*	*brāhmaṇa*	*bhikkhu*		He was fat so he made his nephew Sīha, who was a novice, work for him.	*A.N.*, II, p. 297. *D.P.P.N.*, II, p. 47.
43.	Pingiyānī	*brāhmaṇa*		*upāsaka*	He presented the 500 garments given to him by the Lichchhavis to the Buddha.	*A.N.*, II, pp. 477–80.
44.	Pilinda Vaccha	*brāhmaṇa*	*bhikkhu*			*A.N.*, I, p. 24.
45.	Piṇḍola Bhāradvāja	*brāhmaṇa*	*bhikkhu*		He had special *iddhi* powers.	*A.N.*, I, p. 23; *Cullavagga*, pp. 199–200.
46.	Puṇṇa Mantānīputta	*brāhmaṇa*	*bhikkhu*		He was one of the great disciples and was a nephew of Añña Koṇḍañña. He went away to propagate Buddhism in a district inhabited by fierce people.	*A.N.*, I, p. 24; *K.S.*, III, 89; IV, 34–6.
47.	Bahudhīti	*brāhmaṇa*	*bhikkhu*		He was a very poor *brāhmaṇa* with seven daughters.	*S.N.*,I, pp. 169–71.
48.	Bāvarī	*brāhmaṇa*	Became an *arahant*. (No reference to him joining the *saṅgha*.)		He was a very famous sage who had many disciples. All became followers of the Buddha.	*Sutta Nipāta*, *Khuddaka Nikāya*, I, pp. 419–24; *D.P.P.N.*, II, p. 279.
49.	Bilaṅgaka Bhāradvāja	*brāhmaṇa*	*bhikkhu*			*S.N.*, I, p. 164.

50. Brahmadeva *thera*	*brāhmaṇa*	*bhikkhu*		Son of a *brāhmaṇī*	*S.N.*, I, pp. 141–2.
51. Brahmadeva's mother	*brāhmaṇa*		*upāsikā*		*S.N.*, I, pp. 141–2.
52. Brahmāyu	*brāhmaṇa*		*upāsaka*	He is described as the foremost *brāhmaṇa* of Mithila.	*M.N.*, II, pp. 382–95.
53. Mahā-Kaccāyana	*brāhmaṇa*	*bhikkhu*		He is described as foremost among those who could expound in full sayings which were brief.	*A.N.*, I, p. 24; *D.P.P.N.*, II, pp. 468–9.
54. Mahā Moggallāna	*brāhmaṇa*	*bhikkhu*		Moggallāna was already a *paribbājaka* when he became the Buddha's disciple. Later he rose to great prominence within the *saṅgha*.	*Mahāvagga*, pp. 38–41; *A.N.*, I, p. 23.
55. Bhāradvāja *thera*	*brāhmaṇa*	*bhikkhu*		He was a young pupil of the *brāhmaṇa* Tārukkha. Along with his friend Vāseṭṭha he joined the *saṅgha*.	*D.N.*, I, pp. 198–212.
56. *Mahāsala*	*brāhmaṇa*		*upāsaka*	A wealthy *brāhmaṇa*	*S.N.*, I, pp. 175–7.
57. Mānatthadha	*brāhmaṇa*		*upāsaka*	A proud *brāhmaṇa* who respects no one. Later he falls at the Buddha's feet and kisses them.	*S.N.*, I, pp. 177–8.
58. Mogharāja *thera*	*brāhmaṇa*	Becomes *arahant*		A disciple of Bāvarī	*Sutta Nipāta*, *Khuddaka Nikāya*, I, p. 438.
59. Yamelu	*brāhmaṇa*	*bhikkhu*		These *brāhmaṇas* who had become *bhikkhus* were the object of Buddha's statement that *bhikkhus* should not preach in Sanskrit.	*Cullavagga*, pp. 228–9.
60. Tekula	*brāhmaṇa*	*bhikkhu*			
61. Yasa Kākaṇḍakaputta	*brāhmaṇa*	*bhikkhu*		Played a prominent role in the second council held at Vesāli.	*Cullavagga*, pp. 416 ff. *D.P.P.N.*, II, p. 687
62. Rādha *thera*	*brāhmaṇa*	*bhikkhu*			*A.N.*, I, p. 25; *D.P.P.N.*, II, pp. 730–1.

63. Revata	*brāhmaṇa*	*bhikkhu*		Younger brother of Sāriputta.	*A.N.*, I, p. 24; *D.P.P.N.*, II, p. 753.
64. Lohicca	*brāhmaṇa*		*upāsaka*	A *brāhmaṇa* of Sālavatikā who owned *brahmadeya* land.	*D.N.*, I, pp. 191–8.
65. Vaṅgīsa	*brāhmaṇa*	*bhikkhu*		Told people's future by tapping skulls till he met the Buddha.	*A.N.*, I, p. 24; *D.P.P.N.*, II, p. 802.
66. Vāseṭṭha	*brāhmaṇa*	*bhikkhu*		Along with Bhāradvāja he was a student of Tārukkha. They went to see the Buddha to ask him about who was a real *brāhmaṇa*.	*D.N.*, I, pp. 198–212.
67. Another Vāseṭṭha	*brāhmaṇa*		*upāsaka*		*A.N.*, III, pp. 149, 199; *D.P.P.N.*, II, p. 861.
68. Veṭṭha-dīpika	*brāhmaṇa*		*upāsaka*	A *brāhmaṇa* who asked for a share of the Buddha's relics.	*D.N.*, II, p. 127.
69. Veracc-hāni *brāhmaṇi* [F]	*brāhmaṇa*		*upāsikā*	The *brāhmaṇī* sought the teachings of the Buddha while seated on a high seat. She was told to sit on a low seat before the *dhamma* was taught to her. She is described as a teacher herself.	*S.N.*, III, pp. 111–4.
70. Sakulā *therī* [F]	*brāhmaṇa*	*bhikkhunī*			*A.N.*, I, p. 26; *D.P.P.N.*, II, p. 957.
72. Sāriput-ta	*brāhmaṇa*	*bhikkhu*		He was an inhabitant of Nālakagāma who was already a *paribbājaka* before he joined the *saṅgha*. He was one of the most important disciples of the Buddha.	*A.N.*, I, p. 25; *Mahāvagga*, p. 38.
72. Sundari-ka Bhārad-vāja	*brāhmaṇa*	*bhikkhu*		Sundarika Bhāradvāja asked the Buddha what his *jāti* was. The Buddha replied that even the fact of having originated in a *nīca kula* was irrelevant in the case of a *muni*.	*Sutta Nipāta, Khuddaka Nikāya*, I, pp. 334–9.

73. Sonada-ṇḍa	*brāhmana*	*upāsaka*	A very wealthy and prestigious *brāhmaṇa* who accepted the Buddha's teaching although he did not do so publicly on the ground that his followers would find fault with him.	*D.N.*, I, pp. 97–108.
74. Sobhita *thera*	*brāhmaṇa*	*bhikkhu*		*A.N.*, I, p. 25; *D.P.P.N.*, II, p. 1304.
75. Subha	*brāhmaṇa*	*upāsaka*	Resident of Tudi near Sāvatthi.	*D.N.*, I, pp. 169–82.
76. Vassak-āra	*brāhmaṇa*	feeds the Buddha	Chief Minister of King Bimbisāra and King Ajātasattu.	*D.N.*, II, p. 71.
77. Pokkha-rasādi	*brāhmaṇa*	*upāsaka*	A very rich and prestigious *brāhmaṇa* whose conversion has great demonstration effect. His family also became followers.	*D.N.*, I, p. 65.
78. Piṅgala Koccha	*brāhmaṇa*	*upāsaka*		*M.N.*, I, p. 255.
79. Saṅgār-ava	*brāhmaṇa*	*upāsaka*	Resident of Sāvatthi, described as a *brāhmaṇa* who kept purifying himself.	*S.N.*, I, p. 183.
80. Another Saṅgār-ava	*brāhmaṇa*	*upāsaka*	Resident of Caṇḍalakappa. Declared the Buddha as his teacher.	*M.N.*, II, p. 482.
81. Verañjā *brāhmaṇa*	*brāhmaṇa*	*upāsaka*	He was the object of a long discourse on who is a really spiritual person.	*A.N.*, III, p. 293.
82. Jaṭa Bhārad-vāja	*brāhmaṇa*	*bhikkhu*		*S.N.*, I, p. 165.
83. Suddhi-ka Bhārad-vāja	*brāhmaṇa*	*bhikkhu*		*S.N.*, I, p. 165.
84. Mahā Kammi-ka Bhārad-vāja	*brāhmaṇa*	*upāsaka*		*S.N.*, I, p. 179.

85. Paccanīka	*brāhmaṇa*	*upāsaka*		*S.N.*, I, p. 179.
86. Mātuposaka	*brāhmaṇa*	*upāsaka*		*S.N.*, I, p. 181.
87. Lokāyatika	*brāhmaṇa*	*upāsaka*		*S.N.*, II, pp. 65–6.
88. A *brāhmaṇa*	*brāhmaṇa*	*upāsaka*		*S.N.*, II, pp. 64–5.
89. Another *brāhmaṇa*	*brāhmaṇa*	*upāsaka*		*S.N.*, II, pp. 155–6.
90. A *brāhmaṇa paribbājaka*	*brāhmaṇa*	*upāsaka*		*A.N.*, I, pp. 145–6.
91. Mahā Kassapa	*brāhmaṇa*	*bhikkhu*	Very eminent *bhikkhu* of the *saṅgha* who played a very important role at the first Council of Rājagaha.	*A.N.*, I, p. 23; *D.P.P.N.*, II, pp. 476–83.
92. Chammika	*brāhmaṇa*	*bhikkhu*	After he became a *bhikkhu* he went about making a nuisance of himself with the lay followers.	*A.N.*, III, p. 78.
93. Another *brāhmaṇa*	*brāhmaṇa*	*upāsaka*	Resident of Sāvatthi. He asks the Buddha whether the doer and the experiencer are the same.	*A.N.*, I, p. 145.

GROUP REFERENCES*

94–98. A group of *brāhmaṇas* of Kosala	*brāhmaṇa*	*upāsaka*	They were old, decrepit, but wealthy *brahmaṇas* who came to ask the Buddha what his opinion of the *brāhmaṇa dhamma* was.	*Sutta Nipāta, Khuddaka Nikāya*, I, pp. 311–14.

*For purposes of the statistical analysis we have treated each group reference as consisting of five memebers. This has been done on the basis of a reasonable mean between two references in the Pāli literature. The *Vinaya* refers to a *gāma* as consisting of one *kuṭi* two *kuṭis*, three *kuṭis* or four *kuṭis* (Pārājika, p. 56), and a reference to a small *gāma* consisting of 30 families in the *Jātakas* (Jātaka I, ed. by V. Fausboll, p. 199).

99–103.	A group of *brāhmanagahapatis* of Venāgapura	*brāhmaṇa*	*upāsaka*	Their leader was Vacchagotta and they all became lay followers.	*A.N.*, I, pp. 167–79.
104–108.	*Brāhmaṇagahapatis of* Sāla	*brāhmaṇa*	*upāsaka*		*M.N.*, I, p. 355.
109–113.	*Brāhmaṇagahapatis* of Verañja	*brāhmaṇa*	*upāsaka*		*M.N.*, I, pp. 356–3.
114–118.	*Brāhmaṇagahapatis* of Veḷudvāra	*brahmaṇa*	upāsaka		*S.N.*, IV, pp. 300–3.
119–123.	*Brāhmaṇagahapatis* of Khomadussa	*brāhmaṇa*	*upāsaka*		*S.N.*, I, pp. 183–4.

* * *

1.	Ajita	*khattiya*	*upāsaka*	He was a Lichchhavi	*D.N.*, III, p. 13.
2.	Ajātasattu	*khattiya*	*upāsaka*	King of Magadha who was a parricide.	*D.N.*, I, p. 74.
3.	Avantiputta	*khattiya*	*upāsaka*	King of Madhurā.	*M.N.*, II, p. 316.
4.	Anuruddha	*khattiya*	*bhikkhu*	A Sākyan and kinsman of the Buddha. Also a prominent member of the *sangha*.	*Cullavagga*, pp. 279–81.
5.	Abhayarāja kumāra	*khattiya*	*bhikkhu*	Belonged to a *rāja kula* and was probably King Bimbisāra's son.	*M.N.*, II, p. 71; *D.P.P.N.*, I, pp. 127–8.
6.	Abhaya	*khattiya*	*upāsaka*	A Lichchhavi	*A.N.*, II, pp. 213–16.
7.	Ānanda	*khattiya*	*bhikkhu*	Sākyan kinsman of the Buddha. Closest associate of the Buddha.	*Cullavagga*, pp. 279–81. *A.N.*, I. p. 24.
8.	Udena	*khattiya*	*upāsaka*	King of Kosambī who along with his family, was a supporter of the Buddha.	*Cullavagga*, pp. 412–13.

9.	Upananda	*khattiya*	*bhikkhu*		A Sākyan who was the object of many of the *vinaya* rules.	*Pācittiya*, pp. 50, 123, 129–33.
10.	Kakudha	*khattiya*	*bhikkhu*		A Koliyan who was an attendant of Moggallāna.	*Cullavagga*, p. 283.
11.	Kalāra *khattiya*	*khattiya*	*bhikkhu*		No other details	*S.N.*, II, pp. 43–8.
12.	Kāḷigo-dhā [F]	*khattiya*		*upāsikā*	A Sākyan. Mother of Bhaddiya *thera*.	*S.N.*, IV, p. 338.
13.	Bhaddiya, Kāḷi-godhiy-aputto	*khattiya*	*bhikkhu*		A Sākyan. Listed as chief among those who were of high birth (*ucca kulīna*).	*A.N.*, I, p. 23.
14.	Kimbila	*khattiya*	*bhikkhu*		A Sākyan who went forth along with other kinsmen of the Buddha.	*Cullavagga*, p. 281.
15.	Khemā *therī* [F]	*khattiya*	*bhikkhunī*		Wife of king Bimbisāra. A *bhikkhunī* of great wisdom.	*S.N.*, III, p. 321; *A.N.*, I, p. 25.
16.	Cundi [F]	*khattiya*		*upāsikā*	According to the commentary she was the daughter of king Bimbisāra.	*A.N.*, II, p. 301; *D.P.P.N.*, I, p. 880.
17.	Jeta-kumāra	*khattiya*		*upāsaka*	*rajakula*	*Cullavagga*, pp. 252–3.
18.	Dabba Mallā-putta	*khattiya*	*bhikkhu*		A Mallā. A senior *bhikkhu* who was incharge of apportioning lodgings.	*Cullavagga*, p. 153.
19.	Devada-tta	*khattiya*	*bhikkhu*		A Sākyan—kinsman of the Buddha who was jealous of the Buddha.	*Cullavagga*, pp. 281–4, 300ff.
20.	Dīghaj-ānu Koliya putta	*khattiya*		*upāsaka*	A Koliyan. Object of Buddha's discourse on *kulaputtas*.	*A.N.*, III, pp. 375–8.
21.	Nanda	*khattiya*	*bhikkhu*		A Sākyan and half brother to the Buddha. Chief among those of meditative powers.	*A.N.*, I, p. 25; *D.P.P.N.*, II, p. 10.
22.	Nanda *therī [F]*	*khattiya*	*bhikkhunī*		A Sākyan, chief among those of meditative powers.	*A.N.*, I, p. 26; *D.P.P.N.*, II, p. 24.
23.	Nandiya *thera*	*khattiya*	*bhikkhu*		A Sākyan who features along with Anuruddha and Kimbila in the *Mahāvagga*.	*Mahāvagga*, p. 381; *D.P.P.N.*, II, p. 26.

24.	Nāgasa-mala	*khattiya*	*bhikkhu*		(A Sākyan)	*M.N.*, I, pp. 115–16; *D.P.P.N.*, II, p. 45.
25.	Nandiya	*khattiya*		*upāsaka*	(A Sākyan)	*S.N.*, IV, pp. 339–45.
26.	Pasenadi	*khattiya*		*upāsaka*	King of Kosala who features prominently in the texts; showed deep reverence for the Buddha.	*S.N.*, I, pp. 67–102.
27.	Pukkusa	*khattiya*		*upāsaka*	A Mallā *rājaputta*.	*S.N.*, II, pp. 100–4.
28.	Roja Mallā	*khattiya*		*upāsaka*	A Mallā who was initially indifferent to the Buddha. Ānanda wished that he would become a follower since he was important, so the Buddha drew him into the faith.	*Mahāvagga*, pp. 260–2.
29.	Bhagu	*khattiya*	*bhikkhu*		A Sākyan kinsman of the Buddha who joined along with Anuruddha and Kimbila.	*Cullavagga*, p. 281.
30.	Bodhi-*rājakumāra*	*khattiya*		*upāsaka*	Belonged to a *rāja kula* and had a palace at Suṃsumāragiri.	*A.N.*, II, pp. 318–19.
31.	Bhaddiya	*khattiya*		*upāsaka*	A Lichchhavi who asked if Buddha was a juggler.	*A.N.*, II, pp. 203–7.
32.	Bhumija *thera*	*khattiya*	*bhikkhu*		Belonged to a *rāja kula*.	*M.N.*, II, p. 204; *D.P.P.N.*, II, p. 387.
33.	A Mallā *bhikkhunī* [F]	*khattiya*	*bhikkhunī*		She knocked off a weak *bhikkhu* while she passed him.	*Cullavagga*, p. 388.
34.	Mahā-nāma	*khattiya*		*upāsaka*	A Sākyan who was upset that no one had 'gone forth' into the *saṅgha* from his family. He was a devoted *upāsaka* and was reassured about his future by the Buddha. He was chief among the *upāsakas* who gave good food as alms to the *bhikkhus*.	*A.N.*, I, p. 26.

35.	Mahā-pajāpatī Gotamī [F]	*khattiya*	*bhikkhunī*	Foster mother of the Buddha who was the first *bhikkhunī* to be ordained. (Sākyan)	*A.N.*, I, p. 26; *Cullavagga*, pp. 374ff.
36.	Mahā Kappina	*khattiya*	*bhikkhu*	Belonged to a *rāja kula*. He was a very important membet of the *sangha*.	*A.N.*, I, p. 25; *D.P.P.N.*, II, pp. 473–5.
37.	Rāhula	*khattiya*	*bhikkhu*	A Sākyan. Only son of the Buddha.	*Mahāvagga*, p. 86.
38.	Vaḍḍha	*khattiya*	*bhikkhu*	A Lichchhavi who was notorious for his bad behaviour. He charged Dabba falsely.	*Cullavagga*, p. 213.
39.	Vappa	*khattiya*	*bhikkhu*	Originally a follower of the Nigaṇṭhās. (A Sākyan)	*A.N.*, II, pp. 210–13.
40.	Sarakāṇi		*upāsaka*	(A Sākyan)	*S.N.*, IV, pp. 319–21.
41.	Sīha senapati	*khattiya*	*upāsaka*	Originally a follower of the Nigaṇṭhās. He was asked to continue giving alms to them even after accepting the Buddha as his guide. (A Lichchhavi)	*Mahāvagga*, pp. 248–53
42.	Sumanā rājaku-mārī	*khattiya*	*upāsikā*	Sister of a *raja*. She is listed among the eminent *upāsikās*.	*A.N.*, III, p. 428; *A.N.*, II, p. 299.
43.	Selā *therī*	*khattiya*	*bhikkhunī*	She was called Āḷavikā and belonged to a *rāja kula*.	*S.N.*, I, p. 134; *D.P.P.N.*, II, p. 1289.
44.	Hatthaka	*khattiya*	*bhikkhu*	A Sākyan	*Pācittiya*, p. 3.
45.	Sabbak-āmin	*khattiya*	*bhikkhu*	A Vajjian, one of the oldest *bhikkhus* who participated in the second council of Vesāli.	*Cullavagga*, pp. 425–30.
46.	A Vajjian *bhikkhu*	*khattiya*	*bhikkhu*	A Vajjian.	*S.N.*, I, p. 201.
47.	Tissa	*khattiya*	*bhikkhu*	A Sākyan. He was a nephew of the Buddha's father.	*S.N.*, II, p. 328.
48.	Nandaka	*khattiya*	*upāsaka*	A Lichchhavi minister who exhorts inner purity after listening to the Buddha.	*S.N.*, IV, p. 333.

49.	Kāḷa khemaka	khattiya	upāsaka	They erected *vihāras* for the *saṅgha* at the Nigrodhārāma in Kapilavatthu. They were Sākyans.	*M.N.*, III, p. 174.
50.	Ghaṭāya	khattiya	upāsaka		

* * *

1.	Anātha-piṇḍika	*gahapati*	*upāsaka*	Most prominent *upāsaka* of the Buddha with many *suttas* addressed to him. Listed among the chief donors of the *upāsakas*.	*Cullavagga*, pp. 249–53. *A.N.*, I, p. 26.
2.	A *gaha-pati*	*gahapati*	*upāsaka*	Originally a follower of Ājīvikas.	*A.N.*, I, pp. 201–2.
3.	Ugga	*gahapati*	*upāsaka*	Of Hatthigāma in the Vajjian territory. Best among those who wait upon the *saṅgha*.	*A.N.*, I, p. 26.
4	Ugga	*gahapati*	*upāsaka*	Of Vesāli. Best among those who gave agreeable gifts.	*A.N.*, I, p. 26.
5.	Upāli	*gahapati*	*upāsaka*	Originally follower of Niganṭhas.	*M.N.*, II, pp. 43–60.
6.	Kevaṭṭha	*gahapati*	*upāsaka*	Of Nālandā. He asked the Buddha to perform a miracle.	*D.N.*, I, pp. 183–9.
7.	Jotika	*gahapati*	*upāsaka*	Of Rājagaha. He was the father of Dīghāvu.	*S.N.*, IV, pp. 292–3.
8.	Dīghāvu	*gahapati [putta]*	*upāsaka*	He sent a message to the Buddha through his father Jotika when he was ill.	*S.N.*, IV, pp. 292–3.
9.	Dasama	*gahapati*	*upāsaka*	Gave various gifts and built a cell for Ānanda,	*M.N.*, II, pp. 15–19; *M.L.S.*, II, pp. 14–18.
10.	Nakula-pitā	*gahapati*	*upāsaka*	Very devoted couple who are described as the most intimate of the Buddha's disciples.	*A.N.*, I, p. 26.
11.	Nakula-mātā	*gahapati*	*upāsikā*		*A.N.*, I, p. 27.
12.	Potaliya	*gahapati*	*upāsaka*	Potaliya objected to the Buddha addressing him as a *gahapati* because he had given up the management of property. Later he became an *upāsaka*.	*M.N.*, II, pp. 27–37.

13.	Meṇḍaka	*gahapati*	*upāsaka*	Very wealthy *gahapati* of Bhaḍḍiyanagara who, along with other members of his family, possessed psychic powers.	*Mahāvagga*, pp.254–9.
14.	Mānadi-ṇṇa	*gahapati*	*upāsaka*		*S.N.*, IV, p. 152.
15.	Vijaya-māhiko	*gahapati*	*upāsaka*	Mentioned in a special list of followers.	*A.N.*, III, p. 149.
16.	Vichayo	*gahapati*	*upāsaka*	Mentioned in a special list of followers.	*A.N.*, III, p. 149.
17.	Sandhana	*gahapati*	*upāsaka*	Had 500 followers of his own and features in the special list of followers.	*A.N.*, III, p. 149.
18.	Sigāla-mātā [F]	*gahapati*	*bhikkhunī*	Mother of Sigāla *gahapaṭi*. Chief of those who was released by faith.	*A.N.*, I, p. 26; *G.S.*, I, p. 22.
19.	Sujātā [F]	*gahapati*	*upāsikā*	She was the younger sister of Visākhā. The Buddha taught her the duties of a woman.	*A.N.*, III, pp. 223–5.
20.	Visākhā [F]	*gahapati*	*upāsikā*	Most prominent *upāsikā* of the Buddha. She was conferred eight boons by the Buddha.	*A.N.*, I, p. 27; *Mahāvagga*, pp. 306–10.
21.	Kalyan-bhatta-ko *gahapati*	*gahapati*	*upāsaka*	Provided good alms-food to the *bhikkhus*.	*Cullavagga*, pp. 155–6.
22.	Sigāla	*gahapati*	*upāsaka*	Object of the *Sigālovāda Sutta*.	*D.N.*, III, pp. 139–49.
23.	Soṇa	*gahapati*	*upāsaka*	A *gahapati putta*	*S.N.*, II, pp. 279–84.
24.	A Rāja-gaha *gahapati*	*gahapati*	*upāsaka*	He was a supporter of the *saṅgha*.	*Pācittiya*, pp. 96–7.
25.	A *gaha-pati* who was original-ly an Ājīvika follower	*gahapati*	*upāsaka*	Of Kosambī. He became a lay follower through Ānanda.	*A.N.*, I, pp. 201–3.
26.	Hāliddi-kāni	*gahapati*	*upāsaka*	Of Avanti.	*S.N.*, II, pp. 248–51.

27.	Citta	*gahapati*	*upāsaka*	A very prestigious and learned *gahapati*. He could aspire to be a *cakkavatti*. The *bhikkhu* Sudhamma had to seek his pardon.	*A.N.*, I, p. 26; *Cullavagga*, pp. 32–5.
28.	Sirivaḍ_dha	*gahapati*	*upāsaka*	Of Rājagaha. He was visited by *bhikkhus* when he was ill.	*S.N.*, IV, p. 151.
29.	Sāḷha	*gahapati*	*upāsaka*	Migāra's grandson. He seduced the beautiful *bhikkhunī* Sundarīnanda.	*Pācittiya*, p. 253; *A.N.*, I, pp. 179–81.

GROUP REFERENCE

30. 34.	Pātaligāma *gahapatis*	*gahapati*	*upāsaka*		*D.N.*, II, pp. 68–9

* * *

1.	Ambapāli	*ucca kula*	*upāsikā*	A courtesan (*gaṇika*) of Vesāli who donated the Ambavana to the *saṅgha*.	*D.N.*, II, pp. 76–8.
2.	Kāludāyin	*ucca kula*	*bhikkhu*	He was the son of a minister of Kapilavatthu. According to the commentary he was able to induce the Buddha to visit his father. He is described as the best among those who were good at reconciling families.	*A.N.*, I, p. 25; *D.P.P.N.*, I, p. 589.
3.	Kumāra Kassapa	*ucca kula*. His mother was the daughter of a *seṭṭhi*.	*bhikkhu*	According to the commentary Kumāra Kassapa was brought up by the king since he was born after his mother became a *bhikkhunī*. He was a brilliant speaker.	*A.N.*, I, p. 25; *D.P.P.N.*, I, p. 632.
4.	Cūla Panthakatherā	*ucca kula*, his mother was the daughter of a *seṭṭhi*	*bhikkhu*	He was chief among those who were skilled in mental evolution.	*A.N.*, I, p. 24; *D.P.P.N.*, I, p. 897.

5.	Dhaniya	*gopaka*	*bhikkhu*	Dhaniya was a prosperous owner of cattle and was the object of the *Dhaniya Sutta* in the *Sutta Nipāta*. He is depicted as the picture of contentment till he met the Buddha.	*Sutta Nipāta*, *Khuddaka Nikāya*, I, pp. 271–4.
6.	His wife	*gopaka*	*bhikkhunī*		
7.	Bījaka	*seṭṭhi kula*	*bhikkhu*	Bījaka was the grandson of a very wealthy *seṭṭhi* whose son was Sudinna. He was born after Sudinna's mother pleaded with Sudinna that he should provide the family with an heir otherwise the wealth of the family would pass to the Lichchhavis.	*Pārājika*, p. 23.
8.	Bījaka's mother	*seṭṭhi kula*	*bhikkhunī*		*Pārājika*, p. 23.
9.	Pukku-sāti	*ucca kula*	A monk who died without being ordained (*upāsaka*)	He is described as a *kulaputta* who had been a disciple of the Buddha without meeting him.	*M.N.*, III, pp. 322–32.
10.	Belaṭṭha Kaccāna	*ucca kula*	*upāsaka*	He was a sugar dealer who met the Buddha while travelling from Andhakavinda to Rājagaha.	*Mahāvagga*, pp. 240–1.
11.	Tapussa	*ucca kula*	*upāsaka*	A *vāṇija*. Along with Bhallika he was the first to hear the Buddha's teachings.	*Mahāvagga*, pp. 4–6.
12.	Paṭacārā *therī* [F]	*ucca kula*	*bhikkhunī*	She was the daughter of a *seṭṭhi* but she was the widow of a servant. After many troubles she joined the *saṅgha*. She is listed as chief among those who were proficient in the discipline.	*A.N.*, I, p. 25; *D.P.P.N.*, II, pp. 112–13.
13.	Puṇṇaji	*ucca kula*	*bhikkhu*	A *seṭṭhi-putta* who was a friend of Yasa, son of another *seṭṭhi gahapti*.	*Mahāvagga*, p. 21.
14.	Bhallika	*ucca kula*	*upāsaka*	A *vāṇija* who was an associate of Tapussa.	*Mahāvagga*, pp. 5–6.

15.	Yasa	*ucca kula*	*bhikkhu*		A very delicately nurtured *kula-putta seṭṭhi-putta* whose father was a wealthy *seṭṭhi-gahapati* of Banaras.	*Mahāvagga*, pp. 18–21.
16.	Migasālā [F]	*ucca kula*		*upāsaka*	She was the daughter of Pūraṇa who was the king's chamberlain.	*A.N.*, III, pp. 62–5.
17.	Isidatta	*ucca kula*		*upāsaka*	They were king Pasenadi's chamberlains and were in charge of royal conveyance.	*M.N.*, II, p. 371.
18.	Pūraṇa			*upāsaka*		
19.	A Rājagaha *seṭṭhi*	*ucca kula*		*upāsaka*	He built 60 vihāras for the *saṅgha* in a day.	*Cullavagga*, pp. 239–40.
20.	Raṭṭhapāla	*ucca kula*	*bhikkhu*		He was a very wealthy *kula putta*, who was the only son of his parents. He joined the *saṅgha* after pressurizing his parents to give him permission.	*M.N.*, II, pp. 281ff.
21.	Lady of Veḷukāṇḍa [F]	*ucca kula*		*upāsikā*	She was an exemplary lay woman.	*A.N.*, I, p. 81; *D.P.P.N.*, II, p. 934.
22.	Sudinna Kalandaka putta	*ucca kula*	*bhikkhu*		Very wealthy *seṭṭhi putta* who was requested to provide an heir to the family.	*Pārājika*, pp. 15–24.
23.	Sirimā	*ucca kula*		*upāsikā*	She was the daughter of the courtesan Sālavatī.	*A.N.*, III, p. 428; *D.P.P.N.*, II, p. 1145.
24.	Subāhu	*ucca kula*	*bhikkhu*		They were friends of Yasa and were *seṭṭhi putta's* themselves.	*Mahāvagga*, p. 21.
25.	Vimala	*ucca kula*	*bhikkhu*			
26.	Gavampati	*ucca kula*	*bhikkhu*			
27.	Soṇa Kuṭikaṇṇa	*ucca kula*	*bhikkhu*		A *seṭṭhi-putta*.	*Mahāvagga*, p. 213.
28.	Sona Koḷivisa	*ucca kula*	*bhikkhu*		A *seṭṭhi-putta* of Campa who was very delicately nurtured. He was unused to walking on his bare feet and his feet bled severely. He then reconsidered his decision to join the *saṅgha*. The Buddha taught him moderation in his effort.	

29.	Yasa's father	*ucca kula*	*upāsaka*		*Mahavagga*, p. 21.
30.	Yasa's mother	*ucca kula*	*upāsikā*		
31.	Yasa's wife	*ucca kula*	*upāsikā*		
32.	Sunidha	*ucca kula*	supporter	One of the chief ministers of Ajātasattu who along with Vassakāra invited the Buddha for a meal.	*D.N.*, II, p. 71.
33.	Pañcak-aṅga	*ucca kula*	*upāsaka*	Chief carpenter of Pasenadi.	*M.N.*, II, pp. 212–13.
34.	Mallikā [F]	*ucca kula*	*upāsikā*	Daughter of the chief *mālakāra* (garand maker) of Kosala. She was the wife of King Pasenadi and was very devoted to the Buddha.	*A.N.*, II, pp. 216–17; 321–2.
35.	Visākha of Pañchāla	*ucca kula*	*bhikkhu*	Son of a Pañchāli. He was an enlightened, urbane speaker.	*S.N.*, II, pp. 232–3. *K.S.*, II, p. 190.
36.	Caṇḍa	*ucca kula*	*upāsaka*	A *gāmanī*.	*S.N.*, III, p. 271.
37.	Asiban-dhaka *putta*	*ucca kula*	*upāsaka*	A *gāmanī* of Nālandā.	*S.A.*, III, pp. 276–85.
38.	Maṇicū-ḷako	*ucca kula*	*upāsaka*	A *gāmanī*.	*S.N.*, III, pp. 287–9.
39.	Rasiya	*ucca kula*	*upāsaka*	A *gāmanī*.	*S.N.*, II, pp. 291–9.
40.	Pataliya	*ucca kula*	*upāsaka*	A *gāmanī*.	*S.A.*, IV, pp. 299–311.
41.	Nandaka	*ucca kula*	*upāsaka*	He was a chief minister of the Lichchhavis.	*S.N.*, IV, p. 333.
42.	Dham-madina	*ucca kula*	*upāsaka*	He had 500 disciples of his own.	*S.N.*, IV, p. 348.
43.	A *seṭṭhi putta* of Sāvatthi	*ucca kula*	*upāsaka*	He was a supporter who offered robes to Upananda.	*Pārājika*, p. 305.
44.	A Mahā-maccha (great minis-ter)	*ucca kula*	*upāsaka*	He was a supporter who wished to gift a shelter to the *saṅgha*.	*Pārājika*, p. 367.
45.	Aḍḍha-kāsi	*ucca kula*	*bhikkhunī*	A courtesan: she had to be ordained through a messenger for fear of the	*Cullavagga*, pp. 397–9.

				men who would try to prevent her from joining the *saṅgha*.	
46.	Maha-panthaka *thera*	*ucca kula*	*bhikkhu*	Grandson of a *seṭṭhi*. Brother of Cula Panthaka *thera*.	*A.N.*, I, p. 24. *D.P.P.N.*, II, p. 530.
47.	Bhaddā Kapilāni [F]	*ucca kula*	*bhikkhunī*	She 'went forth' along with Mahāpajāpatī Gotamī and was known as one who could remember previous lives.	*Pācittiya*, pp. 303ff; *A.N.*, I, p. 25.

* * *

1.	Ariṭṭha	*nīca kula* vulture trainer (*gadha bādhi*)	*bhikkhu*	He had the pernicious view that things which are called stumbling blocks (*antarayika dhamma*) are not stumbling blocks at all.	*Pācittiya*, pp. 180–2.
2.	Upāli	*nīca kula*, barber	*bhikkhu*	A barber of the Sākyans who joined the *saṅgha* along with the Buddha's Sākyan kinsmen. He rose to great prominence and became a master of the *vinaya*.	*A.N.*, I, p. 25; *Cullavagga*, p. 281.
3.	Citta	*nīca kula* (son of an elephant trainer)	*bhikkhu*		*D.N.*, I, pp. 158–68.
4.	Kesi	*nīca kula* (horse trainer)	*upāsaka*		*A.N.*, II, pp. 117–19.
5.	Cunda	*nīca kula*, son of a metal-smith worker (*kammāraputta*).	*upāsaka*	He fed the Buddha for the last time at his house. The Buddha fell ill after eating this meal but exhorted the *bhikkhus* not to blame Cunda. He said that Cunda would be blessed with long life, good birth, fame, inheritance and sovereign power in	*D.N.*, II, pp. 98–9.

					the future. Cunda was a resident of the Mallā territory.	
6.	Channa	*nīca kula*, slave (*dāsi putta*)	*bhikkhu*		He was the Buddha's charioteer at Kapilavatthu. After the Buddha's death the *brahmadaṇḍa* (a penalty) was imposed upon him by the *saṅgha*. Later he became an *arahant*.	*D.N.*, II, p. 118; *D.P.P.N.*, I, pp. 923–34.
7.	Tālapuṭa	*nīca kula*, a head-man of actors (*naṭa gāmiṇī*)	*bhikkhu*		He was under the impression that his profession would bring him gains in the future life too but was told by the Buddha that his profession was condemnable. He then joined the *saṅgha*.	*S.N.*, III, pp. 272–3.
8.	Dhaniya	*nīca kula*, potter (*kumbhakāra*)	*bhikkhu*		He built a house of clay for himself and later another one of wood. He took wood from the state's resources and was reprimanded by the king.	*Pārājika*, pp. 51–4.
9.	Bhaggava	*nīca kula*, potter (*kumbhakāra*)		*upāsaka*	The Buddha stayed in Bhaggava's house on one occasion and met Pukkusāti there.	*M.N.*, III, p. 323
10.	Sāti	*nīca kula*, fisherman's son (*kevaṭṭa-putta*)	*bhikkhu*		He held heretical views about the existence of the soul and was reprimanded.	*M.N.*, I, pp. 315–18.
11.	Subhadda	*nīca kula*, barber (*nahāpita*)	*bhikkhu*		He was barber of Ātumā who joined the *saṅgha* when he was old. He had two sons who went around collecting alms from others in order to feed the *saṅgha*. He was probably the same *bhikkhu* who was relieved at the death of the Buddha.	*Cullavagga*, p. 406; *Mahāvagga*, p. 262.

12.	Assa gāmaṇī	*nīca kula*	upāsaka	Although all three are described as *gāmaṇī* or headmen (like Tālapuṭza), their professions are condemned by the Buddha.	*S.N.*, III, pp. 274–6.
13.	Hatha gāmaṇī	*nīca kula*	upāsaka		
14.	Yodhājīvi	*nīca kula*	upāsaka		
15.	A poor tailor	*nīca kula*, tailor (*tuṇṇavāya*)	*upāsaka*	He wished to build a *vihāra* for the *saṅgha* but couldn't because of lack of expertise. He complained that no one bothered to instruct him in the erection of the cell.	*Cullavagga*, pp. 253–4.
16.	A poor *kammakara*	*nīca kula*	*upāsaka*	He took an advance on his wages to feed the *bhikkhus*. He was a resident of Vesāli	*Cullavagga*, pp. 108–9.
17.	A *kumbhakāra*	*nīca kula*	*upāsaka*	He gave alms-bowls to the *bhikkhus*.	*Pārājika*, p. 348.
18.	A *daṅtakāra*	*nīca kula* (ivory worker)	*upāsaka*	He gave neddle cases to the *bhikkhus*.	*Pācittiya*, p. 221.
19.	Bhesika	*nīca kula*, a barber (*nahāpita*)	*upāsaka*	He carried a message to the Buddha on behalf of Lohicca *brāhmaṇa* and was impressed with the Buddha.	*D.N.*, I, pp. 191–3.

* * *

1.	Kuṇḍaliya	*Paribhājaka*	*upāsaka*	He questioned the Buddha on the profit of the Buddha's style of living.	*S.N.*, II, pp. 68–71.
2.	Acela Kassappa (1)	*paribbājaka*	*bhikkhu*	Originally an Acelaka. He joined the *saṅgha* after four months of probation and became an *arahant*.	*D.N.*, pp. 138–49.
3.	Acela Kassappa (2)	*paribbājaka*	*bhikkhu*	He was a friend of Citta *gahapati* to whom he admitted that after 30 years of being a *paribbājaka* he did not know much. He then joined the *saṅgha*.	*S.N.*, III, pp. 267–8.

4.	Timbaruka	*paribbājaka*	*upāsaka*	He questioned the Buddha on the origin of pleasure and pain.	*S.N.*, II, pp. 21–2.
5.	Puṇṇa Koḷiya putta	*paribbājaka*	*upāsaka*	He was an Acelaka who visited the Buddha.	*M.N.*, II, p. 65.
6.	Māgandiya	*paribbājaka*	*bhikkhu*	He was antagonistic to the Buddha initially.	*M.N.*, II, p. 210.
7.	Moliya Sīvaka	*paribbājaka*	*upāsaka*		*S.N.*, III, p. 205.
8.	Vacchagotta	*paribbājaka*	*upāsaka*		*M.N.*, II, p. 189.
9.	Saccaka	*paribbājaka* (A Nigaṇṭha)	*upāsaka*	The *bhikkhus* were invited for a meal by Saccaka. He was supported by the Lichchhavis and was a reputed teacher who was respected by the people.	*M.N.* I, pp. 280–309.
10.	Sabhiya	*paribbājaka*	*bhikkhu*		*Sutta Nipāta, Khuddaka Nikāya*, I, p. 353.
11.	Susīma	*paribbājaka*	*bhikkhu*	He was initially attracted to the Buddha and the *saṅgha* because they were honoured and well looked after.	*S.N.*, II, pp. 102–11
12.	Nandiya	*paribbājaka*	*upāsaka*		*S.N.*, IV, pp. 11–12.
13.	Poṭṭhapāda		*upāsaka*	Questioned the Buddha on the existence of the soul.	*D.N.*, I, p. 168.
14.	Subbhada	*paribbājaka*	*upāsaka*	Last disciple to be ordained by the Buddha.	*D.N.*, II, pp. 115–18.
15.	Sandaka	*paribbājaka*	*bhikkhu*	He was a member of a group of *paribbājakas* (probably Ājīvikās) who accepted the Buddha's teaching even though this meant giving up honour and fame. All the *paribbājakas* with him are said to have done the same.	*M.N.*, II, pp. 211–20; *M.L.S.*, II, p. 202.

Bibliography

ORIGINAL SOURCES

THE PĀLI TEXTS

Aṅguttara Nikāya, ed. by Bhikkhu J. Kashyap, 4 vols., Nālandā Devanāgarī-Pāli series, Pāli Publication Board (Bihar Government), 1959, tr. by F.L. Woodward and E.M. Hare as the *Book of Gradual Sayings*, 5 vols, London, P.T.S., 1932.

Cullavagga, ed., Bhikkhu J. Kashyap, Nālandā Devanāgarī-Pāli Series (Bihar Government), 1956.

Dīgha Nikāya, ed. by Bhikkhu J. Kashyap, 3 vols, Nālandā Devanāgarī-Pāli Series, Pāli Publication Board (Bihar Government), 1958, tr. by T.W. Rhys Davids as *The Dialogues of the Buddha*, 3 vols, London, P.T.S., 1973.

Dhammapada, Khuddaka Nikāya, Vol. I, Nālandā Devanāgarī-Pāli Series, Pāli Publication Board (Bihar Government), 1959.

Dhammapada Aṭṭhakatha, tr. by E.W. Burlingame as *Buddhist Legends*, 3 vols, London, P.T.S., 1969.

Jātaka, ed. V. Fausboll, 5 vols, London, P.T.S., 1963, tr. as *The Jātakas* by H.T. Francis, 5 vols, London, P.T.S., 1957.

Mahāvagga, ed., Bhikkhu J. Kashyap, Nālandā Devanāgarī-Pāli Series (Bihar Government), 1956.

Mahāvaṃsa, ed. by W. Geiger, London, P.T.S., 1964.

Majjhima Nikāya, ed. by Mahapandita Rahula Sankritayan and P.V. Bapat, 3 vols, Nālandā Devanāgarī-Pāli Series (Bihar Government), 1958; tr. by I.B. Horner as *The Middle Length Sayings*, 3 vols, London, P.T.S., 1976.

Milindapañha, ed., V. Trenckner, London, P.T.S., 1962, tr. by I.B. Horner as *Questions of King Milinda*, 2 vols, London, Luzac, 1964.

Nidāna Kathā, tr. by T.W. Rhys Davids as *Buddhist Birth Stories* [Reprint], Delhi, Indological Book House, 1973.

Pācittiya, ed. by Bhikkhu J. Kashyap, Nālandā Devanāgarī-Pāli Series (Bihar Government), 1958.

Pārājika, ed. by Bhikkhu J. Kashyap, Nālandā Devanāgarī-Pāli Series (Bihar Government), 1958.

Paramattha Dīpani ed. by F. Max Muller, London, P.T.S., 1893.

Samanta Pāsādikā, 3 vols, ed. by Birbal Sharma, Nālandā, Nava Nālandā Mahavihāra, 1964.

Saṁyutta Nikāya, ed. by Bhikkhu J. Kashyap, 4 vols, Nālandā Devanāgarī-Pāli Series (Bihar Government), 1959, tr. by F.L. Woodward and C.A.F. Rhys Davids as the *Book of Kindred Sayings*, 5 vols, London, P.T.S., 1952.

Sumaṅgala Vilāsinī (*Dīgha Nikāya Aṭṭakathā*) ed. by Mahesh Tiwari, Nālandā, Nava Nālandā Mahāvihāra, 1974.

Sutta Nipāta, Khuddaka Nikāya, Vol. I, ed. by Bhikkhu J. Kashyap, Nālandā Devanāgarī-Pāli Series (Bihar Government), 1959.

Theragāthā, Khuddaka Nikāya, Vol. II, ed. by Bhikkhu J. Kashyap, Nālandā Devanāgarī-Pāli Series (Bihar Government), 1959, tr. by Mrs C.A.F. Rhys Davids as the *Psalms of the Early Buddhists*, Vol. I, London, P.T.S., 1951.

Therīgāthā, Khuddaka Nikāya, Vol. II, ed. by Bhikkhu J. Kashyap, Nālandā Devanāgarī-Pāli Series (Bihar Government), 1959, tr. by C.A.F. Rhys Davids as the *Psalms of the Early Buddhists*, Vol. II, London, P.T.S., 1948.

I.B. Horner, *The Book of Discipline*, 5 vols, London, Oxford University Press, 1940.

T.W. Rhys Davids and H. Oldenberg, *The Vinaya Texts*, 3 vols [Reprint], Delhi, S.B.E., Vols. XIII, XVII, and XX, Motilal Banarsidass, 1974.

OTHER TEXTS

Ācārāṅga Sūtra, Jaina Sūtras, tr. by Hermann Jacobi, S.B.E., Vol. XXII [Reprint], Delhi, Motilal Banarsidass, 1973.

Kauṭiliya's Arthaśāstra, ed. and tr. by R.P. Kangle, 3 vols, Bombay, University of Bombay, Pt. I (text) 1960, Pt. II (translation), 1963, Pt. III (critical study), 1965.

Aṣṭādhyāyī of Pāṇini, 2 vols, ed. and tr. by S.C. Vasu, Delhi, Motilal Banarsidass, 1962.

Āpastamba Dharmasūtra, tr. by George Buhler, *Sacred Laws of the Āryas*, S.B.E., Vol. II [Reprint] Delhi, Motilal Banarsidass, 1975.

Avadāna Śataka, ed. by J.S. Speyer, Petrograd, Imperial Academy of Sciences, 1902.

Baudhāyana Dharmasūtra, tr. by George Buhler, *Sacred Laws of the Āryas*, S.B.E., Vol. XIV [Reprint], Delhi, Motilal Banarsidass, 1975.

Bṛhadāraṇyaka Upaniṣad, tr. by F. Max Muller, S.B.E., Vol. XV, Oxford, The Clarendon Press, 1881, p. 169.

Gautama Dharmasūtra, tr. by F. Max Muller, *Sacred Laws of the Āryas*, S.B.E., Vol. XIV [Reprint] Delhi, Motilal Banarsidass, 1973.

Kalpa Sūtra, Jaina Sūtras, tr. by Hermann Jacobi, S.B.E., Vol. XXII [Reprint], Delhi, Motilal Banarsidass, 1973.

Lalita Vistara, ed. by S. Lefmann, Halle, A.S. Verlag Der Buchhandlung des Weisenhauses, 1902.

Mahābhārata, ed. by V.S. Sukhtankar and S.K. Belvalkar, Vols. XIII, XV, Poona, Bhandarkar Oriental Research Institute, 1954.

Nirayāvalikā Sūtras, ed. by A.S. Gopani and V.J. Choksi, Ahmedabad, 1935.

Ṛg Veda, tr. by R.T.H. Griffiths, Benares, Lazarus and Co., 1896.

Sūtra Kritāṅga, *Jaina Sūtras*, tr. by Hermann Jacobi, S.B.E., Vol. XLV [Reprint], Delhi, Motilal Banarsidass, 1973.

Tantra Vārtika of Kumarila, Poona, 1910.

Uttarādhyayana, *Jaina Sūtras*, tr. by Hermann Jacobi, S.B.E., Vol. XLV [Reprint], Delhi, Motilal Banarsidass, 1975.

Vāsiṣṭha Dharmasūtra, tr. by George Buhler, *Sacred Laws of the Āryas*, S.B.E., Vol. XIV, Delhi Motilal Banarsidass, 1975.

Vyākaraṇa Mahābhāṣya of Patañjali, ed. by F. Kielhorn, Poona, Bhandarkar Oriental Research Institute, 1962 (first edition 1880).

INSCRIPTIONS

H. Ludders, Berlin, *A List of Brahmi Instructions* [Reprint], Varanasi, Indological Book House, 1973.

Jas, Burgess, *Archaeological Survey of Western India*, Vol. IV, London, Trench Trübner, 1883.

E. Hultzsch, *Corpus Inscriptionum Indicarum*, Vol. I [Reprint], Delhi, Indological Book House, 1968.

Jas, Burgess, *Epigraphica Indica*, Vol. II [Reprint], Delhi, Motilal Banarsidass, 1970.

SECONDARY WORKS

Agrawala, V.S., *India as Known to Pāṇini*, Lucknow, University of Lucknow, 1953.

Alsdorf, L., 'The Impious *Brāhmaṇa* and the Pious *Caṇḍāla*' in L. Cousins *et al.* (eds), *Buddhist Studies in Honour of I.B. Horner*, Holland, Reidel Publishing Co., 1974.

Altekar, A.S., *State and Government in Ancient India*, Delhi, Motilal Banarsidass, 1955.

Ambedkar, B.R., *The Buddha and his Dhamma*, Bombay, Siddhartha College, 1957.

Barua, B.M., *Pre-Buddhist Indian Philosophy*, Delhi, Motilal Banarsidass, 1970.

Basak, C.S., 'The Role of Uruvela Kassapa in the Spread of Buddhism' in A.K. Narain (ed.), *Studies in Pāli and Buddhism*, Delhi, B.R. Publishing Corporation, 1979.

Basham, A.L., *History and Doctrine of the Ājīvikas*, London, Luzac, 1951.

———, 'Ajātasattu's War with the Lichchhavis', *Studies in Indian History and Culture*, Calcutta, Sambodhi Publications, 1964.

Bhandarkar, D.R., *Some Aspects of Ancient Indian Culture*, Madras, University of Madras, 1940.

———, *Ancient History of India* [Reprint], Delhi, Bharatiya Publishing House, 1977.

Bhandarkar, R.G., 'A Peep into the Early History of India', *Journal of the Bombay Branch of the Royal Asiatic Society*, Vol. XX, 1897–99.

Bohtlin, G.K. and Rudolf Roth, *Sanskrit Wörterbuch*, St. Petersburg, Neudruck der Ausgabe, 1855–75.

Bose, A.N., *The Social and Rural Economy of North-East India*, 2 vols, Calcutta, University of Calcutta, 1942.

Bose, N.K., *Culture and Society in India*, Bombay, Asia Publishing House, 1967.

Bougle, Celestin, *Essays on the Caste System*, Cambridge, Cambridge University Press, 1971.

Chakrabarti, D.K., 'Some Theoretical Aspects of Early Urban Growth', *Purāttatva*, Vol. VII, 1974.

———, 'Beginning of Iron and Social Change in India', *Indian Studies Past and Present*, Vol. XIV, No. 4, 1973.

———, 'Iron in Early Indian Literature', *Journal of the Royal Asiatic Society*, No. 1, 1979.

Chakraborty, Haripada, *Asceticism in Indian Culture*, Calcutta, Punti Pustak, 1973.

Chakravarti, Adhir, 'The Federal Experiment in India', *Journal of Ancient Indian History*, Vol. XI, 1977–78.

Chanana, D.N., *Slavery in Ancient India*, Delhi, People's Publishing House, 1960.

Chattopadhyaya, D.P., *Lokāyata*, Delhi, People's Publishing House, 1973.

Chowdhary, Radhakrishna, 'Ownership of Land in Ancient India', *Journal of the Bihar Research Society*, Vol. LIII, 1967.

Coomaraswamy, A.K., *Buddha and the Gospel of Buddhism*, New York, Harper Torchbooks, 1916.

———, *Hinduism and Buddhism*, New York, Philosophical Library, 1943.

———, 'A Royal Gesture and Some other Motifs', *Feestbundel v.d.k. Bataviaasch Genootschap Van Kunstenen Wetenschapen Weltevreden*, Pt. I, 1929.

———, *Temporal Power and Spiritual Authority in the Indian Theory of Government* [Reprint], Delhi, Munshiram Manoharlal, 1978.

Deussen, Paul, *The Philosophy of the Upanishads*, New York, Dover Publications, 1966.

Drekmeier, Charles, *Kingship and Community in Early India*, Stanford, California University Press, 1962.

Dumont, L., 'Kingship in Ancient India', *Contributions to Indian Sociology*, Vol. VI, 1962.

———, *Homo Hierarchicus*, London, Paladin Books, 1972.

Dutt, S., *Early Buddhist Monachism*, Bombay, Asia Publishing House, 1960.

———, *Buddhist Monks and Monasteries of India*, London, George Allen, 1962.

Eliot, Charles, *Hinduism and Buddhism*, London, Routledge and Kegan Paul, 1957.

Fick, R., *The Social Organisation of North-East India in Buddha's Time*, Calcutta, University of Calcutta, 1920.

Fiser, I., 'The Problem of the Seṭṭhi in the Buddhist Jātakas', *Archiv Orientalni*, Vol. XXIV, Praha, 1954.

Fiske, M. Adele, 'Buddhism in India Today' in Heinrich Dumoulin and John. C. Maraldo (eds), *Buddhism in the Modern World*, London, Collier Macmillan, 1976.

Ghoshal, U.N., *A History of Indian Political Ideas*, London, Oxford University Press, 1966.

Ghurye, G.S., *Indian Sadhus*, Bombay, Popular Prakashan, 1953.

Gokhale, B.G., 'The Early Buddhist Elite', *Journal of Indian History*, Vol. XLIII, 1965.

———, 'Early Buddhist Kingship', *Journal of Asian Studies*, Vol. XXVI, 1966.

———, 'Dhamma as a Political Concept', *Journal of Indian History*, Vol. XLVI, Pt. II, 1968.

Gombrich, Richard, *Precept and Practice*, Oxford, Clarendon Press, 1972.

Gonda, J., *Ancient Indian Kingship from the Religious Point of View*, Leiden, E.J. Brill, 1966.

Gupta, S.P., 'Two Urbanizations in India', *Purāttatva*, Vol. VII, 1974.

Hanayama Shinsho, *Bibliography on Buddhism*, Tokyo, Hokuseido Press, 1961.

Heesterman, J.C., *Ancient Indian Royal Consecration*, The Hague, Mouton, 1957.

Hocart, A.M., *Caste, A Comparative Study*, London, Methuen, 1950.

Horner, I.B., 'The Buddha's Co-natals' in A.K. Narain (ed.), *Studies in Pāli and Buddhism*, Delhi, B.R. Publishing Corporation, 1979.

———, *Women Under Primitive Buddhism*, London, Routledge and Kegan Paul, 19030.

Hutton, J.H., *Caste in India*, London, Oxford University Press, 1963.

Izutzu, T., *The Structure of Ethical Terms in the Koran: A Study in Semantics*, Tokyo, Keio Institute of Philological Studies, 1959.

Jain, J.C., *Ancient India as Depicted in the Jain Canon*, Bombay, New Book Company, 1947.

Jayaswal, K.P., *Hindu Polity*, Bangalore, Bangalore Press, 1967.

Jayatilleke, K.N., *Early Buddhist Theory of Knowledge*, London, George Allen and Unwin, 1963.

Jayawickrame, N.A., *Analysis of Sutta Nipāta*, Unpublished Ph.D. thesis, University of London, 1947.

Jha, V.N., 'Varṇasaṃkara in the Dharmasūtras: Theory and Practice', *Journal of Economic and Social History of the Orient*, Vol. XIII, pt. III, 1970.

Jolly, J., *Hindu Law and Custom* [Reprint], Varanasi, Bharatiya Publishing House, 1975.

Jong, J.W., 'The Background of Early Buddhism', *Journal of Indian and Buddhist Studies*, Vol. XII, pt. I, 1964.

Joshi, M.C., 'Early Historical Urban Growth in India: Some Observations', *Purāttatva*, Vol. VII, 1974.

Kalupahana, David J., *Buddhist Philosophy: A Historical Analysis*, Honolulu, University Press of Hawaii, 1976.

Kern, H., *A Manual of Buddhism*, London, The Sheldon Printers, 1932.

Kosambi, D.D., 'Ancient Kosala and Magadha', *Journal of the Bombay Branch of the Royal Asiatic Society*, Vol. XXVII, 1952.

———, 'The Beginning of the Iron Age in India', *Journal of Economic and Social History of the Orient*, Vol. VI, pt. III, 1963.

———, *An Introduction to the Study of Indian History*, Bombay, Popular Prakashan, 1975.

———, *The Culture and Civilization of Ancient India*, Delhi, Vikas Publishing House, 1973.

Law, B.C., *A History of Pāli Literature*, Varanasi, Bharatiya Publishing House, n.d.

Ling, Trevor, *The Buddha*, Middlesex, Penguin Books, 1976.

Lillie, Arthur, *The Life of the Buddha* [Reprint], Delhi, Seema Publications, 1974.

Macdonell, A.A. and Keith, A.B. *Vedic Index of Names and Subjects*, London, Published for the Government of India, 1912.

Malalashekhara, G.P., *Dictionary of Pali Proper Names*, 2 vols, London, P.T.S., 1960.

Mehta, Ratilal, *Pre-Buddhist India*, Bombay, Examiner Press, 1939.

Meillasoux, Claude, 'From Reproduction to Production', *Economy and Society*, Vol. I, No. I, 1972.

Majumdar, R.C., *Classical Accounts of India*, Calcutta, Firma K.L. Mukhopadhyaya, 1960.

Misra, G.S.P., *The Age of the Vinaya*, Delhi, Munshiram Manoharlal, 1972.

Misra, V.D., *Some Aspects of Indian Archaeology*, Allahabad, Prabhat Prakashan, 1977.

Monier, Williams M., *Buddhism* [Reprint], Varanasi, Chowkhamba Series, 1964.

Oldenberg, H., *The Buddha: His Life, His Doctrine, His Order*, London, Williams and Norgate, 1882.

———, 'On the History of the Indian Caste System', *Indian Antiquary*, 1920, Vol. XLIX.

Pande, G.C., *Studies in the Origins of Buddhism*, Delhi, Motilal Banarsidass, 1974.

Rai, Jayamal, *The Rural-Urban Economy and Social Changes in Ancient India*, Varanasi, Bharatiya Vidya Prakashan, 1974.

Rahula, Walpole, *History of Buddhism in Ceylon*, Colombo, Gunasena, 1956.

Ray, N.R., 'Technology and Social Change in Early Indian History', *Purāttatva*, Vol. VIII, 1975–76.

Raychoudhari, H.C., *Political History of Ancient India*, Calcutta, University of Calcutta, 1972.

Rhys Davids, C.A.F., 'Economic Conditions according to Early Buddhist Literature' in E.J. Rapson (ed.), *Cambridge History of India*, Vol. I, [Reprint], Delhi, S. Chand, 1968.

———, *Wayfarers Words*, London, Luzac, 1940.

Rhys Davids, T.W., *Indian Buddhism* [Reprint], Allahabad, Rachana Prakashan, 1972.

———, *Buddhist India* [Reprint], Delhi, Indological Book House, 1970.

———, *The History and Litérature of Buddhism* [Reprint], Calcutta, Sushil Gupta, 1962.

———, *Buddhist Suttas*, S.B.E., Vol. XI [Reprint], Delhi, Motilal Banarsidass, 1973.

———, 'Early History of the Buddhists' in E.J. Rapson (ed.), *Cambridge History of India*, Vol. I [Reprint], Delhi, S. Chand, 1955.

Rhys Davids, T.W. and Stede, W., *The Pāli-English Dictionary*, London, 1959.

Rockhill, W.W., *The Life of the Buddha*, London, Trübner Oriental Series, 1884.

Ruben, Walter, 'Some Problems of the Ancient Indian Republics' in K.M. Ashraf, ed. by Horst Kruger, Delhi, People's Publishing House, 1969, pp. 23–4.

Ryan, Bryce, *Castes in Modern Ceylon*, New Jersey, Rutgers University Press, 1953.

Sahi, M.D.N., 'Stratigraphical Position of the NBP Ware in the Upper Ganga Basin and its Date', *Purāttatva*, Vol. VI, 1974.

Senart, E., *Caste in India*, London, Methuen, 1930.

Sharma, J.P., *Ancient Indian Republics*, Leiden, E.J. Brill, 1968.

Sharma, R.S., *Aspects of Political Ideas and Institutions in Ancient India*, Delhi, Motilal Banarsidass, 1959.

———, 'The Material Milieu of the Birth of Buddhism', paper presented at the 29th International Congress of Orientalists, Paris, 16–22 July 1973.

———, *Material Culture and Social Formations in Ancient India*, Delhi, Macmillan and Co., 1983.

Sharma, Y.D., 'Exploration of Historical Sites', *Ancient India*, Vol. IX, 1956.

Spellman, J.W., *Political Theory of Ancient India*, Oxford, Clarendon Press, 1964.

Spiro, Melford, *Buddhism and Society*, London, George Allen and Unwin, 1971.

Tambiah, S.J., *Buddhism and the Spirit Cults of North-East Thailand*, Cambridge, Cambridge University Press, 1969.

———, *World Conqueror World Renouncer*, Cambridge, Cambridge University Press, 1976.

Talim, M., *Woman in Early Buddhist Literature*, Bombay, University of Bombay, 1972.

Thapar, R., *Aśoka and the Decline of the Mauryas*, Delhi, Oxford University Press, 1973.

———, 'Renunciation: The Making of a Counter Culture?', *Ancient Indian Social History*, Delhi, Orient Longman, 1978.

———, *History of India*, Vol. I, London, Penguin Books, 1962.

———, 'Social Mobility in Ancient India', *Ancient Indian Social History*, New Delhi, Orient Longman, 1978.

———, *From Lineage to State*, Delhi, Oxford University Press, 1984.

Thomas, E.J., *The Life of the Buddha*, London, Routledge and Kegan Paul, 1926.

Varma, V.P., *Hindu Political Thought and its Metaphysical Foundations*, Varanasi, Motilal Banarsidass, 1954.

———, *Early Buddhism and its Origins*, Delhi, Munshiram Manoharlal, 1973.

Wagle, N.N., *Society at the Time of the Buddha*, Bombay, Popular Prakashan, 1966.

Warder, A.K., 'On the Relationship between Buddhism and other Contemporary Systems', *Bulletin of the School of Oriental and African Studies*, Vol. XVIII, 1956.

———, *Pāli Metre,* London, Luzac, 1967.

———, *Indian Buddhism*, Delhi, Motilal Banarsidass, 1970.

Weber, Max, *The Religion of India*, Glencoe, The Free Press, 1960.

———, *Economy and Society*, 2 vols, California, University of California Press, 1978.

Wijesekhara, A., 'Wheel Symbolism in Chakravartin Concept' in A.S. Altekar *et al.* (eds), *S.K. Belvalkar Felicitation Volume*, Banaras, Motilal Banarsidass, 1957.

Winternitz, M., *A History of Indian Literature*, 3 vols, Calcutta, University of Calcutta, 1939.

Yalman, Nur, *Under the Bo Tree: Studies in Caste, Kinship and Marriage in Interior Ceylon*, Los Angeles, University of California Press, 1971.

Zelliot, Eleanor, 'The Indian Discovery of Buddhism: 1855–1956' in A.K. Narain (ed.), *Studies in Pāli and Buddhism*, Delhi, B.R. Publishing Corporation, 1979.

Zimmer, H., *The Philosophies of India*, London, Routledge and Kegan Paul, 1953.

Subject Index

Agriculture, 16–20, 23–26
  cycles of cropping and family organization, 92–3
  and economy, 16
  pastoralism and rice cultivation, 19
  second urbanization and, 20
  similes relating to, 18
  status of occupation of, 112
  use of iron in, 16
  young men of good family and, 102–3
Ārya, 6
Ariyasāvaka, 6, 179
Āśrama grihastha, 40

Bhikkhu
  kinship ties and, 30–1
  lay followers and, 62
  material requirements, 56
  Sākyaputta *samaṇas* and, 31
Bhikkhunī
  bias against entry into *saṅgha*, 31
  distrust of, 33
  entrants from *gaṇa-saṅghas*, 34
  punishment for lapses, 33
  restrictions on, 32
Brahmadeya land, 57
Brāhmaṇa, 39–46
  agriculture and, 43
  asceticism after *brahmacarya* and, 40
  Brahmanical scheme of categorization and, 98–9
  category in religious ethics of Buddhism, 64
  clan-names in *gaṇa-saṅghas* and, 91
  cult of sacrifice and, 37
  laity and, 97, 132
  materialistic tendencies of society and, 42, 64
  performance of *yañña* and, 61
  religion and, 66–7
  saṅgha and, 132–3
  term for spiritually elevated person, 5
Brāhmaṇa-gahapati
  agriculture and, 72–3
  brāhmaṇa-gāmas and, 25–6, 72
  taxes paid to kings and, 72, 133–4
Buddhism
  Asian countries in, 1
  Brahmanism, alternative to, 1, 96–7, 146
  caste-system and, 95–6
  categories in religious ethos of, 64
  doctrinal differences and, 53
  inequality and expanding economy and, 177, 180
  kings' function and role in, 150–76
  Mahars and, 95
  new society and, 97
  privileged strata and, 97
  system of production and, 64
  writing on, 1
Buddhists
  categories and schemes of categorization of, 105, 123
  genesis, myth of, 92
  social origins of, 96
Buddhist Councils, 3, 127–8, 131, 174

Cakkavatti, 6
  as *dhammiko-dhammarāja*, 150, 164–9
  future role of, 173, 176, 181
  responsibilities of, 181
  sculptural representation of, 152
  uposatha observance and, 63
  seven treasures of, 68
  women and, 34
Caṇḍāla
  empirically unverifiable, 106
  low status associated with, 101, 106
caste, 94–5

Dāna, 58–62
Dāsa
  display of envy and, 26, 180

Index of Proper Names